If this world does not have a place for us,
then another world must be made.

— Zapatista saying

This book is dedicated to
the people of the Berkana Exchange,
who *are* making another world.

"If there is any hope for us it lies in rediscovering and recreating community—bringing forth our DNA as social animals into today's world. Do not doubt that this is possible. Do not doubt that the resilience of life-creating conditions is present among us. Indeed, this is exactly what is happening in increasingly diverse social settings. Read *Walk Out Walk On* and see for yourself—and see your self."
—**Peter Senge, author of *The Fifth Discipline* and coauthor of**
   Presence* and *The Necessary Revolution

"Exuberant and galvanizing, this book takes us to where the future is happening. And that is not in the corridors of power but on the grassroots level where a 'trans-local' movement is unleashing human creativity and smarts."
—**Joanna Macy, author of *World as Lover, World as Self* and other**
   books

"This book makes an outstanding contribution to the study of resilience and resilient communities in a world that is increasingly devoid of confidence and trust, one that desperately needs to be reassured that people have the power to claim their right to live and learn. This book will help inspire those warriors without weapons in tackling the issues of food security, education, health, justice, and the sustainability of our environment across the diverse communities that make up our planet Earth."
—**Jim Varghese, Executive Director, Springfield Land Corporation;**
   former Director-General, Government of Queensland; and Member,
   Order of Australia

"A well-told tale of a journey of discovery of the arts of living. Read it with an open heart and it will take you to a soul place far beyond your normal experience. It should be read by everyone who feels an impulse to go abroad to fix the world's poor."
—**David Korten, author of *Agenda for a New Economy*, *The Great***
   Turning*, and *When Corporations Rule the World

"This is a masterpiece, lucid and illuminating. The authors narrate seven great stories of true transformation, inspiration, and leadership."
—Satish Kumar, cofounder, Schumacher College; editor, *Resurgence* magazine; and author of *No Destination, You Are Therefore I Am,* and other books

"We desperately need a new approach to resist prevailing destructive systems and to renew the fabric of community and ecological health. The experiments profiled in this important book embody such visions. I hope their inspiration travels far and wide."
—Helena Norberg-Hodge, author of *Ancient Futures*

"This book gives insight and beauty to what is becoming the new, new world—the world beyond consumerism and all of its side effects. It is an intimate journey through communities and citizens who are creating a future with their own hearts, hands, and relationships. Written with poetic and reflective grace, it moves forward the movement toward communities and economies of gifts, generosity, local control, and care."
—Peter Block, author of *Community* and coauthor of *The Abundant Community*

"This is one of the most poetic, provocative, and powerful books on community-based societal change and coevolution I have read in more than forty years of working with social movements and community development, as well as with large-scale systems change in corporate settings. Deborah and Meg provide unerring conceptual clarity—inviting us to see and sense the deeper dynamics and principles that we can each call on as resources for work in our own local communities and organizations."
—Juanita Brown, cofounder, The World Café, and coauthor of *The World Café*

"The book is a jewel for everyone working to create a better world. Walk out of what you've been doing and walk on to these stories and experiences made rich by reflection. Walk on to deep truths acknowledged here. Walk on to wisdom shared."
—Angela Blanchard, CEO, Neighborhood Centers Inc., Houston

WALK OUT
WALK ON

Other books by Margaret Wheatley

Leadership and the New Science
A Simpler Way (with Myron Kellner-Rogers)
Turning to One Another
Finding Our Way
Perseverance

WALK OUT
WALK ON

A LEARNING JOURNEY INTO COMMUNITIES
DARING TO LIVE THE FUTURE NOW

MARGARET WHEATLEY
DEBORAH FRIEZE

A BERKANA PUBLICATION

Berrett–Koehler Publishers, Inc.
San Francisco
a BK Currents book

Berrett-Koehler Publishers, Inc.
235 Montgomery, Suite 650
San Francisco, CA 94104-2916
Tel: (415) 288-0260   Fax: (415) 362-2512   www.bkconnection.com

Ordering Information

Quantity sales. Special discounts are available on quantity purchases by corporations, associations, and others. For details, contact the "Special Sales Department" at the Berrett-Koehler address above.

Individual sales. Berrett-Koehler publications are available through most bookstores. They can also be ordered directly from Berrett-Koehler:
Tel: (800) 929-2929; Fax: (802) 864-7626; www.bkconnection.com

Orders for college textbook/course adoption use.
Please contact Berrett-Koehler: Tel: (800) 929-2929; Fax: (802) 864-7626.

Orders by U.S. trade bookstores and wholesalers.
Please contact Ingram Publisher Services, Tel: (800) 509-4887; Fax: (800) 838-1149; E-mail: customer.service@ingram publisherservices.com; or visit www.ingrampublisherservices.com/Ordering for details about electronic ordering.

Berrett-Koehler and the BK logo are registered trademarks of Berrett-Koehler Publishers, Inc.

Printed in Canada

Berrett-Koehler books are printed on long-lasting acid-free paper. When it is available, we choose paper that has been manufactured by environmentally responsible processes. These may include using trees grown in sustainable forests, incorporating recycled paper, minimizing chlorine in bleaching, or recycling the energy produced at the paper mill.

Production management: Michael Bass Associates

Book and cover designer: Canace Pulfer

Cover photograph: Aeron Miller

Library of Congress Cataloging-in-Publication Data
Wheatley, Margaret.
  Walk out walk on: a learning journey into communities daring to live the future now / by Margaret Wheatley, Deborah Frieze.
    p. cm.
  "A Berkana publication."
  "Includes bibliographical references and index.
  "ISBN 978-1-60509-731-2
  "1. Communities—Case studies. 2. Community development—Case studies.
  3. Community leadership—Case studies. I. Frieze, Deborah. II. Title.
  HM756.W48 2011
  307.1'4—dc22

                                                              2010053053

First Edition
16 15 14 13 12 11   10 9 8 7 6 5 4 3 2 1

The whole globe is shook up, so what are you going to do
    when things are falling apart?
You're either going to become more fundamentalist
    and try to hold things together,
or you're going to forsake the old ambitions and goals
    and live life as an experiment,
    making it up as you go along.

          —*Pema Chödrön*
          Buddhist Teacher

CONTENTS

PART II: JOURNEYING

PART III: RETURNING HOME

PART IV: REFLECTIONS

WELCOME

OUR INVITATION FOR HOW TO READ THIS BOOK

This looks like a book and reads like a book.
But it can be much more than that.

This book is an opportunity to go on a *Learning Journey*. In these pages, you'll meet people in seven different countries, all of them our friends and colleagues, who have taken on challenging problems that others have been unable to solve. They've discovered enduring solutions and created healthy and resilient communities by working together in new and different ways.

If this were an actual Learning Journey, we'd be traveling together to these communities. We'd get on a plane, propelled by curiosity and a desire to experience ways of thinking and living different from our own. We'd willingly step out of the familiar and discover people in other cultures and places who accomplish their work by relying on beliefs and assumptions quite different from the conventional wisdom.

On a Learning Journey, participants often experience a wide range of emotions: surprise, disbelief, excitement, doubt, joy, reassurance. These strong, contradictory feelings are likely to appear whenever we discover that seemingly unsolvable problems have solutions. All we have to do is change our minds! This is what a Learning Journey offers, even in book form—an opportunity to shake up our thinking, engender new insights, and strengthen our commitments.

We authors have each led several learning journeys. Because we've seen their transformative power, we challenged ourselves to re-create the experience of being in these different communities using only prose and photos. You'll be the judge of whether we succeeded. But it also depends on you. In every journey we've led, everyone has a different experience, even though we're in the same location, meeting the same people. We've learned that we can create the visits, but each participant creates his or her own journey.

For this book to succeed as *your* Learning Journey, we encourage you to think about how best to support yourself as a learner. What conditions need to be present for you to engage fully with the stories, to foster your learning, to reflect on what you just read? We provide the opportunities for immersion, observation, and reflection. But the learning is up to you.

TWO CHOICES FOR HOW TO READ THIS BOOK

A. *You can read this as a Learning Journey*, a provocation that invites you to examine your beliefs and assumptions about how change happens and what becomes possible when we fully engage our communities. *If you choose to journey with us*, start by reading **Part I: Leaving Home**.

B. *You can read this as a conventional book.* We suggest you dig in immediately and begin by reading the story of one community, whichever one attracts you most. However, we need to offer a word of caution. Each visit has been designed to create a sense of immersion—like drinking from a fire hose. This can be overwhelming, at times even disorienting. That's the nature of a Learning Journey—it creates moments when we're no longer sure about something. We authors like this, because we've seen that when certainty collapses, it's often replaced by curiosity. If you're reading through for content and not pausing for reflection at the end of each visit, you may find our approach disconcerting.

STRUCTURE OF THE CHAPTERS (VISITS)

Learning Journeys have four major components, which you'll find in each chapter:

1. **Immersion**. Each visit provides a direct experience inside these communities, through lively prose and many photos. We hope you feel immersed in the stories of these people and places.

2. **Observation**. There are moments when we, as hosts, observe and make visible contrasts between conventional assumptions and practices and those in use in this community. We also take time to explore the major issue this community has dealt with, providing more context. We feel these are core challenges that every community must eventually confront.

3. **Other Examples.** These communities aren't anomalies. In each chapter, we give you a glimpse of what's going on elsewhere, naming other communities and programs that rely on quite similar beliefs and practices to achieve remarkable outcomes.

4. **Reflection**. Each visit ends with a few short essays meant to stimulate your personal reflections. We've learned that it takes time to process any provocative experience, to notice our thoughts and reactions and what they might mean.

We welcome you to this journey!

PART I
LEAVING HOME

This is the setting out.
The leaving of everything behind.
Leaving the social milieu. The preconceptions.
The definitions. The language.
    The narrowed field of vision. The expectations.
No longer expecting relationships, memories, words,
    or letters to mean what they used to mean.
To be, in a word: Open.

—Rabbi Lawrence Kushner

This book takes you on a Learning Journey to places that will inspire, disturb, and provoke you, and to meet people who will delight, nourish, and encourage you. We're glad that you've joined us. We visit seven communities around the world, seven very different cultures, all of which are experimenting with what it means to live the future now. We, the authors, are intimately connected with each of these communities; we've worked alongside them for several years and been transformed by these experiences and relationships.

Our journey takes us to Mexico, Brazil, South Africa, Zimbabwe, India, Greece, and the United States. In each community, we'll experience firsthand what's possible when we change our beliefs about what people are capable of and how change happens. We'll witness communities that rely on everyone to be an entrepreneur, a leader, an artist. These communities trust that these are common human traits, not limited to a few gifted people. We'll meet people who use their ingenuity and caring to figure out how to work with what they have to create what they need.

And as we move from community to community, we'll explore the deeper patterns that link them together, diverse as they are. We'll see how change happens through self-organized efforts that then move across the planet through networks of relationship. We'll see that lasting change doesn't start from the top of a system, but from deep inside it, when people step forward to solve a problem, then move on to the next issue that needs addressing. We'll see how much becomes possible when we abandon hope of being saved by the perfect leader or the perfect program, and instead look inside our community to notice that the resources and wisdom we need are already here.

In every community, you'll meet the Walk Outs Who Walk On. Perhaps you'll recognize yourself in some of them.

WALK OUTS WHO WALK ON

Walk Outs are people who bravely choose to leave behind situations, jobs, relationships, and ideas that restrict and confine them, anything that inhibits them. They *walk on* to the ideas, people, and practices that enable them to explore and discover new gifts, new possibilities.

We learned the phrase "Walks Outs Who Walk On" from our friends in India. They had created a network of young people who chose to leave school. They didn't consider themselves "dropouts," a negative label assigned to them by the school system. They left school because they wanted to be learners, not passive students. They walked on to discover many ways they could contribute to creating change in their world.[1]

Although the phrase may be new to you, think about situations in your life that you've consciously chosen to leave because you knew that to stay any longer would limit you. Whenever we choose to leave behind what confines us, whenever we courageously step forward to discover new capacities, then we can rightfully call ourselves Walk Outs Who Walk On.

The people you meet on this journey have *walked out* of a world of unsolvable problems, scarce resources, limiting beliefs, and destructive individualism. They've *walked on* to beliefs and practices that solve problems and reveal abundant resources. They've created communities where everyone is welcome to learn, grow, and contribute. They've walked out of the greed and grasping of this time, where many individuals try to get as much as they can, and walked on to discover how to create what they need with what they have. And while we visit only seven communities on this journey, there are millions more people like them throughout the world.

When people and communities walk out, they discover they're more gifted and wiser than they believed or had been told, that working together—even in the harshest circumstances—can be joyful, that they can invent solutions to problems that others have declared unsolvable. These communities are creating meaningful change in some of the most difficult political, social, and economic circumstances. They may have little money, few trustworthy formal leaders, and minimal material resources. They may have been told they're "backward" or don't possess the requisite expertise to solve their own problems. Had they accepted current thinking, they would have sat back and waited passively for help to come from the outside—from experts, foreign aid, heroic leaders.

But instead, they walked out. They had the good sense not to buy into these paralyzing beliefs about themselves and how change happens. They walked on to discover that the wisdom and wealth they need resides in themselves—in everyday people, their cultural traditions and their environment. They've used this wisdom and wealth to conduct bold experiments in how to create healthy and resilient communities where all people matter, all people can contribute. Their creativity and hard work make it easier for us to see that a different world is possible.

WHY WE VISIT THESE COMMUNITIES

Margaret (Meg) and Deborah, as your hosts for this Learning Journey, are taking you to meet people and communities we've partnered with for several years through our work with The Berkana Institute.[2] There are many, many other places worthy of visiting, but these are the ones we know well, that we're most intimate with. We're taking you to meet our friends, people with whom we've worked, danced, argued, cried, laughed, consoled, celebrated, and loved. Together, we've explored how self-organization and change happen, we've learned to trust the illimitable power of community, and we've come to realize how important our heritage and cultural traditions are.

Not only do we know these people as friends, but they also know each other well. For several years now, they've worked and learned together, visited one another's communities, shared their discoveries and dilemmas, and gathered annually as a learning community. As we visit each community, you may notice how they weave through each other's lives, how they support each other in deep friendship.

Your experience with these people and communities doesn't have to end with this book. We've created www.walkoutwalkon.net where you can watch videos, hear interviews, and keep informed about where these communities and people are now. Learn more about the *Walk Out Walk On* website on p. 260.)

YOUR HOSTS (THE AUTHORS)

Deborah has partnered with each one of these communities since 2004. She's led Learning Journeys to Mexico, Brazil, South Africa, and Zimbabwe. In this book, she's written each of the seven visits, wanting you to experience what it feels like to be there, getting to know these communities and their pioneering work. All of these relationships were developed through the Berkana Exchange (an initiative of The Berkana Institute), a community of friends and a community of practice that has worked together over several years and that continues to actively engage and support one another. The people Deborah writes about have become her extended family, an intimate learning community that is inventing new solutions to the issues she cares about most—such as food security, ecological sustainability, and economic self-reliance.

Meg Wheatley and Deborah Frieze

Meg has worked with most of the people you'll meet, in gatherings and Berkana-hosted events around the world. She's been on the ground in the communities in South Africa, Zimbabwe, and the United States and led three Learning Journeys to South Africa and Zimbabwe. From her experiences with these communities—as mentor, student, steward, friend—she's learned firsthand about the power of community and self-organization. (It is these people and communities who've informed her work over the past several years; their stories and examples appear in her articles and books.) Meg's contribution here is to prepare you for the journey and to guide the reflections that, hopefully, lead you to think more deeply about your experiences and what might be changing in you as a result. Throughout the visits, both Deborah and Meg make visible the patterns and beliefs that connect these diverse communities.

SEVEN HEALTHY AND RESILIENT COMMUNITIES

We define these places as *healthy and resilient communities* because they have learned to trust themselves to find their own solutions and take control of their own future. They develop greater capacities and become smarter over time as they learn what works and how to work together. They become confident that they can deal with whatever problem confronts them next. In the face of hunger, poverty, ill health, environmental degradation, and economic injustice, they respond, adapt, invent. That's what makes them healthy and resilient.

Healthy and resilient communities take on big issues, those that all communities eventually must deal with—food, economics, education, leadership, environmental challenges. To give you a taste of what's ahead on this journey, here's a brief description of where we're going and the focus for each visit:

Mexico: From Scaling Up to Scaling Across. Taking things to scale doesn't happen vertically through one-size-fits-all replication strategies. We'll visit *Unitierra*, a new form of university, and the *Zapatistas*, a populist movement for self-determination. In both places, there's a deep, unshakable belief in the power of people to claim their right to live and learn as they see fit. We'll observe how their experiments move horizontally, scaling across villages and nations, *trans-locally*, as many diverse people learn from their discoveries and are inspired to try their own.

Brazil: From Power to Play. Most leaders believe that it's their job to motivate people, that without their directive control, no work gets done. The most common way to motivate people is through external means, using punishment and reward. We'll experience *Warriors Without Weapons*, where play, not power, evokes people's passion, creativity, and motivation to work hard on seemingly overwhelming challenges.

South Africa: From Problem to Place. Today's approach to social change posits that large and complex issues must be addressed one by one, with institutions and experts who specialize in that particular problem. We'll explore tiny *Joubert Park* in Johannesburg, where people have created changes in education, public safety, arts, ecology, food, and more using the principle of *start anywhere, follow it everywhere.*[3]

Zimbabwe: From Efficiency to Resilience. Conventional attempts to solve problems of scarcity focus on efficiencies—attempting to do more with less by cutting budgets and staff, minimizing resources, optimizing outputs. *Kufunda Learning Village* has achieved resilience in a time of total systems collapse by choosing a different approach. They engage in a wide range of small local actions that give them the capacity to continuously adapt to an unpredictable and chaotic world.

India: From Transacting to Gifting. The transactional culture of today promotes self-interest and scarcity; people strive to take as much as they can and accumulate more than they need. In a gift culture—common in many traditional societies—generosity prevails and money loses its power. *Shikshantar* is experimenting with gift culture, replacing mindless growth with the confidence that we have what we need.

Greece: From Intervention to Friendship. In our pursuit to find what works, we seldom notice how disempowering it is when we look for answers from experts and best practices created elsewhere. At the *Art of Learning Centering* at Axladtisa-Avatakia, participants walked out of dependence on experts and learned to trust the capacities and creativity available in friendship to address their community's needs.

United States: From Hero to Host. When a community stops waiting for a hero to save it, it discovers internal resources and solutions to solve otherwise intractable problems. People in Columbus, Ohio, are walking out of heroic leadership and walking on to a new "operating system" of using conversational processes to address complex problems, such as health care, homelessness, poverty, public safety, and more.

These seven communities are very different from one another—different cultures, histories, and environments. But beneath these interesting and important differences, they share a common identity as Walk Outs Who Walked On.

THE ROLE WALK OUTS PLAY IN CREATING CHANGE

Walk Outs Who Walk On play a crucial role in societal change. They use this time of dissolution and failing systems to create and experiment with new ways of working and organizing. In doing their pioneering work, they rely on the fact that people's capacity to self-organize is the most powerful change process there is. They've seen how local efforts can emerge into larger, transformative changes when they connect with other local efforts. They've confirmed Margaret Mead's brilliant statement that the world changes by dint of small groups of dedicated people. And they've demonstrated that when people know where they come from—their traditions and culture—they develop strength and stamina. These pathfinders have

come to understand that living is a synonym for learning: they experiment, take risks, fail, succeed, make it up as they go along, and offer compassion and forgiveness to each other.

When any of us experiment with walking on, we're able to discover potential that we couldn't see before we freed ourselves from constraints. It's motivating to discover these hidden capacities and see how they serve us to accomplish good work. It's essential that we feel motivated, that we have faith that we're doing the right work, because whenever we use ideas and approaches that don't conform to the world's expectations, we're going to meet with resistance.

At Berkana, we use a map (co-created with our global family of friends and colleagues) to describe the predictable dynamics that are bound to occur between those pioneering the new and those preserving the old. We've used it for many years in diverse organizations and communities and now rely on it to know what to expect when we decide to walk out and walk on.

All systems go through life cycles. There's progress, setbacks, seasons. When a new effort begins, it feels like spring. People are excited by new possibilities, innovations and ideas abound, problems get solved, people feel inspired and motivated to contribute. It all works very well, for a time.

And then, especially if there's growth and success, things can start to go downhill. Leaders lose trust in people's ability to self-organize and feel the need to take control, to standardize everything, to issue policies, regulations, and laws. Self-organization gets replaced by over-organization; compliance becomes more important than creativity. Means and ends get reversed, and people struggle to uphold the system rather than having the system support them. These large, lumbering bureaucracies—think about education, health care, government, business—no longer have the capacity to create solutions to the very problems they were created to solve.

When a system reaches this stage of impotence, when it becomes the problem rather than the solution, we as individuals and communities have a choice. Either we struggle to fix and repair the current system, or we create new alternatives. New alternatives can be created either inside or outside the failing system. But if we choose to walk out and walk on, there are two competing roles we're called upon to play: We have to be thoughtful and compassionate in attending to what's dying—we have to be good hospice workers. And we have to be experimenters, pioneers, edge-walkers. Playing these dual roles is never easy, of course, but even so, there are enough people brave enough to do so.

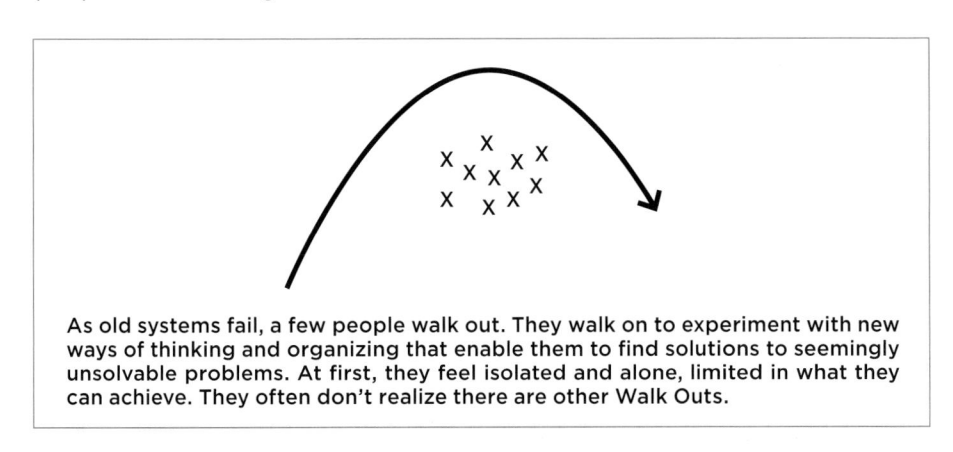

As old systems fail, a few people walk out. They walk on to experiment with new ways of thinking and organizing that enable them to find solutions to seemingly unsolvable problems. At first, they feel isolated and alone, limited in what they can achieve. They often don't realize there are other Walk Outs.

Skilled hospice workers offer comfort and support to those at the end of their lives far beyond attending to physical needs. They help the dying focus on the transition ahead, and encourage them to see what their life has taught them—what wisdom and values shine clearly now that the distractions are gone.

Walk Outs need to do this kind of hospice work on ourselves. Even as we stop struggling to fix things, even as we reject the status quo, we don't leap empty-handed into the future. We need to consciously carry with us the values and practices that feel essential. What have we learned, what do we treasure as the means to create good work, fulfilling lives, meaningful relationships? From our many experiences—the battles, victories, disappointments, successes—we need to glean our hard-won wisdom and preserve it at all costs. This is what we'll most need as we walk out and walk on to give birth to the future.

Inside dying systems, Walk Outs Who Walk On are those few leaders who refuse to work from the dominant values that permeate the bureaucracy, such things as speed, greed, fear, and aggression. They use their formal leadership to champion values and practices that respect people, that rely on people's inherent motivation, creativity, and caring to get quality work done. These leaders consciously create oases or protected areas within the bureaucracy where people can still contribute, protected from the disabling demands of the old system. These leaders are treasures. They're dedicated, thoughtful revolutionaries who work hard to give birth to the new in very difficult circumstances.

And then there are those who leave the system entirely, eager to be free of all constraints to experiment with the future. You'll read their stories in the next pages. But even though they might appear to have more freedom than those still inside, they encounter many challenges that restrict their actions. Old habits and ways of thinking constantly rear up on their path. It's easy to get yanked backward, or to doubt that this is the right direction. It takes vigilance to notice when these old ways of thinking block the path ahead.

Pioneers have to expect to feel ignored, invisible, and lonely a good portion of the time. What they're doing is so new and different that others can't see their work even when it's staring them in the face. These are difficult dynamics to live with, especially when you know you've done good work, that you've solved problems that others are still struggling with. This is why it's so important that pioneers work as community, encouraging one another through the trials and risks natural to those giving birth to the new in the midst of the breakdown of the old.

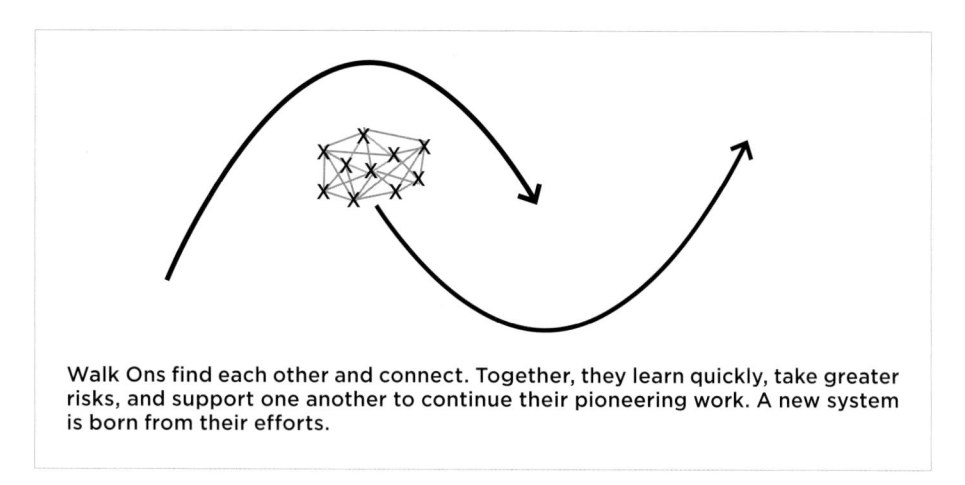

Walk Ons find each other and connect. Together, they learn quickly, take greater risks, and support one another to continue their pioneering work. A new system is born from their efforts.

If you've walked out of confining situations, you've probably experienced at least some of these dynamics. They're easily observable in the lives of innovators and courageous leaders everywhere. They'll be quite notice-able in the stories you're about to read as we journey through these seven communities. In each visit, we'll see how these difficult dynamics lose their power as we work together in community. It's so much easier to keep walking on when we're in the company of kindred spirits.

Before we move on to Mexico, we'd like to talk about packing. How can you travel light but ensure that you have all the essentials for a rich learning experience?

PREPARING TO LEAVE HOME

A Learning Journey can be judged successful by how much it destabilizes and challenges our worldview. If we take the risk to step into a world very different from our own, we discover that our particular way of seeing is incomplete, that there are many more ways to see and interpret what's going on in life. We can discover that judgments and assumptions often limit our ability to see new possibilities.

Most traditions and cultures have initiation rituals that require setting out in order to be transformed. We willingly and bravely undertake a quest. We leave the comforts and safety of home, travel to strange and unfamiliar lands, and are welcomed to return only after we've discovered answers to our quest that we're prepared to put into practice.

This Learning Journey in book form might not seem to be asking that much of you. You're probably reading this in familiar surroundings. But don't be fooled. You won't be tested by the demons and dragons of old, but you might well be confronted by your beliefs and assumptions, internal demons that may rear up to block your path, or warn you to turn back, preventing you from reaching lands of new possibility.

THE COURAGE TO QUEST

Quests begin with a yearning that won't let us go. These questions of profound longing can be deceptively simple: "Why can't people be more kind?" "Why can't we work together better?" "Why are so many people unhappy?" "Does life have to be so hard?"

Behind these questions—perhaps the reason we're brave enough to ask them—is a deep intuition that things could be better, that life doesn't have to be this way. This sense that more is possible can propel us beyond the safety of our daily routines, the security of our habitual ways of thinking, and send us out into the world to find answers.

Leaving home takes courage. We have to be brave enough to explore our questions, to cultivate our dissatisfaction with the present state of things, to notice what disturbs us, what feels unfair, terrible, heartbreaking. We have to be unafraid to look reality in the eye and notice what's really going on. If what we see opens our hearts, this is a good thing, because that's where our courage is found. With open hearts, we can bravely begin searching. We can go into the world with our questions, carried by our yearning to find a simpler and more effective way to live life and to benefit more people.

Here are a few questions that we offer to engage you as a learner. They're designed to help you notice what you notice in your world. Among all possible information and situations, we only observe a miniscule percentage of what's happening. As you notice what gets your attention, you can also see your filters.

What issues consistently get your attention? Which ones make you angry? Which ones make you excited?

Have you glimpsed or experienced a future that inspires and motivates you?

Who do you want to be for this world? What is the contribution you hope to make?

Are you willing to risk being changed by this journey?

PACKING FOR THE JOURNEY

As with any journey, it's better to pack light. For this particular trip, since you're sitting someplace comfortable, the only baggage you need to attend to is what you're carrying in your mind. By this stage in our lives, we each have a well-developed lens for viewing the world. We began constructing this lens as young children from the beliefs and assumptions taught by our families and culture. Throughout most of our lives, we polish and refine this lens with our experiences—the good, the bad, the ugly, the sublime.

As we rush about our lives, preoccupied with tasks and responsibilities, it becomes easy to forget that how we see the world is just one of many possible interpretations. We settle into our opinions and judgments, and assume that everyone else sees things the same way. But if this were true, we wouldn't get into arguments or difficulties with our partners, colleagues, leaders.

When we enter a new culture, we can expect to feel surprised, confused, disrupted. These are promising feelings, because they offer us a choice. Either we can retreat to the safety of our familiar opinions, or we can become curious. If we're willing to be disturbed, we can try to let go of our judgments and confess that we don't understand what we're seeing.

Confusing moments are wonderful opportunities to observe our minds more closely. If something's provoked or startled me, it's because I assumed something different was true. I thought things worked like this, but now I'm not so sure. . . .

- I thought material well-being made people happy, yet I'm sitting with people who have no material goods and we're feeling very happy, just because we're together, sharing stories.
- I expected that good community leaders had to be formally trained and developed, yet here I am meeting dozens of people, some with no education, who are bright and capable leaders, skilled at engaging others and getting work done.
- I believed that social entrepreneurs were a rare breed of people, yet here everyone I meet seems to have ideas and is thinking about the next project or dream.
- I assumed that our methods of planning, budgeting, and strategizing were necessary to get anything done, yet here I'm meeting highly motivated people who are accomplishing great work without doing any of those activities.

As we journey together, we encourage you to welcome those moments when you feel confronted, surprised. Each one is an opportunity to see your own mind, to notice your beliefs and assumptions. And to be open to change.

Now let's begin.

A LEARNING JOURNEY INTO COMMUNITIES

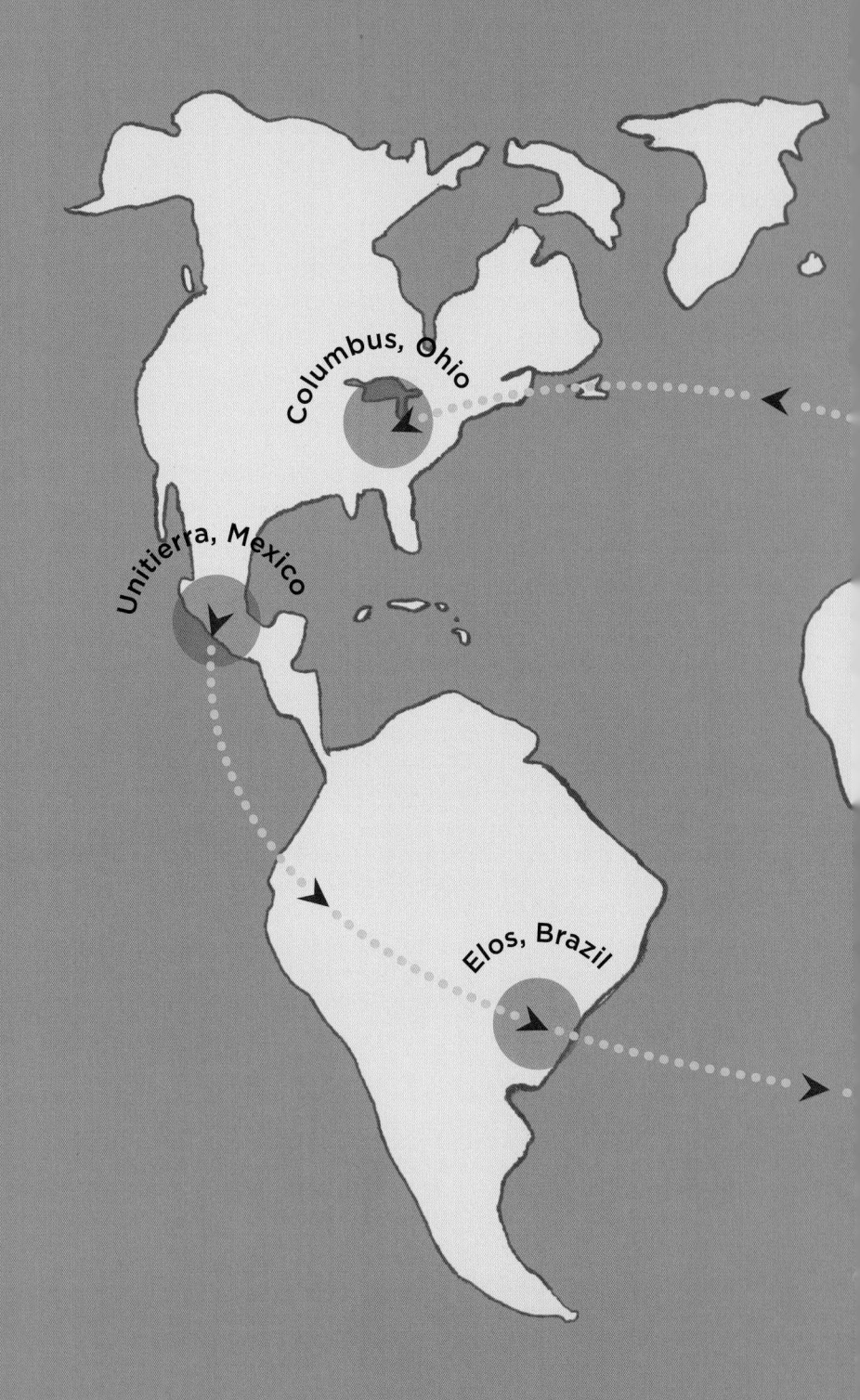

DARING TO LIVE THE FUTURE NOW

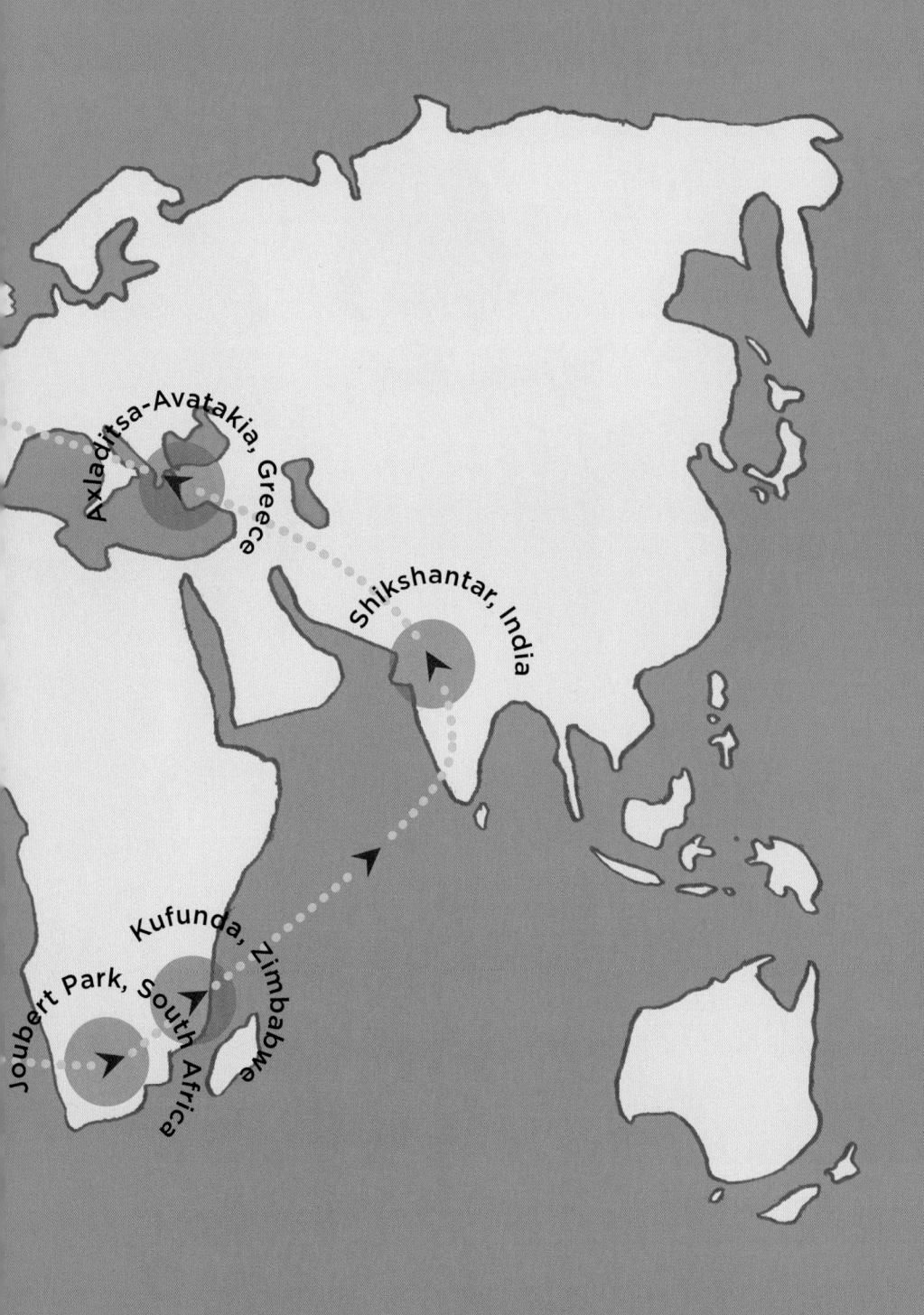

PART II
JOURNEYING

UNITIERRA, MEXICO
FROM SCALING UP TO SCALING ACROSS

We are rehearsing the beginning of the construction of a new world, a good one; a world in which many worlds can be together.

—*Zapatista saying*

There are stories in this woman's eyes that gaze out at you from beneath the black ski mask that guards her face. There are layers of stories that have accumulated over time, like molting skins. This one began on January 1, 1994, when the Zapatista army rose up against the Mexican government to protest the launch of NAFTA (the North American Free Trade Agreement)—an act, the Zapatistas believed, that would endanger indigenous peoples' rights to their land and sacrifice their autonomy and traditional way of life in the name of progress. This first story uncoils itself when you arrive at this woman's village of Oventic, about forty miles from San Cristóbal de las Casas, the sixteenth-century Spanish colonial city of Chiapas, Mexico. *The Mexican government wants to control me, but I am Tzotzil, descendent of the Mayan people. I was here long before the Mexicans.*

There is another story in her eyes just beneath the first that tells you she is a survivor. *My land was colonized when the Spaniards came. I have survived the diseases you brought with you. I have labored under your command. But I am still Tzotzil, descendent of the Mayan people. I was here long before the Spanish.*

And another. *I fought against the Aztecs and lost, and now I pay tribute to them. But I am still Tzotzil, descendent of the Mayan people. I was here long before the Aztecs.*

FROM SCALING UP TO SCALING ACROSS

I am Tzotzil, a cultivator of corn. I live in harmony with many other ethnic groups that share our fertile highlands. Our languages are different. Our traditions are different. But we honor one another's culture. My land and culture are rich—no matter that you tell me I am poor.

I am Zapatista, I am Tzotzil, I am Mayan, I am Olmec, the bearer of the mother culture of Mesoamerican civilization. All of this is who I am. If you come to my village, you must learn who I am.

THREE STRANDS

Everything for everyone, nothing for us; we are the road, then, we must follow ourselves.

—Zapatista saying

In the beginning of the world, the Goddess of the Moon taught women to weave. She gave them designs in their dreams, and they plaited the strands of time, space, and the forces of nature. Time itself traveled on multiple paths, weaving a paradox of linear and cyclical passages in its wake. This is a Mayan world, a Mesoamerican intermingling of the material and the supernatural, the pragmatic and the magical. If you find yourself lost, stay where you are and surrender: You have entered a different land.

And so your journey here in Oaxaca and Chiapas, the two southern-most states of Mexico, will weave three strands. Observe the wisdom of *Zapatismo*, that philosophy of resistance that is rooted in the indigenous heritage of place. Listen for the sound of *Unitierra*, a name claimed by those who embrace autonomy and friendship. Follow the movement of *bicimáquinas*, the inventive bicycle-powered machines, as they ramble through Mexico and beyond.

Watch for all these. Whenever one is in the foreground, know that the others are here, too, in the background. Like the image of the vase and the two faces—wherever you put your attention, that's what you'll see. But know that everything else is present also.

Is it too much? Mexico is like this. It is not the land you've been trained to see: *Men with long mustaches wearing sombreros. Dirty streets with drug deals on dark corners. Bandidos, tequila, machismo. Farm workers. Violence. Corruption.* That is a Westernized caricature being lived out today in the stories that travel northward. And we in the north spin back the mythical antidote of fighting crime and corruption with development, of advancing and creating wealth so that citizens can obtain higher and higher levels of consumption.

There's another Mexico, says Mexican anthropologist Guillermo Bonfil Batalla: the *México profundo*, a land formed by a great diversity of people who are the bearers of ways of understanding the world and of organizing human life that have their origins in Mesoamerican civilization.[4] They speak many languages and honor many traditions. Over millennia, they have created and re-created their culture, adjusting to foreign pressure by assimilating some practices and spitting others back out. Their land is sacred, as it is the resting place of their ancestors, and they will organize to sustain it—which at times means they must fight, and at times means they must become invisible.

As we journey through this land, we also will move in and out of time. Sometimes you will think you're in the present, only to discover you're actually mining the past, and then suddenly the spirit of the future has made its presence felt. What is happening to time? You can't track it here.

Which is why Mexico is the perfect place to explore the question of how small changes become large ones—how systems get to scale. Because when we seek to scale things up, we move vertically, we presume linear time, we build on what has come before. But constant forward progress is an illusion. In reality, life is cyclical, undulating in loops and waves, two steps forward, one step back—and a whole lot of steps sideways.

This Zapatista woman will reveal her story, but not her face. You will be introduced to her by Sergio Beltrán of Unitierra, your host in Oaxaca and Chiapas.

FROM SCALING UP TO SCALING ACROSS

My first visit to Oaxaca was in May 2006. As an American, I thought I knew Mexico. I'd been there before, I'd entered into the lives and stories of many Mexicans, I'd read up on the issues and challenges between us and our southern neighbor—NAFTA, immigration, the war on drugs. I'd studied Mexico's rich indigenous heritage, learned about Mayan culture, visited its astonishing ruins.

And yet, all I had ever experienced was what Guillermo Bonfil Batalla calls the *imaginary Mexico*, a nation developing itself in the image of the West, suppressing its Mesoamerican heritage. In Oaxaca and Chiapas, encountering indigenous people is not a historical or anthropological exercise. The *Mexico profundo*, a civilization other than ours, is as contemporary and real as anything Western civilization has created—it's just, as the Zapatistas say, another world. It's a world that governs itself differently, organizes around collective work, recognizes its interdependence with the land. It's a world that has evolved its systems of health, education, and economy throughout centuries of learning.

After several trips to Mexico and experiencing many different expressions of human creativity, I am left with the question: Which kind of world am I contributing to creating?

Deborah

RECLAIMING THE FREEDOM TO LEARN

Take any bus headed north on Heroico Colegio Militar street in downtown Oaxaca. Get off at Escuela Naval Militar. Walk four blocks to the right. Turn right at Azucenas. Three-quarters of a block down on the left-hand side, you'll find a former private home painted terracotta brown that has high windows with metal bars. Go inside.

Welcome to Universidad de la Tierra, Unitierra for short. This is a space in which magic happens. It looks absolutely ordinary, doesn't it? That's because magic is invisible.

Over here on your left is the coffeepot and the telltale stains of mugs left too long unattended. On your right is the main room with the long table dappled in sunlight that pours through the cane ceiling. There are more rooms in the back and a set of stairs leading up to the roof.

Three young men are crouched over a computer screen; they are editing a film about the 2006 teachers' strike that led to a populist uprising in Oaxaca City. Another two friends in a dark corner lean in toward each other, their heads nearly touching as their voices rise in a heated discussion, punctuated by words like *autonomía*, *democracia,* and *libertad* (autonomy, democracy, and liberty). A young woman sits alone folding small rectangles of chocolate into paper envelopes. These are students of this university. They have no teachers, they follow no curriculum, and they receive no degrees.

It is hard to explain something that is daily rewritten.

This is the explanation offered by Sergio Beltrán, your host at Unitierra. His grin is earnest and mischievous, just like this peculiar place that is equal parts prankster and sage. Learners at Unitierra follow a self-directed path. They choose a topic, find learning partners, and proceed at their own pace. At any given time, Unitierra simply is that unique cocktail of energies that are flowing through the space, re-created every day through learners' experiences and interactions. What unites the learners is a belief that learning is practiced for the sheer joy of it—rather than to acquire certification or secure a job. Learning occurs when we engage with the world, in friendship with others, using our hands and wits and reflecting on our discoveries.

Some see Unitierra as a social movement, a protest to dominant forms of schooling that are leaving many young people behind. Sergio sees it more as a mood, a way of doing and thinking that provides another option to learners who are seeking to discover things for themselves. Learning is not about getting it right or becoming the expert; it is about creating an environment of conviviality, discovery, and joyfulness.

Never mind explaining it—let's take a look. Walk back toward the stairwell that takes you to the roof. The first thing you'll encounter is a human-sized wooden cabin with a decorative mandala embedded in the side wall. A single step leads up to a platform that sits atop a steel drum and some plastic jugs. Inside is a dry composting toilet, one that separates liquid and solid waste—both of which can be used as fertilizer. Separating the two forms of waste reduces odors and flies, making these toilets more suitable for indoor use. This one was built by the CACITA crew, whom you'll meet later, and has since evolved into a new, portable design that surfaces at workshops and festivals so people can learn about an alternative approach to handling their waste.

Next to the dry toilet is the *bicibomba*, a bicycle-powered water pump that has transformed the daily work of RASA, the group of friends who have commandeered the rooftop for their explorations in urban agriculture. Short for Red Autónoma para la Soberanía Alimentaria (Autonomous Network for Food Sovereignty), RASA is connecting urban gardeners throughout

Oaxaca who are learning how to produce food through back-yard and rooftop gardens. Now, instead of having to tap electricity to access water on the roof, a member of the RASA team goes for a spin on the bicibomba to pump water directly to the roof. The water travels in little rubber cups attached to a rope running through a PVC pipe and is then dumped in a reservoir. Once you arrive upstairs, behold the bounty of urban agriculture. Tomatoes, cucumbers, carrots, squash, and beans grow in planters made from discarded vegetable crates and empty water bottles. Peas and lettuce are sprouting in bisected PVC tubing. Be careful not to stumble over the giant solar roaster. It's made from welded metal and mirrors, and it churns out the roasted cacao beans of Chocosol organic chocolate that tastes like sunshine and joy and the Lacandón jungle where the cacao beans grow.

RASA is not only about inventing technologies for urban agriculture. It's about weaving together people who wish to reunite *Oaxaqueños* with their food sovereignty, which means their right to decide for themselves what they eat and their ability to produce it. They do this by inviting people to share their skills, to garden together, and to have a good time. In the language of Unitierra, what RASA is up to is *co-motion* rather than *promotion:* spreading ideas through contagion rather than pushing people in a particular direction.[5] Co-motion is walking at the pace of the other, rather than at whatever pace you want to go. It is a horizontal movement that begins with being rooted in your own purpose and place, and then connects with others who are rooted in theirs. There is no monolithic approach to this work, there is no centralization of power, there is no ownership of ideas. Instead, the network is engaged in continuous creation and re-creation, in self-discovery, and in adaptation.

RASA grows food and flowers in discarded containers on Unitierra's roof. The *bicibomba* pumps water up to the rooftop garden.

RASA is not Unitierra—if you're thinking of Unitierra as a thing, as an institution—but it is an impeccable expression of Unitierra's beliefs and purpose, a cluster of people and ideas that together are reclaiming the freedom to learn. And so is CACITA, as we're about to discover.

THE PIRATE SHIP

Mexico has its metaphors all mixed up, you might think, as Drakula welcomes you to the Pirate Ship, which is some sort of junkyard candyland where boys wander around like lords of the flies, and you're certain you've fallen down the rabbit hole (or at least taken the blue pill). This is CACITA, the Autonomous Centre for the Intercultural Creation of Appropriate Technologies, and it floats on an 8- by-20-meter piece of property in San Pablo Etla, about twenty minutes from Unitierra.

Here, on this tiny parcel of land, you discover that there are bicycle-powered machines, solar ovens, dry compost toilets, humanure and vermicomposting (ways of harvesting organic waste as fertilizer), rainwater catchment systems, small-scale urban agriculture and ecobuilding projects, recycled alternative fuels, and even a bit of wind power. Originally conceived in conversations among friends at Unitierra, CACITA is another expression of the commitment to strengthening the autonomous learning capacity of people, communities, and neighborhoods to generate economic and social self-sufficiency.

With its wind-ruffled tarp for shade and its slanted roof and walls assembled from a patchwork of billboards, siding, and fractured paneling, the Pirate Ship wields its nickname with pride—and more than just visual integrity. This is a place of constant motion, where a crew of clever men experiment just beyond the margins of conventional life. Rumors spread about Captain Drakula, whose real name may be Eric, and you overhear in whispers words like "bodyguard" and "Subcomandante Marcos"—it might be best not to ask any questions.

Chivo, short for "dirty goat," is brandishing a machete and offering you chunks of coconut that he's hacked off in an expression of hospitality. At night, he sleeps on sacks of cacao beans stacked five feet high, filling his dreams with solar-roasted chocolate ground by bicycle power and distributed from Oaxaca all the way north to Toronto.

One of the members of this motley crew is Daniel Perera, a Guatemalan who sounds like an American, lives like a Mexican, and travels like a nomad. Altogether too handsome for his own good, Daniel is our trans-local protagonist. *Trans-local,* you ask? Let us explain.

Suppose that there are no universal solutions to global problems—like poverty, hunger, or environmental destruction. Suppose that the kind of large-scale systems change that many of us have been yearning for emerges when local actions get connected globally—while preserving their deeply local culture, flavor, and form. What if people working at the local level were able to learn from one another, practice together, and share their knowl-edge—freely and fluidly—with communities anywhere? This is the nature of trans-local learning, and it happens when separate, local efforts connect with each other, then grow and transform as people exchange ideas that together give rise to new systems with greater impact and influence.

And so Daniel tells you a story that begins in Guatemala, where he met Carlos Marroquín of Maya Pedal. Carlos and his colleagues conceived of bicimáquinas back in 1997, when they recognized that salvaged bicycles could be reconstituted into human-powered machines that grind corn and cacao, pump water, sharpen metal, blend beverages—and ultimately wash clothing, generate electricity, plow soil, and saw wood. Maya Pedal's in-tention was to contribute to environmental conservation while supporting local family economies. Its commitment was to give away all its knowledge freely so that many other friends and partners could participate in the evolution and diffusion of the ideas.

Daniel returned to Oaxaca City carrying a few photos and the concept of a *bicimolino,* a bicycle-powered mill, that could help ease the task of grinding cacao beans that he, Chivo, Drakula, and a few others were using

At the Pirate Ship, a crew of clever men experiment just beyond the margins of conventional life. Drakula repairs a *bicimáquina.*

to make solar-roasted Oaxacan chocolate. What he did not carry with him was a blueprint—or any design documents at all, for that matter—on how to build the bicimolino. Based on Daniel's memory, a few rough photos and a spirit of bricolage (a do-it-yourself process of assembling something out of the materials at hand), the trio set about making it up. The early models were clunkers—heavy, slow, and not exactly a smooth ride. But over time, through ongoing experimentation and occasional input from Carlos, the bicimáquina designs became increasingly graceful and more complex. The CACITA crew offered their designs to youth in villages and schools, leaving behind the models that the learners built so they could continue to adapt and improve them until bicimáquinas began appearing like scattered seeds among communities throughout Oaxaca and Chiapas.

And beyond. In fact, Daniel has been invited to India to carry the bicimáquina seed even farther afield. But before you hear the next part of his story, we'll travel onward, south to San Cristóbal de las Casas in Chiapas, where we'll encounter a second Unitierra.

The term *trans-local learning* arose in conversation with the members of the Berkana Exchange. We were talking about being a global learning community, connecting our projects from Mexico to Brazil to India to Zimbabwe and beyond. But something didn't ring quite true. For many of us, the word *global* implied universality, a single solution, product, or ideology that could be applied anywhere, regardless of place, people, or culture. This was the "global" of multinational corporations, of free trade, of economic development. We were not against globalization; in fact, we believed that the only way large-scale change could happen is by inviting ideas and resources to flow around the globe. But we believed that for an idea or innovation to be meaningful and lasting, it needed to arise from the unique conditions of people and place. As Meg Wheatley often reminded us at our gatherings, people only support what they create.

We embraced the term *trans-local* to represent what happens when people carry an idea from one place to another and set it loose in a new local environment, allowing it to emerge into something entirely different. We would learn together trans-locally by offering one another our stories, experiments, and dreams—like Daniel, who in his journey to India carried with him the idea of bicimáquinas, rather than the how-to manual for building the machines.

Deborah

FROM SCALING UP TO SCALING ACROSS

ANOTHER WORLD IS POSSIBLE

This second Unitierra—Unitierra-Chiapas—resides deep in the heart of the land that gave birth to *Zapatismo*, the movement that believes it is possible to create a world in which many worlds can be embraced. It goes by the name CIDECI, the Center for Indigenous Training.[6]

It is impossible to avoid noticing the politics of this place. As you approach the entryway to CIDECI, a buoyant mural proclaims its allegiance with the Zapatista movement: a two-story building of turquoise and red brick bursts into view, populated with brown faces and white eyes that peer out over bandanas and through ski masks; the bold red star of the EZLN flag (EZLN stands for Ejército Zapatista de Liberación Nacional, the official name of the Zapatista Army of National Liberation) cradled in the hands of community. Even the campus generator radiates ideology on its muraled walls: *"Luz y fuerza libre—autonomía para iluminar la esperanza."* Free light and power—autonomy to illuminate hope.

San Cristóbal was one of four cities that the Zapatistas seized in January 1994. Although the Mexican army swiftly pushed them back into the countryside, the movement and its spirit burrowed into the soil of this place, where it has been tenderly cultivated by the local people, many of whom are indigenous. Here, says CIDECI founder Dr. Raymundo Sánchez Barraza, is the nutrient content of the soil on campus: *resistancia, autonomía, sobrevivencia, reciprocidad, democracia radical. Radical democracy* rejects established political power, working instead with the forces of self-determination. *Reciprocity* rejects market forces in favor of a gift culture that exchanges learning for love and labor. *Surviving* and *resisting* are the roots of social movements all over the world that have sustained their indigenous heritage in the face of dominant forces that develop and commodify culture.

Yes, says Raymundo, an impassioned and grave man in his sixties who occasionally pounds the table with his fist, another world is possible. And it is young indigenous learners who are building it. More than eight hundred of them come each year to this Unitierra, most of whom walked out of school or had none to start with. There are no formal educational requirements; there is no tuition. But students here must maintain the space, offering their time to clearing trails, tending the rabbits and ducks, preparing meals, putting in windows. They may come for fifteen days, or a month, or a season, or a year. They may live here or go back home to their pueblo. They'll decide what they learn, although they'll likely begin with something practical, like woodworking, welding, farming, baking, weaving, or typing. The pedagogy, says Raymundo, is learn to *do*, then learn to *learn*, then *consider the other in his or her entirety*. The purpose is afterward to go back home to strengthen their local community.

He tells you this in a spacious courtyard room with bright yellow columns and sunlight streaming in. You sit around the edges of a heavy, wooden table decorated with Mesoamerican motifs that has been carved by the woodworking students. Nearly everything on this campus is made from natural materials—wood, brick, adobe, stone—that have been lovingly crafted by learners. The campus itself oozes vitality, nestled as it is into the lush green of a mountainside and dotted with log cabins, flower gardens, greenhouses, beehives, and colorful textiles. There is even a bici-bomba down by the pond that pumps water to the wells. And murals, everywhere murals, matched in their radiance only by the traditional dress of the women learners, with their dark blue or green shifts beneath a lacy pinafore of ribbons—red, yellow, green, pink, and blue.

To name is to make visible. CIDECI was operating long before they claimed the name Unitierra-Chiapas. But when they spoke with their friends in Oaxaca City, they recognized themselves in the other. *If knowledge is being produced and disseminated here*, they asked, *then aren't we a university, too? A university without shoes, of course, a shoeless university just from below.*[7] (This is a reference to the Barefoot movement, which has its roots among health workers in China and became the inspiration for the Barefoot College, a trans-local movement pioneered in India to give the rural poor—the "barefoot"—an opportunity to experiment with their own solutions to poverty and inequity.)

Unitierra-Chiapas is steeped in *Zapatismo*. Here, indigenous students learn to "consider the other in his or her entirety."

FROM SCALING UP TO SCALING ACROSS

And it was so. CIDECI became another Unitierra. Nothing had to change. There were no transactions. There was no written agreement. No one got involved in merging accounts, reconciling practices, or reevaluating policies. There was simply a declaration: We share a commitment to cultivate learning, friendship, and communal self-care. We each do this in our own best way.

Other places have claimed Unitierra's name. There is Unitierra-Istmo, located in the narrow stretch of land that separates the Gulf of Mexico from the Pacific Ocean. In Mexico City, another group had been at work on alternative learning models long before it, too, christened itself Unitierra. And a fifth Unitierra today is emerging among Chicano (U.S. citizens of Mexican descent) communities throughout California.

This is *scaling across*: releasing knowledge, practices, and resources, and allowing them to circulate freely so that others may adapt them to their local environment. The appearance of Unitierra in its many different forms is a powerful example of self-organization, where people working from the same principles create practices that reflect the uniqueness of their community and culture. This horizontal phenomenon of scaling across may have something to do, perhaps, with the surprising popularity of the Zapatista movement.

AN ARMY THAT FIRES WORDS

Sergio of Unitierra has arranged your papers for a visit to Oventic, one of the Zapatista autonomous communities. In the hour's drive from San Cristóbal, you climb deeper into the rolling highlands of central Chiapas, passing homesteads and sloped cornfields. The heavy mist makes everything luminously green—pine and oak forests interrupted by limestone springs fed by underground rivers. As you climb into the clouds, you pass signs reading, "You are in Zapatista Territory in rebellion. Here the people rule and the government obeys."

Your entry is not certain: When you arrive, you will be interviewed by the Junta de Buen Gobierno, the Council of Good Government, to determine whether you will be received. For this is a rebel region, one of five *caracoles* that make up the heart of the Zapatista movement. The *caracol* is the spiral shell of the snail or conch, and in Mayan legend it was used to alert villagers to evil. For the Zapatistas, the caracol is where they claim their autonomy, where they organize the world they wish for. It's also the place from where their message goes out to the rest of the world—and so they do receive us. We will carry their message far beyond the Chiapas highlands.

A wide road cuts a steep path through the village, lined with small square homes made of wooden planks topped with corrugated tin roofs. Their facades are the billboards of the movement, featuring bold murals that proclaim the slogans of Zapatismo—and broadcast the services inside. You stand now in front of the Casa de Junta del Buen Gobierno, waiting to be received.

You are offered a seat on a long wooden bench. Two women and two men in black ski masks sit behind a table. Against the wall behind them is a black Zapatista flag with hand-sewn red satin lettering spelling out *Democracia, Libertad, Justicia* (Democracy, Liberty, Justice) over the EZLN red star. They ask about the reason for your visit. Someone responds, *I am here to learn so that I can share your story.*

You are welcome here and sent to meet two members of the political council, who will tell you the story of this place—its history, its ideology, its practices. They tell you about the central health clinic that provides free treatment and medication. They tell you about the school, where the lessons have been designed by the community, and the older students become teachers of the younger ones. They tell you about the cooperatives for coffee and handicrafts, where women work collectively to sell their textiles. You visit each of these places, and at every stop, their story is told to you anew.

The more you hear the story, the less sense it may make. You are assaulted by one paradox after another. *"The mountains told us to take up arms so we would have a voice. It told us to cover our faces so we would*

Oventic is blanketed in murals and signs. This one reads, "You are in Zapatista Territory in rebellion. Here the people rule and the government obeys."

FROM SCALING UP TO SCALING ACROSS

have a face. It told us to forget our names so we could be named. It told us to protect our past so we would have a future."[8] Here is an army that fires words instead of weapons, a revolutionary group with no interest in seizing power, a people who make themselves invisible so as to be seen.

Are you lost, are you lost in this place? It's a story that defies logic. And yet somehow this story has wound its way around the world like few others. This provincial movement has mobilized people in more than a hundred countries to initiate meetings and projects; two Italian villages declared themselves Zapatistas, saying that the Zapatista struggle is also their own[9]; the internationally known rock band Rage Against the Machine took up the cause in their music and on concert tours, calling upon audiences worldwide to declare solidarity. The poetry of the movement—gifted through more than two hundred essays and twenty-one books authored by Subcomandante Marcos—has blazed across the Internet. Yes, Zapatismo has attracted the anarchists, the agitators, and the malcontents. But it also has attracted those who yearn for participatory democracy, for civic engagement, for egalitarianism, and for social justice.

Something about this movement has stirred humanity's imagination. What if that something is invisible? What if a movement spreads, not because we can replicate the conditions from here to there, but because of something entirely unseen? Let's pause now to take a look at the deeper pattern.

FROM SCALING UP TO SCALING ACROSS

French winemakers use the term *terroir* to describe the unique characteristics that place bestows on each varietal. It is what makes us desire champagne from France, coffee from Kenya, cigars from Cuba, and sourdough from San Francisco. The word itself means something like "a sense of place," which emerges from the unique qualities of soil, climate, and topography. Just ask any Napa winemaker who's ever tried to imitate a Burgundy or Chianti, and they'll tell you: Cultivate the same grapes, use the same techniques, follow the same timing—and your wine is guaranteed to taste nothing like the original.

Modern winemakers have learned to embrace the notion of scaling across: the movement around the world of winemaking practices and techniques that have preserved deep reverence for the uniqueness of place, for the gift of terroir that today has generated bountiful flavors, styles, and vintages on five continents.

But respect for the invisible forces of place—to which we could add its social and cultural heritage—is hardly conventional wisdom when it comes to taking things to scale. More often, in fact, we find ourselves confronted with the suppression of the local—consider the uniformity of any Starbucks, McDonald's, or Wal-Mart. From Seattle to Singapore, we homogenize culture by subsuming local flavor through standardization and replication. This is what *scaling up* is about: We patent a product, standardize a process, franchise a formula. That's the recipe for success in a global economy that idolizes—and idealizes—growth. Take, for example, this quote from *Harvard Business Review* about scaling up:

> [There are] five steps for successful replication. First, make sure you've got something that can be copied and that's worth copying. Second, work from a single template. It provides proof of success, performance measurements, a tactical approach, and a reference for when problems arise. Third, copy the example exactly, and fourth, make changes only after you achieve acceptable results. Fifth, don't throw away the template.[10]

Scaling up creates a monoculture that relies on replication, standardization, promotion, and compliance. It's easy to make the case for this strategy in the context of consumer culture. Businesses all over the world encourage people to consume their beverages, buy their merchandise, watch their movies. Despite the fact that community is inherently local, most people engaged in community change nonetheless aspire to follow in the footsteps of big business by scaling up, expanding programs, and rolling out offices in new geographies. They pursue the coveted strategy of disseminating best practices, which holds that what has been invented and perfected in one place can be parachuted or transplanted into another. This view assumes that organizations are machines, and to improve them, we just need to swap out the old parts for new and improved ones, or install new software. In other words, conventional wisdom tells us to use the same irrigation, measure out the same slant of hillside, and plonk down our grapes. And then somehow we're surprised when the wine tastes bad.

Fortunately, community is nothing like a machine, and citizens rarely surrender their autonomy to the experts' advice. In fact, it only takes a little bit of digging to discover that even in corporations, exchanging best practices often doesn't work. What does work is when teams from one organization travel to another and, through that experience, see themselves more clearly, strengthen their relationships, and renew their creativity. Like a Learning Journey, these are the visits that disrupt our old ways of seeing and widen our view of what's possible.

Trans-local learning is exactly how Maya Pedal and Unitierra and the Zapatistas are spreading their word. The bicimáquinas are traveling the world as a product without a patent, a machine without a manual. Friends and strangers alike are invited to adapt and evolve the designs, to find new uses for the concept. Unitierra has done the same with its name, which spreads through Mexico based on a set of beliefs about learning, autonomy, and community—and a commitment to the local, to the unique properties of place. Zapatismo has wound its way into the hearts of many peoples around the world—even though, or perhaps because, all they wish for is the right to choose how to live at home.

Scaling across happens when people create something locally and inspire others who carry the idea home and develop it in their own unique way. But releasing our grip on its shape can be difficult, which is exactly what Daniel, whom we met at the Pirate Ship, is discovering in his journey through India.

When I was in business school, "scaling up" was how most of us thought about growth. We understood it to mean adding more parts where the parts all look the same. And we assumed that most systems were ripe for replication, that one size could fit all. It hadn't occurred to me at the time that this approach was problematic—especially in the context of communities.

Many times in the process of sharing Berkana's story, I have been asked to explain how we intended to take our work to scale—that is, what aspect of our programs could be replicated from one community to the next? I, too, yearned for an easy and efficient way to demonstrate that our work was having a meaningful impact. I, too, wished that the notion of scaling up could be applied to people and communities.

But a single model cannot account for the differences between urban and rural communities or between Mexicans and Americans. In the context of community change, our work is to foster networks of relationships through which ideas and beliefs can travel, adapt, evolve, and grow. We're not ignoring scaling up; we're resisting it because we've found that for most communities, it doesn't work. Scaling across invites communities to learn from one another and solve their own problems in their own particular way.

Deborah

SCALING ACROSS FROM MEXICO TO INDIA

Behind our black mask,
Behind our armed voice,
Behind our unnameable name,
Behind us, who you see,
Behind us, we are you.

Behind we are the same simple and ordinary men and women,
who are repeated in all races,
painted in all colors,
speak in all languages
and live in all places.

The same forgotten men and women.
The same excluded,
The same intolerated,
The same persecuted,
We are you.

—*Subcomandante Marcos*[11]

Daniel had been invited to India by Manish Jain of Shikshantar, a learning center based in Udaipur, Rajasthan. A friend and learning partner of Unitierra, Manish had visited Oaxaca in 2006 and was eager to explore the use of bicimáquinas in his community. Shikshantar was immersed in its own experimentation around *kabaad se jugaad*, the transformation of garbage (*kabaad*) into things that are useful, durable and beautiful—such as solar cookers, handicrafts, clothes and bags. *Jugaad* is ingenuity, an invitation to the imagination to play and invent new solutions using whatever is right in front of you. For Shikshantar, bicimáquinas seemed a promising new expression of this spirit of kabaad se jugaad.

For Daniel, the learning exchange was an opportunity to spread the bicimáquina word, Johnny Appleseed–like, to a whole new continent. But it didn't go exactly as planned. It was quite a shock, for instance, to discover that in India there are no bicycles to spare for conversion into stationary machines!

Here are Daniel's reflections, in his words:

I'm excited to announce that we have developed a new and improved *bicilicuadora* (bicycle-powered blender). People here call it the "cycle-mixie," and there are two wonderful novelties about it: It is *much* cheaper than the one we've been making in Oaxaca and Guatemala, and—this is the best part—it still functions as a bicycle! We're confident that people anywhere can think of and create new applications and local adaptations out of this simple and clever technology.

I'm really impressed by the way we built it. Frankly, I was skeptical when I asked Panji, Vishal, Nirmal and Ram where the tools were, and they brought out a screwdriver, a handsaw, a file, a couple of wrenches, and a hammer. I've gotten used to working in a fully equipped workshop in Oaxaca that has a large work table, welding machine, vertical drill, table saw, angle grinder and the standard instruments you find in a toolbox. At CACITA, we usually ask for these conditions to be met prior to organizing any workshop. This was going to prove to be quite a challenge.

At Shikshantar, the starting point was inverted. We began by asking, "How can we build a cycle-mixie with what we have?" rather than, "Where do we get what we need in order to build the *bicilicuadora* I know how to make?" As a result, the machine we built was entirely new, and the workshop became more than technology transfer. It was a creative process of people locally adapting a tool in a way that made sense to them. I'm now confident that we could do this even with more complex machines, such as the *bicibomba*.

A few weeks later, we designed and built a new and improved bicycle-powered washing machine and launched it during a *mela* [fair] last Saturday. Based on a Maya Pedal design, we wanted it to be lighter, simpler, cheaper, and more effective. I think we pulled it off. The most satisfying part of this process is to know that it has triggered something that is just beginning: a collaborative effort that I hope will transcend borders, oceans and the vast distances that separate us. I intend to maintain this working discussion and playful dialogue with Panji and Vishal—from Mexico and Guatemala to India and back. My hope is that we can continue to imagine, develop and put to use new prototypes, share ideas, give each other advice and support in working with low-tech, appropriate tools, and continue to reflect together on the role of technology in development.[12]

Is it difficult to imagine that a dozen bicimáquinas will ever amount to anything? That five Unitierras can alter the landscape of education? Too often, cynicism trumps evidence. Because there is story after story after story of small local actions that scaled across—without planning, without control—and became large-scale movements. And nobody could have predicted that those small beginnings would lead to great changes.

What these many success stories reveal is that change happens differently than many of us imagine. It doesn't happen from top-down support, or elaborate plans, or from the best-practice or franchise model. It happens as small local efforts create and develop solutions that then travel freely through networks of relationship. Each community works from the same principles, yet what manifests from local ingenuity are designs and innovations that look very different and that are beautifully adapted to work well in their own environment.

This is often how change happens—even those huge, global successes that receive prestigious awards. In 2004, Wangari Maathai won the Nobel Peace Prize for her work in organizing the Greenbelt Movement, which had planted over thirty million trees in Kenya and East Africa. Wangari was a biology professor at the University of Nairobi in Kenya. In a meeting with other Kenyan women, she learned that the fertile and forested land of her youth had been devastated. All the trees had been cut down for coffee and tea plantations. Local women had to walk miles for firewood, and the water had become polluted with chemicals and run-off from the plantations.

She knew that the solution to the plight of these women was to plant trees, to reforest the land. So she and a few women decided to begin immediately. They went to a large park in Nairobi and planted seven trees—five of which died. (The two that survived are still there today.) Their initial success rate was 28.5 percent, discouraging by anybody's standards. But they didn't give up. They learned from that experience, and the women carried their learnings back to their villages. Gradually, they became skilled at planting trees. Other villages saw what they were doing, learned from them, and, over time, a large network of villages became skilled at tree planting. In less than thirty years, thirty million trees were flourishing in six hundred communities, in twenty nations. By 2009, forty million trees had been planted. Villages now have clean water, shade and local firewood, improved health and community vitality.

Daniel and Shikshantar friends construct a *cycle-mixie*, a bicycle-powered blender that still functions as a bicycle.

FROM SCALING UP TO SCALING ACROSS

Here is perhaps a more familiar story of scaling across, when an idea starts in one place and works its way around the world. In 1935, when alcoholic Bill Wilson took a business trip to Akron, Ohio, he asked another alcoholic, Dr. Bob Smith, to help him stay sober. Two years later, one hundred members of Alcoholics Anonymous were following a twelve-step program to recover from addiction. Today, membership is estimated to have topped two million people in more than one hundred thousand groups across the globe. AA doesn't try to organize or control its members; it has no central authority. Instead, new groups form as individuals step forward to start hosting conversations in their own communities. These groups are linked together by their commitment to AA's core organizing principles, out of which arises each group's unique local experience.

The Transition Towns movement, which we'll learn more about during our visit to South Africa, is an accelerated story of scaling across. The first official "Unleashing" of a Transition Town—a community devoted to taking on the twin challenges of peak oil and climate change—occurred in Totnes, England, in September 2006. In just over a year, the Transition model spread to fifty other towns and cities throughout the United Kingdom. As of July 2010, there are more than 321 communities in 15 countries that are participating in the movement.[13]

When we start our small local efforts, we never know where things might lead. We don't know if bicimáquinas and Unitierra will lead to larger-scale changes. What we do know is that scaling across, where good ideas and innovations travel trans-locally through networks of relationship, is the way that lasting change happens in our complex, relationship-rich world.

LEAVING THE ZAPATISTAS

Have you forgotten where you are? These stories have come to you while resting in the Zapatista caracol of Oventic, that place between the worlds that reminds us to be alert, writes Subcomandante Marcos, "to the rightness of the worlds which people the world."[14] The Zapatistas are claiming the right to live in their world—no more, no less. For this, they must be faceless; for this, they must be nameless. Whether or not the government grants these people their autonomy, they will persevere, as they have been doing since the Spanish came, since the Aztecs came, as they are doing today.

Before you descend from this misty highland village, the Zapatistas will make one request of you: Will you remember their story? Will you let it remain in your heart and provoke your imagination? Will you tell it to others? For that is the reason they accepted your request to visit their village and learn about their world. As you look back into the eyes of the Zapatista woman who gazes at you from behind her black ski mask, she wants to know, will you recognize that she is you?

MOVING INTO REFLECTION

It's time now to slow things down and take time for reflection. If this were a real Learning Journey, if we'd just been together in Mexico, we'd gather after dinner to contemplate our day's experiences and share feelings and thoughts. For this journey in book form, consider how you might create reflective space for yourself—putting the book down for a while, flipping back to look at photos or settling in with a cup of coffee or tea. Whatever supports you to engage in reflection.

At the start of this journey, we described beliefs and assumptions as a kind of baggage. We all have thick, well-polished lenses for interpreting what we see and experience, otherwise we couldn't get through a day, make a decision, or participate in society. But as we get busier, move faster, and generally are more distracted, we often stop noticing that there are other versions of reality. It takes slowing down and reflecting on our experiences to notice that there are many ways to live life, to understand situations, to solve problems.

As we visit each community, it's our goal to create sensory overload. We'll feel satisfied as authors if you're stimulated by people and experiences, surprised by strange ideas and practices, perhaps even overwhelmed at times by what's new and different.

Our personal experience with leading journeys has led us to expect great swings of emotions—joy into sorrow into grief into laughter into beauty into despair into compassion. We've discovered that these contrasting emotions, with all their discomfort and paradox, are the ones that open us to real learning. In this swirling maelstrom of conflicting feelings, we get cracked open. Our familiar ways of seeing suddenly don't feel so clear or so right.

If you're feeling provoked, disturbed, confused, surprised, now's a good time to reflect and contemplate what these feelings might mean and where they might lead you.

.

We invite you to settle in and dwell in the richness of the people, stories, and ideas you've just encountered in Mexico.

SCALING UP

We've just been in the company of people who are inventive and hard-working, passionate about what they're doing. And we witnessed how their inventions and ideas traveled across the world, inspiring others to be creative and claim for themselves what they needed.

Think about how you and your colleagues feel when you create something that excites you, when you've discovered a new process, idea, or model that solves a recurring problem. If what you've discovered is a solution to a problem that plagues many people, what do you do? Most of us want to get it out to as many people as possible, as quickly as possible so that everyone can benefit.

In Western culture, we're encouraged to scale up our good idea to have the greatest influence. We're directed, even funded, to create manuals, training programs, franchises, templates, transferable business models. The primary focus is to create easily replicated models and then disseminate them. This process is based on the assumption that whatever worked here will work there—we just need to get it down on paper and train people in how to be us.

If only it were that simple.

Scaling up relies on another assumption, one that is fervently believed, but rarely true in experience. The assumption is that people do what they're told. So instructions get issued, policies get pronounced. When we don't follow them, bosses just create more. When we still fail to obey, we're labeled as resistant or lazy. Consider your own experience. How do you feel when someone presents you with a finished plan or outline, when the steps, the curriculum, the process are set down in great detail? Do you gratefully accept it, excited to implement it to the letter of the law? Or do you poke holes in it, noticing where it needs changing, where you disagree? How many times do you just file it away, never to look at it again? Have you ever been so opposed to a plan or program that you quietly sabotaged it?

If you've done any of these things, you're just like the rest of us. People don't support things that are forced on them. We don't act responsibly on behalf of plans and programs created without us. We resist *being* changed, not change itself.

This is the fatal flaw of scaling up. Its methods destroy the very energies necessary for taking things to scale—people's creativity and curiosity, our desire to learn and contribute, and the satisfaction we experience when we're engaged together in mutual discovery.

When have you been given someone else's plans
or practices and told to just implement them?
How did you respond?

SCALING ACROSS

Unitierra, the Zapatistas, Daniel of the bicimáquinas—these stories illumi-nate a radically different approach to taking things to scale. They each began as small local efforts that moved trans-locally through networks of relationships. Each new place adapted, changed, grew the original idea into something else. As more people joined the experiments, large-scale change emerged.

This is how sustainable change happens in this networked, interconnected world. A few people focus on their local challenges and issues. They experi-ment, learn, find solutions that work in their local context. Word travels fast in networks and people hear about their success. They may come to visit or engage in spirited communications. There's usually a lot of energy in these exchanges: Visitors are curious to learn what's been accomplished, and those who did the work are eager to tell their story. But these ex-changes are not about learning how to replicate the process or mimic step-by-step how something was accomplished. Even if people want to know exactly what went on, this isn't the information that's most useful. Any attempt to replicate someone else's success will smack up against local conditions, and these are differences that matter.

People often say, "We don't want to waste time reinventing the wheel." But we *do* need to reinvent the wheel. And it's never a waste of time. What we learn from others' successful innovations is that wheels are possible. What others invent can inspire us to become inventive, can show us what's achievable. Then we have to take it from there.

People eagerly support those things we've had a hand in creating; we're motivated to keep going by discovering for ourselves what works (and what doesn't). Engaged with others in problem solving, inventing, and learning, we discover that we're creative, caring, intelligent. When we have the chance to meet with other wheel inventors, our energy, confidence, and boldness grow and grow.

As we connect with others and discover solutions to our problems, our small local efforts can emerge into large-scale change. And then we have the satisfaction of no longer feeling strange or being labeled as foolish dreamers, mavericks, and crackpots. Our pioneering methods become accepted, normal even, just the way things get done around here.

This is scaling across—we start locally, then connect with others. We learn and experiment together, focused on figuring out what works. After years of inventing, risking, failing and learning, our approaches and inventions take root in many places and are accepted by large numbers of people. This is how the Zapatista movement ignited people's spirits around the world. This is how you plant forty million trees in Africa.

Do you know of small efforts that grew large
not through replication, but by inspiring
each other to keep inventing and learning?

FROM SCALING UP TO SCALING ACROSS

WHY CHANGE HAPPENS

The only reason change happens on this planet,

the only reason change ignites across networks,

the only reason Daniel's invention finds new forms

      as he carries it from Mexico to India,

the only reason Unitierra succeeds in creating joyful universities,

the only reason Zapatistas speak to the hearts of millions,

the only reason seven trees planted in Kenya blossom across Africa

      into forests of forty million. . . .

The only reason these changes happen is because of people.

People who discover they're creative and caring.

People who know others are like them, creative and caring.

People who learn to trust themselves and everyone else.

People who know that dreams only manifest when shared.

People who pour time and love into creating

      the places where ever more people,

          no matter how oppressed or beaten down,

            no matter how beaten down,

              will step forward and

      confidently, predictably, miraculously

      discover their true human spirits.

Are you a Zapatista?

ELOS INSTITUTE, BRAZIL
FROM POWER TO PLAY

On the warrior's path, it is up to you to discern which threads have been woven by divine hands and which have been woven by human hands. When you begin to discern the difference, you become a *Txucarramãe*— a warrior without weapons. . . . When you discover what you have been doing with your life and how it is you dance through the world, little by little you let go of your weapons, those creations made to kill creations. Suddenly, you discover that when we stop creating enemies, we extinguish the need for weapons.

—Kaká Werá Jecupé
Indigenous teacher in Brazil

Berequetê!

Edgard Gouveia Júnior is the kind of man who chases blue butterflies. Despite his 6-foot, 5-inch volleyball player's frame, you'd more expect to see him cavorting around an elfin forest than rebuilding dilapidated housing in the slums of Santos, Brazil. And yet, for Edgard, the most hapless parts of Brazil's impoverished *favelas* are as magical as any elfin forest.

Berequetê!

Sixty warriors stand in a circle. Edgard shouts out the directions, and you find yourself waving your arms in the air, rolling your knees in circles and wiggling your rear to the beat of the wild syllables that cascade off your tongue.

Berequetê!

Sixty warriors reach around the circle to grab the closest right ankle that hovers nearby. You are hopping around the room on one foot each, like a giant, hobbled millipede.

Berequetê!

Sixty warriors advance toward the center of the circle until you are standing shoulder to shoulder, squeezed into position like some sixty-cylinder engine. Edgard tells you to turn to the right, which you do, and then sixty left feet step another few inches toward the center to tighten up the circle even more. And then you sit down. Chaos breaks out as warriors scream and shout and tip over and stand up again, and then you're all stepping another left foot toward the center until you can find a sturdy set of knees to land on and now you're all waving your arms wildly in the air as you shuffle forward in micromovements, chanting:

Berequetengue, tengue, tengue! Berequetengue, tengue, tengue! Berequetengue, tengue, tengue! Berequetengue, tengue, tengue!

The word means nothing. Not a thing. You just sing it for the sheer mouth feel, the delight of exotic sounds. You play this game, dancing and swaying and moving around the room, hands encountering heads, hips rebounding off knees, shoulders and elbows and wrists shimmying. It gets inside of you, this movement. This sound. This touch. This rhythm. This beat. This game.

This dance is Brazil.

In January 2007, my friends at the Elos Institute invited me to come to Brazil to play a thirty-day game. (I participated in ten days of it.) We would all become *Txucarramãe*, Warriors Without Weapons, people who dance in the face of despair, who create beauty amidst decay. Here's what they promised: We would *play* to change the world. And the world where we were going to play was Paquetá, a small community beset by poverty, unemployment, drug abuse, and homelessness.

I was skeptical. Would this be yet another example of outsiders arriving to save a victimized populace? Another case of people with greater power and influence coming to the rescue of the weak and the needy?

I had underestimated my friends. The purpose of this game was not to help, save, or fix anyone else. The purpose of this game was to discover how play unleashes everyone's creativity, how it invites us to see what's possible rather than what's so. In this game, it would be the residents of Paquetá who would discover and build their dreams. I would have the privilege of playing alongside, learning how a community becomes healthy and resilient, not when it gains access to power and wealth, but when it discovers that its creativity and capacity were there all along.

Deborah

THE WAY OF THE WARRIORS

Do you want to play at transforming the world?
Everybody wants to and can change the world! It can be done with play, with a free and spontaneous spirit, without suffering, and with confidence that your efforts will make a difference!

—*Invitation to the* School of Warriors Without Weapons

This is your invitation to a thirty-day game, a boot camp for building dreams. Every day, you'll wake up at 6 A.M. and journey into the *cortiços*, the impoverished neighborhoods of Santos's decaying former city center, where you'll work for ten hours a day alongside community members who wish to create with you a place of beauty that meets the community's needs. You'll spend your evenings in teams that compete to see who can serve a dinner that is truly *espetacular!*—festooning the dining space with woven garlands and floating flowers, the dishes with decorative herbs and garnishes. Some nights, you'll sit for hours around the Fire Council, sharing what you've learned and what you're committed to learning. Then you'll seal that commitment by declaring yourself, *My name is Deborah and I say, Hey!* And through the flickering 3 A.M. darkness, fifty-nine voices will answer you back with a resounding *Ho!* that reminds you how much more is possible when you have a whole community standing with you.

This is the philosophy of serious play created by the Elos Institute, an organization based in Santos, Brazil, cofounded by Edgard Gouveia Júnior, Rodrigo Alonso, Mariana Motta, Natasha Gabriel, and Alexandre Esteves. Elos, which means "links," describes their work as helping people recover their ability to dream and find the will to realize these dreams with others. They work with people from high-risk urban and traditional communities in the São Paulo area, and through the Warriors Without Weapons program, with youth and social entrepreneurs from four continents. They believe that everybody wants to—and can—transform the world. And that we can do it voluntarily, cooperatively, and joyfully.

The five met in architecture school and formed Elos in 2000 after they had finished a project renovating the city's run-down fishing museum. The project allowed them to contribute to the revitalization of the city's waterfront district and to experiment as architects with a unique approach. Rather than rely on the inspiration of one or two visionary architects, they would design the space based on a more collective wisdom, surfaced through community conversation, cooperative games, and a spirit of play. From that experience, a vision arose: They would design a program that would match architecture students who want to build things—rather than merely model them—with communities that believe they lack the skills to

Edgard Gouveia Júnior with Paquetá community member Roberto Bernacio. Children are locked in their basement home while their mother goes to work.

FROM POWER TO PLAY

build the structures they need. And so they launched the first Open Summer University, Universidade Aberta Verão, which later evolved into the Escola de Guerreros Sem Armas, the School of Warriors Without Weapons.

It is now January 2007, and we're attending the third Warriors Without Weapons program, where warriors from sixteen countries are gathering in Santos. They are architects, engineers, students, managers, and nonprofit workers. Some of them have advanced degrees; others never finished school. The youngest is seventeen; the eldest, thirty-four—with a few older friends hovering around the edges. They have come to partner with community members from Paquetá, a once affluent neighborhood near the port that for more than thirty years now has been in a state of disrepair. This is a neighborhood of *cortiços*, old buildings that were once owned by wealthy Portuguese families and then deserted and rented out to poorer people, who sublet them to even poorer folk. In this building, twenty-three families share one toilet. When it rains, the wall becomes a waterfall, so the family moves the cabinet to the middle of the room until the sun comes back. In the blackened space underneath that stairwell, an old woman pays rent to sleep—that's her home. See those children peeking out from behind the iron bars at street level? They'll appreciate it if you say hello and reach through the bars to touch their fingers. Their mother works during the day and has nowhere safe to send them, so she locks them in the sweltering heat of their concrete basement home until she returns at night.

Elos is determined to challenge our beliefs about what's possible when communities play together. For this is the place where, for the next thirty days, we'll open our hearts to discover what dreams are waiting to be released.

THE ROOM OF THE SALTED CIRCLES

This is the room of the salted circles that repel knee-deep layers of dirt, asbestos, syringes, and excrement.

This is the room where drug deals happen and homeless men shelter. Murders are committed here. Notice how the light tunnels through the cracked and buckling roof, refracting off broken glass. See in the corner, under that accidental skylight, how the rainwater pools in a lagoon of sludge.

This is the room where you spend only fifteen minutes every day. You are cleaning this space, shoveling layers of shit and broken dreams onto pallets and dragging them out into the sunshine. Our task seems impossible. We will never finish. But finishing isn't the point; this is a daily practice, a ritual designed to cultivate sacred spaces of possibility in the face of toxicity and despair.

This is Apene, an 11,195-square-foot abandoned apple warehouse in Paquetá, where our training as warriors begins.

With a soft voice and gentle smile that provides comfort in the darkness, Rodrigo tells you that this place is a symbol of how we can confront catastrophic human and environmental degradation. This is the perfect place to build another dream, he promises. To have a healthy social fabric, we need healthy public spaces. When we restore a degraded public space, we restore our connections to each other and to our community. We make the impossible possible.

But you mustn't be reckless. Apene is a dark place, and you must honor its shadowy power. You must protect yourself—not only with face masks and gloves and by washing your shoes after you exit, but also with ceremony. Before beginning, we gather round outside under the still-bold late afternoon sun for a circle dance, a celebration of light and of life and of each other. It is a counterpoint to Apene's desolation. And then we enter. At the close of our work, we turn again to one another, this time indoors, stepping into one of the columns of light that pierce through the ceiling. At the center of the circle stand a plant, some earth and water, and a lit candle. Someone pours salt in the ever-widening circles of a mandala and then offers a song or prayer for healing, sometimes in Portuguese, other times in Swahili, Urdu, English, Swedish, or Spanish. We are calling upon all the traditions we know—upon all the ancestors of our multicultured community—to absolve this place of its history, to help us do this work. For it seems no one else is coming to help.

For fifteen minutes every day, the Warriors will shovel layers of dirt, asbestos, syringes, and excrement to clean this abandoned warehouse. They protect themselves with circles of salt and song.

FROM POWER TO PLAY

NO ONE IS COMING TO HELP

Brazil is the economic and political powerhouse of South America. It is the fifth largest country in the world, has the fifth largest population, and is the world's eighth largest economy, surpassing Canada and Russia, and is more than five times the size of South America's next largest economy, Argentina.[15]

It is also one of the most economically unequal countries in the world. The top 10 percent of the population earns nearly 50 percent of the national income. More than fifty million Brazilians—approximately 32 percent—live on less than $2 a day.[16] Most of them are scattered among the *favelas* and the *cortiços*, the slums and shantytowns that emerge wherever the marginalized populations of Brazil—usually, the darker skinned Brazilians of African descent—can find a place to erect their haphazard shelters. They take long bus trips to work, if they have any work at all. They send their children to failing public schools that use their limited resources to tackle illiteracy and truancy rather than facilitating learning. They endure the twin economic engines of prostitution and the drug trade that fuel their neighborhoods. And they survive in an environment of violence in a country whose crime rate is among the highest in the world.

But the blight of the urban poor is far, far away from the chic neighborhoods of the Brazilian well-to-do, who send their children to private schools, drive around in private cars, and have private security services. They enjoy the fantasy of Brazil, a sensory explosion that has been exported around the world: the luscious images of white-sand beaches and scantily clad women, the pounding beats of samba and capoeira that blast down your spine and slam into your hips, the toffee-like scent of Brazil nuts and the sickly sweet smells of overripe fruit. Perhaps it is the fruit that reveals the most about Brazil, the endless, infinite variety of fruit—*abacaxí, açai, cupcuaçu, graviola, jabuticaba, maracujá, pitanga, taperebá, uva, umbú.* Brazil, the most fecund of nations, where you can taste a different fruit every day of the year. Brazil, a land of relentless fertility.

Like Brazil's fruit, nobody knows exactly how many favelas there are, or how many people live in them. What we do know is that their growth is also relentless, and that there are enough of them to assume that when it comes to transforming life in a favela, no one is coming to help. Instead, the residents of Brazil's tenements must rely on their own fertile imaginations, their own capacity to generate the possibility of a different world.

Which is why Edgard, Rodrigo, and Mariana are inviting the residents of Paquetá, its children, parents and grandparents—those who have been branded illiterate, apathetic, and in need—to attend a two-day urban planning conference.

THE OASIS GAME

Do you want to play a game?

More than 150 people have already arrived at SESC, the Social Service of Commerce Center, our meeting space in downtown Santos, and are itching to start playing the Oasis Game. This game will take two days to play, and there's excitement in the air. Small children are running around the perimeter of the large meeting space, chasing each other up and down the stairs to the open-air second level. Parents and grandparents from Paquetá shake hands and exchange kisses with neighbors from a few blocks down the road. Some get introduced to the local government representatives who are circulating in the crowd, while others are given hearty hugs by the warriors who have already been roaming around their community for three weeks. We are ready to begin.

This game opens with a circle dance, and there's Edgard, his head poking out above the crowd from the center of the room, talking you through the movements that will begin to connect us to one another. The purpose of this game, he tells you, is to *play at changing the world*. In our case, that's Paquetá, and our challenge in the next two days is to envision, design, and begin building oases there—places where we find joy, beauty,

On Day One of the Oasis Game, we dream. On Day Two, we build.

connection, and cooperation, where we create a culture of caring for the planet, starting with our neighborhood. Places that are as spectacular as stumbling across an oasis in the desert.

This is a charrette (a creative process used by designers to rapidly develop solutions), and today, our task is to build models of oases using the tools of the architect's trade: cardboard and colored paper, markers and pens, pins, scissors, glue, tape, rubber cement, fabric, and fimo clay. Of course, every game has rules, and Edgard offers these four:

1. Whatever we build has to be simple, accessible, and easy.
2. It can't cost anything—whatever tools and materials we might need, we'll have to find a way to obtain without paying for them.
3. The product has to be something that we create collectively and with our hands. (It can't be an idea.)
4. It has to meet a real need in the community—*as defined by the community.*

We have a head start on that last point, since the warriors have been engaged in conversation with the community for the past three weeks, and ideas have been popping. There are few public community spaces in Paquetá, and now there's talk afoot of turning Apene—that shadowy space of broken dreams—into a cultural center, starting with relocating the bright red seating of an abandoned cinema down the block. Other folks have been dreaming of a garden and playground where children can escape from the relentless concrete of the cortiços. A third group wants to explore how to organize the cardboard collectors (people who collect and resell cardboard waste) to form a cooperative to combat exploitative pricing. No matter that this last option violates Edgard's Rule Number Three—the group wants to forge ahead anyway.

You are given a choice of where you want to go and find your way to the children's garden project—*jardim das crianças*. You and about fifteen others—half warriors, half community members—head upstairs to a space that has a table and plenty of standing room. Hands of all colors and ages reach into the materials box and start pulling out tools with which to draw, cut, roll, stick, and twist. There isn't a plan, exactly. Nonetheless, order breaks through the chaos as a line of putty trees appear to provide a shaded area; a matchstick swing set dwells near the blue clay pond; felt grassy areas provide open space for soccer and other games; and bright orange fimo rocks point the way through the labyrinth of activities. Participants have come and gone over the past three hours, the ranks of garden planners at times swelling to more than thirty and ebbing to only five or six. But what you have now is good enough—because when you're playing a game, nothing has to be perfect—and ready to be presented to the community. Tomorrow, you'll go to the site of the proposed jardim das crianças and begin building it.

Games are universal. There isn't a culture on Earth that hasn't developed traditions for teaching people how to create, imagine, and build, how to play roles and make believe, how to test our physical, mental, and emotional limitations. Games transform the landscape of our environment: a familiar room is now a castle, an abandoned square becomes a battlefield. We play games because they're fun, not because we're trying to be realistic, practical, or efficient. Games invite us to let go of our resignation and our sense of limitation—and simply to start dreaming, creating, and imagining. In the words of Brazilian educator Paulo Freire:

> I am convinced that in order for us to create something, we need to start creating. We cannot wait to create tomorrow, but we have to start creating. I am sure that in trying to create something inside of history we have to begin to have some dreams. If you don't have any kind of dream I am sure it's impossible to create something.[17]

When we play, we're in a constant process of discovery, experimentation, risk-taking, and creation. We tinker. We invent. We dream and we imagine and we make believe until it's time to go out there and build the world we dream of.

JARDIM DAS CRIANÇAS

Walk a few blocks down from Apene, and you'll find the site designated for the jardim das crianças, the promised children's garden. *It can't be true!* Where once stood a multistory home, its arched façade proclaiming its colonial Portuguese heritage, now towers a pile of refuse and rubble more than eight feet off the ground. You duck your head to pass through the entryway and scramble up the forty-five-degree slope into a world that's like nothing you've ever encountered. There, in front of you, is a yellow brick road of trash, beckoning you to follow its path. You step gingerly on headless teddy bears and cracked pipe fittings, rotting banana peels, crusty yogurt containers, and stained coffee mugs. Baked in Brazilian sunshine, the stench is staggering. Up ahead is a tiny shelter, no bigger than a doghouse with a makeshift plywood roof perched against a remnant of a brick wall. Smoke is pouring from the darkened space. *Someone lives here!*

A man crawls out of the shelter to check you out. It is impossible to tell his age. He tells you about his home—how about fifteen years ago, there had been a fire and the landlord let the tenement fall into disrepair; how the squatters gave it up after four years and the site became a neighborhood garbage dump. Now he is the only one left, and he points you toward the back half of the old building and invites you to explore.

You shuffle past the shelter and gasp at the beauty that explodes in front of your eyes: an Emerald City of life—carpets and walls and rafters of green dotted with splotches of pink. Jungle vines reach skyward and twine around ancient fortress walls. Birds nest in hidden crags that once formed rafters. Even this place can't resist Brazil's dogged commitment to create life. A jardim das crianças here? Absolutely. Yes.

So you begin with these mountains of trash, attacking them with pickaxes and shovels, gaining on them by only inches per hour. Today, five children show up to help you collect the loosened bricks that will become the stairway entrance. Tomorrow, they'll bring ten more children along to help build the garden and then ten more after that, including an eleven-year-old boy nicknamed Boizinho who wants to man your wheelbarrow. From that day on, he'll be there in the garden every day, waiting to greet you and spending the day by your side, working and playing and singing songs with you—no matter that you don't speak a word of Portuguese.

Each day, more workers will appear, neighbors bearing gifts of shovels and wheelbarrows and the sweat of their labor. One day, bags of sand and sod will be dropped off—nobody knows by whom—so you can lay down a lawn and create a sand garden. A pile of old vinyl records is discovered,

Somewhere beneath eight staggering feet of trash, a *jardim das crianças* is waiting to be born.

WALK OUT WALK ON

which the children paint and hang off of old crossbars to create luminescent chandeliers. This oasis has magic in it—a magic that beckons people to stop by, to contribute, to create something beautiful together.

There is no blueprint for this garden. There are no foremen. Everything is a constant process of discovery and creation. Messes happen. Sometimes one person builds half a wall and then someone else comes along and tears it down to start another. Redundancy happens. There is chaos and confusion—and there is also laughter and joy and pride. There is wild self-expression as children design their own rock gardens and declare that the jungle must be preserved, for it offers places to climb and to hide. Yes, there are architects among us. There are urban planners and permaculture farmers. We have *expertise*. But instead of relying on our expertise, we all pitch in wherever we can, and a community is rediscovered. Together, we become garbage collectors and ditch diggers and bricklayers—side-by-side with the eight-year-olds and eighty-year-olds who will be visiting this garden every day.

Working in the children's garden, I had taken on the task of creating the entryway. Day after day, I dug down through the mountain of trash until it was low enough to build a brick stairway. Others came and went, but I had made this my project, an effort I was in charge of, had a vision for, and was committed to completing.

Imagine my frustration one morning when I saw that dozens of the bricks I had painstakingly laid had been removed and repositioned. Someone else had a different idea about this staircase, and he had gone ahead and begun rebuilding.

Of course, I was infuriated. This new approach would slow us down! We might not finish! And where had he been anyway during the hard days of digging through the trash? After all, this was *my* stairway.

Gently, he explained to me how his approach would stabilize the stairway and make it last longer. How with a few more hands, we'd be able to get it done quickly. And that without the hard work I had already put in, he would not have seen what he could create.

Yes, play creates chaos and redundancy and confusion. But it also creates the space in which we invent together, we inspire each other, and we talk through our differences. I continue to be grateful today for the messes we made in the children's garden.

Deborah

FROM POWER TO PLAY

RECIPE FOR CURING URBAN BLIGHT

The heat and the stench and the heavy lifting of clearing the garden are too much to bear through the midday sun, so it's time for a break. First, pay a visit to the street vendor who will cut a hole into a young coconut just big enough for a straw and send you off to a shady spot to sip on that revitalizing water. Now, let's reflect together on what we're witnessing because it's turning the conventional approach to the urban poor on its head.[18] Take a moment to consider the recipe of the old, familiar model, on the right.

When the old recipe is used, you may be surprised to discover what's happened to your creation twelve months down the road or so. No one is using the community center or someone has ripped the planks off the benches in the public square. This is to be expected—no one bothered to ask the community members what they thought their needs might be. No one invited them to talk about their own dreams and experiment with bringing them to fruition. And now, hundreds of thousands of dollars—perhaps millions or even billions—have gone down the proverbial sewer. Again.

There must be a reason this scenario repeats itself time after time after time in cities and towns and villages all over the world. There must be some assumptions that we can drag out of the shadows and tease apart so as to avoid this repetition. Assumptions like:

- The answers exist out there—*and the experts have them.*
- To get things done, you need people of power and influence to champion your cause.
- Plan ahead and stick to your plan.
- Nothing gets done right unless you're in control.
- Don't ask for other people's opinions.
- We don't have time to experiment and tinker around.
- We mustn't fail! (And when we do, find someone to blame.)

Where did these beliefs come from? They didn't arise from our understanding of who we are as human beings, people who want to learn and contribute, who are best motivated by challenge and hope. These beliefs expose the dominant worldview that the universe, and people, are best understood as machines. In a machine, nothing happens without an external designer, without manipulation and control. Machine-world leaders fear that if people and situations are left to themselves, chaos results.

Curing Urban Blight: An Old-Fashioned Recipe for Community Activists

Ingredients
- Impoverished and needy community
- Charismatic local activists
- Building or public square that can be torn down
- City council members with poor listening skills
- Decision makers who don't live in the neighborhood but control the distribution of goods and services
- Guilt-stricken local funding agency
- Benevolent architects and engineers

First, forge a coalition of leaders among local neighborhood associations, such as churches, ethnic groups, political organizations, and labor unions. You can count on this very small number of leaders to represent a very large number of community members.

Next, identify your enemy. Look for people who control the ownership and distribution of resources in your community, such as city council members, landlords, businesses, and politicians. Before you start, make sure this enemy actually has the resources and authority to address your concern.

Make yourselves as unified as possible. Create a standardized message that any member of your leadership team will repeat robotically. Any deviation from that message may be exploited by your detractors.

Get visible. Gain public sympathy by casting a spotlight on your urban blight, thereby forcing the decision maker's hand. You must be seen as victims of discrimination—be that economic, social, racial, or political. You'll want to keep a muzzle on any members of your community who have the skills to resolve the problems themselves, such as architects, engineers, and construction workers. If you're seen to be able to solve your own problems, you'll likely not get the resources you need.

If you're successful, then some good-willed architecture firm (also not from the neighborhood) will win the rights to design your new community center or public square, eager to display its commitment to corporate social responsibility. In due time, there will be a ribbon-cutting ceremony. This should be attended by the mayor, or someone of equal authority, who will bestow *gravitas* on your event. A picture of the mayor and the charismatic community leaders will be in tomorrow's newspaper.

Leaders have to take control, assert their will, use their political power, and push ahead to get results. How the leader uses power can be either subtle or brutish, but it's unquestioned that such power is necessary to accomplish anything, to bring order out of chaos.

In the logic of this kind of power, people need to be forced to do work through either rewards or threats. People get rewarded if they are compliant and obedient, if they don't ask questions or challenge the status quo. Creativity and new ideas are construed as a threat to authority; better to use old, familiar solutions repetitively, even when they don't work. People who work in this machine-like environment *do* begin to behave as machines, robotically performing tasks, convinced they're not creative, waiting for experts and entrepreneurs to tell them what to do.

In the logic of play, people are invited to break rules, experiment, innovate, and be original. Can you remember how you played as a child? If you were like most children, you delighted in opportunities to be off balance, to relinquish control, to be surprised. You pushed the edge to see just how far you could go—and it was no big deal when you toppled over. In fact, the more errors you made, the more you learned how to solve problems— like maintaining balance. You tried things out for no other reason than because they were new. When you got your hands on an object, your first question was "What can I do with that?" not "What is it for?" As adults, we like to categorize things: a paperclip is a paperclip; a box is a box. For a child, a paperclip is a lock picker, a cherry-pit remover, a booger-hunting device, a lightning rod for elves. Play returns us to a state in which we can see what's possible—not what's so. When we look through the eyes of play, we see a children's garden; when we look through the eyes of power, we see only trash.

The Oasis Game disrupts the power differential between the urban poor and the professional problem solvers by putting them side-by-side and handing them a basket of crayons and rubber cement. Edgard, Rodrigo, Mariana and the rest of the Elos team have walked out of the notion that we need to leverage power to produce results. They have walked on to the belief that creativity is in everyone, play unleashes that creativity, and if we want to create a healthy and resilient community, we need to invite the members of that community to play together. When we play, everything once again becomes possible.

Elos is in good company these days when it comes to walking on to play. Over the past decade, a new movement of people has emerged around the world who, like children, recognize that a paper clip is never just a paper clip. What do you see when you stumble across a stack of old newspapers, used CDs, empty beer cans? Most of us see trash. But not these people. They fold newspapers into window blinds, craft CDs into lampshades, twist empty beer cans into earrings, and weave the pop tabs into handbags. They are upcyclers, and they transform trash into treasure.

Upcycling[19] is the practice of inventing beautiful, useful, and surprising products out of waste materials—such as water pumps from salvaged bicycles (which you learned about on our journey to Mexico), solar cookers made from discarded suitcases and car windshields (which you'll discover on our journey to India), and jewelry crafted out of soda cans and plastic bags. It is distinct from recycling in that the recycling process often requires large energy inputs and generates unrecoverable and unusable by-products, such as sludge, dross, and toxic compounds. Upcyclers challenge themselves to reinvent the world by playing with its waste. They construct homes out of discarded auto tires filled with rammed earth. They host "Trashion Shows" featuring dresses made from bird feed bags, vinyl records, and discarded Santa beards. They build compost toilets out of plastic bottles, coffee tables out of phone books, chairs out of campaign posters. The list goes on and on—and at an exponentially accelerating rate. In 2006, a Google search on "upcycling" generated fewer than ten resources. In 2010, that leaped to more than 217,000.[20] Upcycling is exploratory, playful, filled with make-believe. It is rooted in the spirit of bricolage that calls forward the tinkerers, the dreamers, and the inventors.

It is the tinkering and the dreaming itself that motivates us to act. Instead of being overwhelmed by the mountain of trash or the downtrodden neighborhood or the exploitation of power, we are inspired to experiment,

An upcycled handbag made out of soda and beer can pop tabs by Aerin Dunford of Oaxaca, Mexico. Boots made from plastic bags by Chilean designer Camila Ladra.

FROM POWER TO PLAY

to try out new ideas, to take ourselves a little less seriously. We do not have to conform to what we already know. Play invites us to explode the boundaries, to distort the familiar. There is no failure in play; we're not trying to get it right. We are not even trying to solve our problems. No, what we're doing when we play is exploring our dreams.

A CIRCLE OF JOY

Do you remember when you first set foot in Apene, that tragic warehouse filled with the detritus of our disposable culture? It was only thirty days ago, and now a dream that seemed impossible, implausible, has borne fruit. For the Warriors Without Weapons are an audacious crew, and they dared to plan a fiesta—a block party for the whole community—inside this seemingly untamable space. From several blocks away, you can hear the heavy bass drums of the local samba school beating out the sixteenth notes of that uniquely Afro-Brazilian dance that is shaking and shimmying its way toward you. The parade goes on and on, a brilliantly plumed bird with an ever-lengthening tail of newcomers who join the festivities. They are the children who imagined the garden, the grandmothers who painted signs, young jobless men who muscled away piles of debris, the vendor who offered coconut water, and the gardener who donated wheelbarrows. They are the neighbors who only watched from a distance and the businessmen who laughed at the warriors' folly, but they are here now, magnetized to this collective dream, ready to discover what is being unveiled.

Warriors demonstrate their improbable success at transforming Apene into a community center. Edgard and the children of Paquetá celebrate their new garden.

What is being unveiled is the Centro Cultural Paquetá, a community center where people can gather to tell stories, play games, watch movies, and rediscover one another. Graffiti artists have emblazoned the outside walls in bold murals of green and purple; small circles of trees and flowers in tiny raised beds adorn the concrete. Inside is a cavernous clean and empty room, one whose concrete floors have been scoured with mops, whose walls have been savaged by high-pressure hoses, and whose air has been tenderly blessed with songs and prayers. The old cinema's red leather seats, scrubbed to gleaming, line up facing a curtained theater scene chalked onto the wall.

There is no trace left of the oppressive, fear-filled energy that inhabited this space thirty days ago. Something sacred has restored this room, now absolved of its history. Can you feel it on your skin? The community members seem to. As they file in from the raucous celebrations outside, a hush descends. Edgard stands in the center of the room, quietly inviting each of us into the sacrament of a final circle dance, this oldest and most universal of dances. Boizinho, the boy you worked with in the garden for days on end, rushes over to stand by your side. He is happy and tearful and clinging to you in anticipation of separation. Hand-in-hand-in-hand around the periphery of the room, concentric circles take shape as people who have connected across language and culture find one another. One circle whirls to the left, the other to the right. We move together into the center and release back out again, a giant heart pumping open and closed, open and closed. We are dancing to "Kumbalawé," the Cirque du Soleil song that proclaims:

> Kumbalawé mana, kumbalawé mana
> Urulimé
> Kumbalawé mana, kumbalawé mana
> Urulimé
> Teku mande m´bala, teku mande m´bala
> Teku mande
> Kumbalawé mana
> Kumba teku mande

As with *Berequetê,* the words mean nothing. Not a thing. They spin us around the room, embracing the community in spirals of gratitude and joy and the sorrow of parting. They are a final benediction from Edgard, our alchemist: May the spark of life shine in you through the darkest of places.

FROM POWER TO PLAY

POWER

In the cortiços we just visited, bright possibilities grew from the rubble of human poverty. When the community recognized that no one was coming to help, they didn't just resign themselves to that fate. With the encouragement of friends and people who believed in them, they began working together in new, playful ways. They exercised leadership that encouraged people to step forward, that revealed people's innate motivations to create and contribute. As a result, they discovered that those living there—the old, the homeless, the children, the neighbors—were capable of contributing in wonderful, transforming ways to their community.

Their approach to leadership stands in stark contrast to the more familiar ways leaders use power. In physics, power is defined as the rate at which work gets done. This works fine for machines, but it has no relevance for humans. Yet many leaders assume that people *are* machines, that we can be programmed, motivated, and supervised through external force and authority. This "command-and-control" leadership smothers basic human capacities such as intelligence, creativity, caring, dreaming. Yet it is the most common form of leadership worldwide. When it doesn't work, those in power simply apply more force. They threaten, cajole, reward, punish, police, legislate.

People resist the imposition of force by withdrawing, opposing and sabotaging the leader's directives. Those in charge then feel compelled to turn up the pressure and apply even harsher measures. They seldom notice that it's their controlling leadership that creates these difficult and unruly behaviors. And so this destructive cycle continues to gain speed, with people resenting leaders and leaders blaming people.

This cycle not only destroys our motivation, it destroys our sense of worth. We lose sight of our skills, we forget that we're creative, we come to believe what those in power say about us, that we're lazy, useless, worthless. This destruction of the human spirit is readily visible in places like Paquetá and any community or country where people have suffered from oppression. It's also visible in rigid hierarchies where people, confined to small boxes, can't remember when they last felt good about themselves or confident in their abilities.

WALK OUT WALK ON

Power of this kind has a predictable outcome: it breeds powerlessness. People accept the message they've heard so consistently, that they're helpless without a strong leader. They become dependent and passive, waiting for a leader to rescue them, and their growing dependency leaves leaders with no choice. They must take control if anything is going to get done.

Warriors Without Weapons consciously abandoned the familiar weapon of control. They reached playfully inside the community and discovered that they had what they needed, the human spirit that can never be extinguished, even in the darkest places.

Have you had personal experience with
command-and-control leadership? How did it impact
your motivation, relationships, effectiveness?

PLAY

Here are contrasting voices about what's possible—or not—in doing the work of community change.[21] Which voices sound most familiar?

Do you want to play at transforming the world? It can be done with play, without suffering, with confidence your efforts will make a difference!

> This work is very important. It's very hard. You'll need a lot of help. You'll need the government. I'll connect you with some experts I know who could help you. Where's the money coming from?

What does this community need? What do you care about? Here are some materials—pens, paper, cardboard, pins, glue, crayons. Dream a garden, design a community center. But before we begin, come, join hands and dance.

> It's impossible. No one cleans up a filthy warehouse working fifteen minutes a day. What's all this ritual and ceremony? They can't really believe their ancestors are helping them, can they? Why do they ask illiterate poor people to do urban planning? Inviting them here is just a sham. We know what to do. Where's the plan? Send those noisy children away—they're distracting us.

Almost no one here is used to seeing anything good happen. So people from outside our neighborhood come to help even though they have nothing to gain from it and nothing to do with our suffering. It's been wonderful to see everyone working together and for our community to start to be more united.

> This is a terribly difficult project. How's the Master Plan coming along? Do we have all the necessary permits? Why don't these people do what we ask? They just sit in their squalor, waiting for us to help them. No wonder they're poor—they can't do anything for themselves.

Why do I feel so happy doing this backbreaking work day after day? I'm not getting much sleep but I have more energy now than ever!

WALK OUT WALK ON

I'm tired. I don't know how much more I can take. I'd like to help, I really believe in this project, but I'm exhausted. And truth be told, it's not working. I just heard about another project that sounds much more interesting. . . .

We are going to fight until the end to see these projects through. What we've done here will attract people to the other projects some people in the community don't believe can be done. We showed here that the impossible is possible. It's like we've discovered a gift inside ourselves, something that we already had.

Where have you encountered these voices in your life?
How have you responded to them?

WE'VE FORGOTTEN WHO WE ARE

When did play become estranged from work?

> A manager fills out an employee attitude survey. One question asks: How often do you have fun at work? He replies: Not Applicable.

Why do we place more value on struggle than on ease?

> Joseph Campbell, a wise mystic and scholar, said that we can identify our gifts by noticing what is easiest for us to do. He advised you to "follow your bliss." Few people understand what he was talking about.

How did we let darkness become more important than light?

> By 1998, psychological journals had published more than forty-five thousand articles on depression. They had published only four hundred articles on joy.[22]

Why do we deny that humans need to celebrate?

> Cave paintings from thousands of years ago depict our ancestors dancing, not sitting in meetings.

How did we forget who we are?

> Play is not a foolish waste of time.
> Play is not a mindless diversion from work.
> Play is how we rediscover ourselves.
> Play is how we ignite the human spirit in which our true power lies.

Do you want to play at transforming the world?

JOUBERT PARK, SOUTH AFRICA
FROM PROBLEM TO PLACE

We belong in a bundle of life. We say, "a person is a person through other people." It is not "I think therefore I am" [but rather] "I am human because I belong." I participate, I share.

—*Archbishop Desmond Tutu*

It's a carnival! There are giant puppets, clowns, jugglers, and mimes running willy-nilly all over the park in brilliant splashes of orange, yellow, green, blue, and pink, teasing children and tossing about balloons, bowling pins, flags, and flowers. Dancers and singers and theater troupes are warming up in different corners of the park, readying themselves for their performances. The Zulu dancers, attired in animal skins, head rings, ceremonial belts and ankle rattles, prepare *indlamu*, a traditional war dance accompanied by drums. Two young men face off, each raising one foot high overhead and slamming it down to the ground in a display of the warrior's might. A troupe of gumboot dancers wearing miners' thick rubber boots are stomping out the rhythms of a Morse code for miners who were forbidden to speak to one another. A children's choir warms up their voices in the intricate harmonies of *isicathamiya,* a style popularized internationally by groups like Ladysmith Black Mambazo. A percussion ensemble lays out their *djembes* in preparation for a drumming workshop. You can give the djembe a try, nestling it between your legs as you kneel on the ground. If you beat your palm and fingers together against the center of the goatskin drumhead, you'll make a low-pitched bass note; strike the rim and you'll make a midrange tone; relax the fingers against the rim for the high-pitched slap. After only ten minutes, your palms will be red and smarting, fingers swollen and pumping with blood. The percussion ensemble will play all day.

People are scattered everywhere on the grass, dark splotches against a green canvas, accented with the irrepressible purple blooms of jacaranda trees. Lovers stretch out, napping in the sun. Old women sit on a bench sharing a meal of *pap* made from maize. On a giant chessboard

Zulu dancers and children perform at the Ziyabuya Festival in Joubert Park.

FROM PROBLEM TO PLACE

South Africa is the most overwhelming place I've ever fallen in love with. Not overwhelming for the conventional reasons—too much poverty, crime, misery. It's overwhelming because of its complexity. It's overwhelming because in every story I heard, in every place I visited, in every person I met, there seemed to be just as much to celebrate as to grieve. It's as if the deep wound of its history as a brutal apartheid state is covered up by only the most fragile layer of new skin—one that is still transparent and vulnerable to infection.

Joubert Park was my first stop in Johannesburg in 2004. I had been warned that it was unsafe, a broken-down green space in the heart of the inner city. I went there in the company of Dorah Lebelo, the director of the GreenHouse Project. Yes, there were still shootings in Joubert Park. It was still a transient community of people passing through on their way, they hoped, to something better. There were still innumerable problems—unemployment, homelessness, HIV, illiteracy. But my first impression of Joubert Park was of something entirely different.

When we arrived, the Zulu dancers were rehearsing for the Ziyabuya Festival. They weren't in costume, just the ordinary jeans and T-shirts of young South Africans, standing around joking casually with one another like youngsters anywhere. But as soon as they moved into formation, their energy shifted. Their posture was uplifted, their movements confident and bold. As they celebrated their heritage in the midst of this scarred landscape, I could sense that the past they were drawing on was fully present in them today.

South Africa always confronts me with the full range of human experience—our most glorious triumphs and contemptible atrocities. It is a place where the past and the present are inextricably intertwined. Which is why we begin our journey to South Africa with its history, so we can know where we are today.

Deborah

laid out in long, flat bricks on the ground, a few men reposition thigh-high knights and pawns. Toddlers tumble off swings to run after the ice cream vendor when he rings his bell. Photographers carry sandwich-board signs displaying portraits, wedding photos, and family shots, offering visitors a memory for ten rand.

This canvas is framed with a thin black line, a fence. Beyond the fence is chaos—cars blaring, people rushing about, pedestrians, cops, workers, beggars, drug peddlers, children. People are frenetic, on edge, restless. Inside the fence, there is joy, vitality, well-being. Perhaps two thousand people will pass through this place today to participate in the Ziyabuya

Festival. They will celebrate the parade of floats, dancers, and percussionists, beating out music with their drums and their bodies and their voices. They will celebrate their African culture and heritage; they will celebrate this place called Joubert Park—no matter that it is in the middle of Johannesburg's Central Business District, one of the most dangerous neighborhoods in one of the most dangerous cities in the world.

We are here because this tiny place no bigger than a football field carries in its earth the entire history of South Africa: its rich beginnings as the mother of us all and its rape by colonizers from the North; the horror of apartheid and the triumph of humanity; the heartbreak of broken dreams and the tenacity of those who are building the future. We are here because there is something for us to learn from Joubert Park about the power of place. You will learn this from the photographers who banded together to stop crime in the park, from the mothers who refused to tolerate vulnerability for children, and from the artists who inspired teenagers to express their anger through art rather than violence. You will learn this from the environmentalists who planted a refuge of green in the urban wasteland. But all this will happen later today. First, you must know where you are. You must hear the story of what has come before, for Joubert Park has triumphed over its history by knowing itself deeply and by communing with its past, its present and its vision of the future.

Indaba, my children, as they say in South Africa.[23] *Come gather around the fire and listen to the story of Joubert Park.*

JOUBERT PARK SINCE THE BEGINNING OF TIME

Credo Mutwa, renown Zulu *sangoma* (shaman or healer) tells this story about the origin of the Zulu people: [24]

> In the beginning nothing existed but the Fertile Darkness, floating on the invisible River of Time. There was no sun, there were no stars, nor the light of the moon; no earth, no place to stand, no vegetation, no waters, no roaring ocean, no brooks or rivers, no animals, no people. Nothing existed but nothingness and a darkness that overspread all.
>
> But there was a trouble, a stirring in the darkness, a desire arose in the River of Time for the Fertile Darkness to give birth to something out of nothing. It was a strange mating, between Time and Nothing, but from it came one tiny spark of Living Fire.
>
> And the Living Fire was consciousness. "I am," the spark wailed, "I AM!" In its fury and loneliness, it fed upon the Nothing and the Fertile Darkness,

FROM PROBLEM TO PLACE

and so it began to grow a great blaze. Nothingness felt this Something, and wished to destroy it. It sent cold to overwhelm and destroy the spark of fire.

But all living things resist whatever threatens their very life, and so the spark grew brighter, and fought against the cold and the darkness. And since that time there is also the eternal battle of Fire and Ice, of light and of darkness, throughout this universe. The Wise Ones know that this is a battle that must always be fought but never won. Only the Great Spirit, Unkulunkulu, may watch over such a titanic struggle and remain calm, for the battle goes this way and that, and all life struggles in its embrace.

As you listen to this story, look up—do you see *imPhambano*, the three warthogs of Orion's belt chasing one another across the shimmering night sky? The Milky Way, thick as mealie pap porridge and wheeling across the black horizon, feels so close it's no wonder some Africans say they descend from the stars. Beneath your feet is the richest continent on the planet—earth filled with diamonds and gold that will one day be ripped from their native soil, earth that will one day give birth to all of humanity.

Know this place as your Mother, for Africa is where we began. One day, humans will leave Africa and colonize the rest of the world.

Africa will colonize the rest of the world.

•• • ••

Indaba, my children. Listen to the story of how the world came back to Africa.

It was the seventeenth century when the first Dutch Boers trickled in to farm the land. The battles began: colonizers from the North against the mighty Zulu warriors, against the Xhosa, the Bapedi, the Venda, against the Basotho, the Tswana, the Tsonga, the Ndebele. But one event eclipsed all others. It was a Sunday in March 1886 when an Australian gold miner chanced upon the bountiful deposits of the Witwatersrand gold reef, set up camp where today stands Johannesburg's Central Business District, and transformed this quiet area of open veld into what would become the financial and commercial hub of sub-Saharan Africa.

The new Union of South Africa—which was formed after the British and the Boers settled their own war-torn rivalry for South Africa's riches—would need a lot of mining labor to extract its tremendous mineral wealth. The government solved its need for miners by relocating blacks to separate mining towns, further institutionalizing the racism already entrenched among South Africa's white colonizers.

A mere one year after gold was discovered, a piece of open veld stretching down to the railway line was set aside to become Joubert Park. In 1895, this is how Thomas Richard Adlam, son of the park's designer, described it:

> We cycled on the paths, climbed trees, ran across the lawns (except on Saturday afternoons and Sundays), and had our secret dens and hiding places in thick shrubberies and in the rockery. The pond was a favourite resort. The island, in the centre, thickly covered with shrubs and pampas grass, was perfect for the game of Robinson Crusoe. Sometimes we threw strict orders to the winds and waded to the island, getting trousers leg wet, though turned up to the limit. We used to sail our toy steamboat there; when its propeller got tangled in the weeds, that was an excuse for wading in the pond.[25]

For the next ninety-seven years, this idyllic, verdant park would be a playground for lucky white boys and girls.

•••••

Indaba, my children. Listen to the story of how apartheid strangled our humanity. Through much of the twentieth century, the area in and around Joubert Park was haunted by two different worlds, one for Whites and one for Blacks. Here are glimpses of these different worlds, as apartheid strengthened its hold.

It's midday and the park is full. Office workers and shop clerks from nearby businesses eat brown-bag lunches on *slegs blanke* benches— reserved for whites only. [26]

> For blacks, it is a crime to sit on a Whites Only bench. As Nelson Mandela recalls in his autobiography, *Long Walk to Freedom*, "It is a crime to walk through a Whites Only door, a crime to ride a Whites Only bus, a crime to use a Whites Only drinking fountain, a crime to walk on a Whites Only beach, a crime to be on the streets past eleven, a crime not to have a pass book and a crime to have the wrong signature in that book, a crime to be unemployed and a crime to be employed in the wrong place, a crime to live in certain places and a crime to have no place to live."[27]

In the northwest corner, the Victorian conservatory is replete with ferns and exotic flowers. Goldfish swim among the lily pads in the indoor pond.

On the northeast side, children flock to a small house filled with games and toys that hosts after-school programs. And in the south, the magnificent Johannesburg Art Gallery attracts patrons to its world-class Flemish and Dutch collections.

> December 5, 1956. Nelson Mandela, Walter Sisulu, and 154 other freedom fighters are arrested for treason and jailed at the Fort, a bleak, castle-like compound notorious for its brutality, no more than a ten-minute walk from Joubert Park. Throughout the struggle against apartheid, tens of thousands of people—men, women and children—are tear-gassed, beaten, shot, tortured, banned, imprisoned, and exiled.

Ladies recline on picnic blankets beneath umbrellas, sipping tea with gloved hands. Pensioners move knights and pawns around the chessboard embedded in the earth, while children splash around the fish pond surrounding the fountain which sprays them with cool mists of water when they get too close.

> 21 March 1960. Nineteen black boys and girls—and fifty adults—are mown down as they flee from a peaceful anti-apartheid protest in Sharpeville, an hour's drive from Joubert Park. Most are shot in the back.

On Sundays, a military band fills the bandstand, and movies are shown in an open-air theater, which occasionally also hosts ballets and plays. At Christmastime, the park is transformed into a Disney-like world of colored lights and statuettes featuring fairy-tale characters such as Snow White and the Seven Dwarfs. Families sing along with the Christmas carols piped in through overhead speakers.

> 1963 marks the beginning of more than twenty years of forced removals that push 3.5 million blacks out of urban areas and into bantustans, homelands reserved for black tribes. The most notorious removal is Sophiatown, the cultural center of Johannesburg's urban black community less than six miles from Joubert Park. The government bulldozed homes, uprooting more than sixty thousand people who are dumped like rubbish onto unwanted land. Many families are split up when the government's rigid race classification identified some family members as colored and others as black, forcing them to live in different townships.

The park closes every evening at 6 P.M., signaled by the ringing of a bell. White residents return to their expensive high-rise apartments overlooking the park.

> Black people, who are allowed to work and shop in the neighborhood but who are not allowed to live here, must vacate the area and travel home to the townships, a long distance from Joubert Park. Every day, they bear the indignity and the disenfranchisement of being classified as less-than-human in the land of their birth.

> *This is the pattern of apartheid, a system of segregation that, in the words of Nelson Mandela, was diabolical in its detail, inescapable in its reach, and overwhelming in its power.*[28]

•• • ••

Indaba, my children. The Rainbow Nation is born!

April 27, 1994. Already by 5 A.M., the queues to vote in the national election are snaking through Joubert Park. Old people, young people, people with disabilities, workers, mothers—people of every age and color, though very few whites, are standing together, waiting, excited, happy, tense. It is four years after Nelson Mandela was released from prison, ten thousand days after he entered. On this day, the African National Congress will win the national election and Mandela will become South Africa's first black president. Welcome to the nonracial, united, and democratic new South Africa based on one person, one vote.

The Rainbow Nation is born. And to the surprise of the entire world that watches this tortured nation transition to black power, it chooses to forgive. Nelson Mandela leads his countrymen in walking side-by-side with their oppressors, recognizing, as Archbishop Desmond Tutu phrases it so beautifully, that for South Africans, there is no future without forgiveness. Here's how the Archbishop describes the power of forgiveness:

> *Ubuntu* is very difficult to render into a Western language. It speaks of the very essence of being human. When we want to give high praise to someone we say, *"Yu, u nobuntu"*; "Hey, he or she has *ubuntu.*" This means they are generous, hospitable, friendly, caring and compassionate. They share what they have. It also means my humanity is caught up, is inextricably bound up, in theirs. We belong in a bundle of life. We say, "a person

is a person through other people." It is not "I think therefore I am." It says rather: "I am human because I belong." I participate, I share. . . .

To forgive is not just to be altruistic. It is the best form of self-interest. What dehumanizes you, inexorably dehumanizes me. Forgiveness gives people resilience, enabling them to survive and emerge still human despite all efforts to dehumanize them.[29]

This is the magic of South African resilience: They know that we belong in a bundle of life.

•• • ••

Indaba, my children. Listen to the story of our hearts breaking yet again.
After decades of being prohibited by apartheid from living in the city center, in the 1990s blacks from all over South Africa and beyond migrate to Johannesburg seeking opportunity. With the city's central train station just blocks away, Joubert Park is the first port of entry for new arrivals in Johannesburg, attracting waves of migrants and immigrants from Nigeria, Mozambique, Zimbabwe. The change is sudden and dramatic, and with it comes a surge of crime, homelessness, prostitution, and drugs. *Tsotsis*, young thugs carrying switchblades and running in gangs, pass through the park with impunity, helping to raise Johannesburg's murder rate to more than eight times the world average.[30] Joubert Park swiftly becomes a no-go zone.

Inside the park, things look different now. Everywhere, there are bodies stretched out among the garbage and the filth—some are passed out or resting; others live here during the week and go home on weekends; still others have nowhere else to go. According to those who live here, every so often someone is stabbed, gunshots ring out, babies are abandoned to freeze to death in the cold winter nights.

The Victorian conservatory is empty; the once magnificent fountain is dried up. The Johannesburg Art Gallery is nearly deserted as patrons are afraid to venture into the park, and those who live there are unaware of its treasures.

Around the perimeter of the park, things go from bad to worse. It's now a commercial ghost town. Businesses fled the city center in the 1980s to relocate to the white northern suburbs, fearing that vengeance would erupt with the end of apartheid. In their place, hawkers, hustlers, and trolley pushers line the streets trying to rustle up business. Masses of *kombis*, the minivans that serve as informal taxis, clog the streets and sidewalks until they overflow with commuters heading back to Soweto and other nearby townships. The old high-rise buildings that border the park have fallen into disrepair, becoming a slum-lord playground for overcrowding and exploitation of a desperate and transient population. It is impossible to calculate the population in the neighborhood—it could be as many as ten thousand people living in the twenty-four city blocks around the edge of the park.[31] More than 20 percent of the area's residents are under the age of twenty, many of whom hang out in the shadowy corners of the park sniffing glue and benzene.

This is not the promise of the new South Africa. It is heartbreaking, a hopeless place where dreams crumble into the dust left behind after all the gold has been stripped out.

Indaba, my children. Now you know what has happened here. Now you are ready to experience Joubert Park.

WHERE TO START?

Do you want to try to fix this place? Let's see, which problem would you like to solve first? Take your pick. How about HIV? One in every four people in this neighborhood is infected with the disease.[32] Crime? South Africa has among the world's highest per capita rates of murder, rape, robbery and assault.[33] Unemployment is closing in on 30 percent—again, far higher downtown.[34] Or perhaps you'd rather start with poverty? Urban decay? Drugs? Child rape? Teen violence? Lack of schooling? Illiteracy?

In Western culture, we've refined the practice of problem solving. We've learned to identify and label the deficiency—here are the failing schools; these are the broken families; this is the abusive corporation. We've developed squadrons of professionals trained to break down problems into their component parts, and then to resolve, reform and eradicate them. These are the well-intentioned social servants who are reengineering our schools to produce learning, our hospitals to produce health, our police to produce safety, our legal systems to produce justice. We approach problems one by one and invest in specialized institutions to deal with each of them.

Unfortunately, the proposed solutions that come from these institutions often have little to do with the people who live in the community;

they have to do with the professionals who come to solve the community's problems. The citizens themselves become clients, needy people who are acted upon by wiser outsiders. In his book *The Careless Society,* John McKnight writes, "Human service professionals with special expertise, techniques and technology push out the problem-solving knowledge and action of friend, neighbor, citizen and association. As the power of profession and service system ascends, the legitimacy, authority, and capacity of citizens and community descend. The *citizen* retreats. The *client* advances. The power of community action weakens. The authority of the service system strengthens."[35]

So it goes in city after city, region after region, nation after nation. As problem solvers, we have extended our fingers into the planet's every nook and cranny, probing for knots and tight spots that need our healing touch. Professionals and volunteers alike embrace assignments in war-torn and troubled places with a spirit of service and good will, hungering to give their gifts.

And yet, the growth of the problems we yearn to resolve continues to outpace our skills at problem solving. What's more, we argue with each other about which approach will be most effective, convinced that each problem (education, economic security, health care, good governance, etc.) can be solved in isolation. We seek simple solutions, but the challenges of community are deeply interdependent and complex. They are part of a whole system. When we seek to solve our problems through segmentation, we always create unintended consequences—thus more problems. Does this sound familiar? Have you ever been asked to solve one problem only to discover that the solution itself spawned several new ones?

If we were to proceed in Joubert Park in the conventional way, we'd be debating which problem to tackle first. Prepare to be surprised, for the starting place was simply the moment when a few people stepped forward to act, to create a better future. The starting place, as Archibishop Tutu says, begins with the recognition that "we are bound together by our caring humanity, a universal sense of *ubuntu. . . .* Then we experience fleetingly that we are made for togetherness, for friendship, for community, for family; that we are created to live in a delicate network of interdependence."[36]

It is the delicate network of interdependence in Joubert Park that gives rise to great change—and to the practice of starting anywhere.

START ANYWHERE, FOLLOW IT EVERYWHERE

Getting to Joubert Park is no easy task. Even if you arrive by private car, you'll have to wend your way through the frenzied city streets, past the hawkers and hustlers who still crowd the sidewalks and spill over into the traffic. In every direction are the telltale signs of urban neglect—the rubbish and the noise and the hopeless eyes of loiterers with nowhere to go. The perimeter of Joubert Park still feels tense, unpredictable. People warily eye one another, waiting for something to happen. They are watching you, too.

As you enter the park, a photographer greets you, his Nikon and a whistle slung around his neck, watchful eyes registering every person who passes in and out of this gate. He is on patrol, a member of the Photographers Association that formed in response to rising crime in the park. Recognizing that people won't come to have their picture taken if the park doesn't feel safe, the photographers organized their own neighborhood crime watch, nabbing muggers and snapping photos of stabbings to hand over to the police.

Start anywhere. There are dozens of photographers throughout the park. They were the first to self-organize to reverse the park's rampant deterioration in the 1990s. Their small efforts paved the way for something new to emerge—the possibility that Joubert Park could, once again, be a place where children run and play.

Follow it everywhere. As you approach the northeast corner of the park, you see an octagonal building painted in the traditional Ndebele style: vivid red, gold, blue, and green geometric shapes outlined with thick

Neighborhood children come to Lapeng to play in the park. The Creative Inner City Initiative invites inner-city youth to express themselves through art and music.

FROM PROBLEM TO PLACE

black borders. In the playground just outside, forty children are holding hands in a big circle, chanting a song. The ladies tending the children are mostly volunteers, many of them local mothers of the children in the program. They invite you indoors in hushed voices to glimpse the little ones who are sprawled on mats spread out on the floor, napping.

This is Lapeng ("at home" in Tswane) Family and Childhood Center, a day care–cum–empowerment center that began in 1997 to create a space for early childhood care that had been nonexistent for black children. Most of the preschool children in the neighborhood still spend all day shuttered for safety inside the stale spaces of the high-rise tenements surrounding the park. This is in violation of children's rights, Lapeng proclaims: the right to jump, the right to play, the right to enjoy sunshine and fresh air, the right to hear birds sing.

Early on, the Lapeng team recognized that caring for sixty-five children daily wasn't sufficient to create a systemic shift in the welfare of local families. High levels of unemployment, illiteracy and insecurity among parents continued to create instability at home. So they began to invite unemployed parents to participate more actively in caring for the children, adding classes in literacy, math and science, art and Montessori training. Local mothers learned to start their own day care centers. Teenagers began to drop by Lapeng in the afternoons to teach the toddlers simple math and colors. Lapeng took responsibility for coordinating the Ziyabuya Festival because they believed in the powerful effect that arts have on building self-esteem and connecting youth to their culture. They dared to celebrate the gifts of South Africa's artistic heritage in the heart of its most despondent neighborhood.

In 1998, Mathibedi Nthite finished art school and came to Joubert Park as a volunteer to coordinate the Ziyabuya Festival. Soon after, she joined Lapeng full-time as an administrative assistant and, by 2004, became the organization's director. A spirited young woman in her early thirties with two children of her own, Mathibedi is passionate about the role of the arts in educating children and uniting families and communities. She and her colleagues recognized that the festival could catalyze yet another Joubert Park initiative—one that would unite inner-city artists with a place in need of beauty.

The Creative Inner City Initiative (CICI) was launched in April 2002 to invite inner-city youth who were struggling with drug abuse, gangs, and crime to express their frustrations and dreams in creative ways—through street theater, painting, welding, textile printing, mosaics, sign making, and more. Originally planned as an eighteen-month initiative, CICI was housed in an old school building just outside the park, where youth would gather to hang out, experiment with new skills, or just tell their stories. The purpose was to build the capacity of local artists, connect them with one another, and trust that those networks of relationships would strengthen over time, creating a local web of support. That web ultimately engaged more than eight hundred artists and performers.

The opportunity to beautify the park wasn't the only thing that Mathibedi noticed as she worked with children and families at Lapeng. She also noticed how many of the parents at Lapeng had arrived from the rural areas and yearned to be able once again to grow their own food. As they struggled to find jobs and feed their families, they bemoaned their wasted gardening expertise they'd cultivated since birth. "Then by God's grace," Mathibedi declares, "The GreenHouse Project came in!"

WE'VE GOT WHAT WE NEED

Joubert Park may seem an unlikely setting for one of Africa's most progressive green initiatives, but against all expectations, The GreenHouse Project proudly sprawls across the northwest corner of the park. Pick your way through a maze of green: chicken-wire barrel gardens of vegetables that burst through their side walls and pour out the top in a form of vertical agriculture; raised brick beds with row after row of spinach, lettuce, tomatoes, carrots, onions, potatoes, and herbs; aromatic compost piles of straw and organic waste fermenting into richly fertilized soil. Two young boys race through, pushing wheelbarrows. A couple of elderly men rake up straw that has gathered in the pathways. A woman harvests corn that

Crops grow out the tops and side walls of barrels in a form of "vertical agriculture." The park's old potting shed was converted into the GreenHouse Project office.

FROM PROBLEM TO PLACE

she will bring over to Lapeng for the children's lunch. She is part of the urban agriculture co-op whose member organizations have plots in the garden. Others come here to learn the skills of vertical agriculture so they can grow food at home on their balconies and rooftops. Every inch of space is in use—growing food and replenishing soil, capturing rainwater and cleansing graywater (recyclable wastewater), developing eco-friendly buildings, conserving energy and recycling waste.

Claiming its space in Joubert Park in 2002, The GreenHouse Project is an ambitious effort to create a holistic approach to environmentally friendly city living. A young woman with intense eyes and a wide grin comes rushing at you, already talking a mile a minute. This is Dorah Lebelo, the impassioned director of the project, and you'll need to give her all your attention if you want to keep up. Immediately, she launches into an explanation of the deeper purpose of her work. "What we're doing here at the GreenHouse is about empowering people so they can realize that they've already got the knowledge," she says. "They have once lived like this; they have once grown their own food; they have once built their own houses; they have once fetched their own water; they have once dealt with their own waste."[37] Dorah knows this personally. She herself moved to Joubert Park in 1997 as a new arrival from Limpopo, South Africa's northernmost province. She stayed two years during the area's peak crime period, then moved to a northern suburb only to return to Joubert Park four years later as part of the GreenHouse team.

What Dorah learned living in a rural community she's now applying to life in the city. "We start from a place of abundance—knowing that we've got what we need—and we operate from that," she says. "We're not looking to other people to solve our problems; we work to maximize our own potential."

Evidence of this belief abounds in the imaginative and thrifty reuse of the park's neglected structures from its apartheid years. The old potting shed was a small, damp rectangular building constructed of brick and asbestos that provided access to three long hothouses. This would become the GreenHouse's main office—and a demonstration of community engagement and green-building principles. The bulk of the materials that had to be dismantled were set aside for reuse. Rubble from the demolition was used as a porous substrate for the "willow wall," a living fence designed to purify and release graywater. Old steel radiator pipes were rewelded into light fixtures. Broken pieces of glass were fitted into a mosaic decorating the front steps.

New construction materials were natural, renewable or secondhand. The GreenHouse team invited the community to participate in Learn and Build courses, where they constructed the straw-bale wall that anchors the conference room. They experimented with a dung-finished earth floor, but they ultimately couldn't get the recipe quite right and settled for pine boards. They made natural paint from various combinations of cottage cheese, builder's lime, and pigment powder.

The office is fitted with water-free compost toilets, rainwater harvesting systems, and a solar water heater and stove to cook staff lunches. Dorah directs your attention to what looks like a metallic satellite dish attached to a bicycle. She giggles as she explains how they've sent staff members cycling around the neighborhood, selling hot dogs and popcorn cooked on the solar panel of this sun-powered hot dog stand.

Before leaving the office, Dorah introduces you to Mabule Mokhine— soon to be her successor at The GreenHouse Project (as she shifts her attention toward the role of women in climate change policy). Born in Soweto, Mabule had contributed to founding a community-based organization that had partnered with the GreenHouse long before he joined its staff. In contrast to his high-speed colleague, Mabule is soft-spoken and reflective, and while his head is often absorbed in social theory, his hands are most at home in the soil and recycling—growing food and transforming waste.

Together, Mabule and Dorah lead the way to an unfinished construction project, the renovation of the old Victorian conservatory. Tall pillars of timber surround shade walls constructed of straw-bale and hydroform

Dorah Lebelo has been with The GreenHouse Project since it first arrived in Joubert Park in 2002. Her successor as project director is Mabule Mokhine.

FROM PROBLEM TO PLACE

bricks made of 5 percent cement and 95 percent compressed clay and sand. This will be a two-story conference center and exhibition space and an important future source of income for The GreenHouse Project.[38]

The final stop on your tour is the recycling center which opened for business in March 2006. Managed by a workers' cooperative of fifteen people from the neighborhood, the center sorts paper, plastic, bottles, tin, and glass. In the morning, the workers go out into the neighborhood clad in bright yellow overalls to collect recyclables and raise awareness about the importance of reclaiming our waste.

Critics have suggested that the effort is wasted on a community such as Joubert Park, whose population is more concerned with surviving than saving the environment. But Dorah sees the two concerns as interdependent. "If we want to create sustainable communities, we are going to have to look at things in a holistic way," she explains. "We just cannot come and say, 'Oh, my responsibility is health, and I'm just going to come here and only look at health. I'm just going to give these people drugs and help them survive AIDS.' You need to look at what it is they are eating and where they are living. What kind of houses are they living in? What kind of energy are they using? It's not only about one thing. Once you start addressing this, it's going to lead you to that. Once you own that one, it's going to lead to another." She's interested in how we can look at people's lives holistically—the whole system—rather than just one problem at a time.

The Photographers Association. Lapeng. CICI. The GreenHouse Project. These are only part of the whole system that today forms Joubert Park. There's also the Youth Empowerment Network that connects at-risk youth; the Joubert Park Neighborhood Network to provide information on

Interdependence is the essence of Joubert Park. Community members recognize that producing food, educating children, and providing jobs are inextricably linked together.

WALK OUT WALK ON

tenant rights and citizen engagement; the Joubert Park Public Art Project, a collective of artists working to revitalize the inner city and integrate the Johannesburg Art Gallery (JAG) into the community. And of course, there is the transient community of residents, migrants, and immigrants for whom Joubert Park is the port of entry to the rest of South Africa. Things change quickly in Joubert Park, and for that reason, the organizations that provide the community's only sense of continuity need to stay very connected, at times gathering every month to catch up on one another's work and reflect on the latest challenges in the park. Together, they steward the health and well-being of those whose lives are touched by Joubert Park.

Start anywhere, follow it everywhere. It started with the small act of photographers figuring out how to secure their livelihood. As the park became more secure, people's attention turned toward the children; with day care established, people could focus on the parents; as the parents learned to read and obtain employment, attention shifted to the youth. And so on. No one planned this process. The professional problem solvers would hardly have recommended that a start-up child care center begin teaching adults mathematics, or that a ragtag band of entrepreneurial photographers become the catalyst for a systemwide transformation. Nonetheless, a conversation that began among a few men led to a level of collective engagement that would transform Joubert Park from resignation and despair into hope and possibility. This is the pattern of systems change: We act locally, inside the intricacies of a place. We achieve success in one area, and then we notice where to pay attention next.

This recognition of interdependence is the essence of Joubert Park. At lunchtime, everyone gathers in The GreenHouse Project's straw-bale boardroom for a freshly harvested, solar-stove-cooked bowl of vegetable soup. The GreenHouse staff is here, as is Mathibedi from Lapeng, friends from the Youth Empowerment Network and the garden volunteers. This is a family, and they take the time daily to be together, to listen to the stories and dreams that are emerging in the ever-changing place that is Joubert Park. Doreen Khumalo, a local mother and GreenHouse staffer who prepared today's lunch, shares her story. "I started at the crèche where I used to take my child," she recalls. "I saw a space where I could plant and they allowed me to plant there. I got food from there, children from the crèche got food from the garden, and mothers at the crèche got food, too. It was a crèche for unemployed mothers. That's where GreenHouse saw me. Then I came here and volunteered for three years. Then I got a job. That's why you see me here."[39]

When the meal is finished, Dorah quietly shares with you her own understanding of Ubuntu, which is lived out daily in the harsh landscape of downtown Johannesburg. "We operate from the fact that I am because you are," she reflects. "You've got to be okay for me to be okay. Together, we can make it."

A PLACE-BASED APPROACH TO PROBLEMS

Here—on this tiny parcel of land no bigger than a football field that carries in its earth the entire history of South Africa—here, a community has dared to turn to one another to create a sense of safety, care for its children, educate its adults, empower its youth, grow its own food, and make wise use of its own waste. Joubert Park is a place that knows itself as a community, that works with what is present, not what is absent. It is a place that expects leadership to burst forth from the many, not be controlled by the problem-solving few.

Our instinct as problems solvers is to notice when a great solution has emerged and try to capture it, as if it were a sapling that we could uproot

When I was first introduced to the phrase "Start anywhere, follow it everywhere" in 2002, it had an immediate impact on me. I had recently quit my job as a consultant, where I was often hired to design a road map for clients to travel from their current state to some desired future. One reason I had quit was because I realized that the journey never unfolds the way we say it will. Not only does life come along with its unplanned detours, but too often those of us designing the road maps are not part of the landscape. Time after time, we would misread—or simply miss—its contours and signposts.

What struck me about "Start anywhere, follow it everywhere" was its invitation to relinquish our bird's-eye view in favor of having our feet on the ground, traversing territory with which we have become deeply familiar. This is what I witnessed in Joubert Park over the years. Through their intimacy with this place, Dorah, Mabule, Mathibedi, and others inside Joubert Park can see who else is here, which resources are showing up, what's calling for attention now. They aren't trying to solve the problem of homelessness; they're figuring out how to support homeless people in Joubert Park. They're not trying to eliminate illiteracy; they're teaching their neighbors to read. In Joubert Park, solving problems always begins with knowing where we are.

Deborah

and replant in any barren landscape. Dorah was invited to do just that in 2004, when she was approached by a community group in Hillbrow, a neighborhood equally afflicted with poverty and crime next door to Joubert Park. They, too, had a park, and they wanted to know if Dorah and her colleagues could fix up their area the way they had done their own. "I told them that it would be hard for us to replicate what happened because that community is not the same," Dorah recalls. "Of course, we can share experiences, and in listening to our experiences you might pick up some things that will help you to start an initiative that is similar to this one. But because of the nature of the relationships and the kind of people that have been involved, you can't duplicate what happened in Joubert Park in any other place." She invited them instead to join her in Joubert Park to listen to their stories, share resources and ideas, and create learning relationships. But she was emphatic that the local community would have to discover its own path. "The people have to do it by themselves," she says. "It can't come from those who don't live what's happening day to day in the area."

As outside observers, one impoverished inner-city park may look the same as any other. We try to make sense of difference by looking for what's familiar, by relying on the uniformity of our experience. So we neutralize the uniqueness of place, cleansing it of its ecological and cultural ancestry. It becomes easy to believe that what works here will work there, that what is good for these people will be good for those people. That if we've solved a problem in one place, the same solution should be implemented in another. That we should scale up instead of scale across.

Yet somehow the uniqueness of place regularly breaks through. When we know a place intimately, we experience its aliveness in many dimensions. We are connected to its past and its present, to the people who live there today and those who have passed through before, to its native ecology and that which has been added or destroyed, to the structures that have been built upon its ground and those that have crumbled back into its earth.

Each place is an interdependent web of relationships, which is why you can start anywhere. There is no right place to start. It is only when we're inside a system that we can begin to know its dynamics. And even then, we can never predict how that system will respond to our efforts. It is only *after* we disturb the system that we can see its interconnections and what our next work could be—which is why a day care center decides to teach adults literacy. From the outside, the problems of Joubert Park seem to need lots of programs and professionals; only from the inside can we see how the photographers, mothers, artists, and gardeners are capable of self-organizing to weave together a resilient community.

Everything that has come before in Joubert Park—its beauty and hope, destruction and despair—contributes to what it is today. The power of this place is irrepressible, pulsing with its heritage of myth, music, dance, and tragedy. How absurd to waltz in from beyond its borders with our problem-solving skills and dictate how this place should be cured of its ills. Dorah and her colleagues in Joubert Park have walked out of a problem-based approach to place and walked on to a place-based approach to problems.

Start anywhere, follow it everywhere.

UNLEASHING TRANSITION TOWNS

Do you fear that the work of Joubert Park is too small? That it can never have an impact on the rest of South Africa? After all, walk only a block or two beyond its borders, and you'll find little has changed. And yet, the power of acting locally to heal one place—to bring it into whole-ness—has the potential to sweep through a far larger system in ways that we may neither see nor predict.

If we look beyond Joubert Park, we'll find stunning illustrations of this. Take, for example, the Transition Town movement, which began in the English town of Totnes. In October 2005, environmentalists Rob Hopkins and Naresh Giangrande started to host a series of talks and film screenings in this town of eight thousand about the twin challenges of peak oil and climate change.[40] Less than a year later, they gathered 350 people together for the "Official Unleashing of Transition Town Totnes," an event that would ignite the town with a deluge of initiatives and explorations: Feeding Totnes, the Energy group, the Health and Medicine group, Oil Vulnerability Auditing, the Local Government Liaison Group, the Economics and Livelihood Group, the Heart and Soul Group. The town launched the Totnes Pound, a paper currency designed to encourage people to support local businesses. It launched a seed exchange, a local food directory, tree planting, an arts group, a storytelling event, a business swap shop. Everyone in the community was invited to contribute their gifts, to take the *start anywhere* of the Unleashing and *follow it everywhere*.

Meaningful work is like a wildfire. Just over a year after the Unleashing, the Transition Town movement had spread to fifty other towns and cities through the United Kingdom. As of July 2010, 321 towns in 15 countries have officially proclaimed themselves Transition Towns. The movement is about the power of place-based change. Each and every one is engaged in a messy, emergent, self-organizing process filled with experimentation and uncertainty stretching out to every aspect of local life. There are no predefined solutions, no deference to outside expertise. Nothing captures the essence of this "community-scale" work better than the movement's own "Cheerful Disclaimer" writ large on its website:

> Just in case you were under the impression that Transition is a process defined by people who have all the answers, you need to be aware of a key fact.
> We truly don't know if this will work. Transition is a social experiment on a massive scale.
> What we are convinced of is this:
> • if we wait for the governments, it'll be too little, too late
> • if we act as individuals, it'll be too little
> • but if we act as communities, it might just be enough, just in time.
> Everything that you read on this site is the result of real work undertaken in the real world with community engagement at its heart. There's not an ivory tower in sight, no professors in musty oak-paneled studies churning out erudite papers, no slavish adherence to a model carved in stone.
> This site, just like the transition model, is brought to you by people who are actively engaged in transition in a community. People who are learning by doing—and learning all the time. People who understand that we can't sit back and wait for someone else to do the work. People like you, perhaps. . . .[41]

People like the citizens of Joubert Park. People, says Dorah, who recognize their inherent capacity as human beings to be as creative, imaginative and committed as their community calls on them to be. "I am a leader because there are people around me who believe in me," she says. "I don't exist outside my community; they create me. And I in turn create them by believing in their leadership, by trusting that we have everything we need to create the world we wish for."

This, too, is Ubuntu, an invitation to each and every one of us to recognize that we are inextricably bound up together in a bundle of life.

FROM PROBLEM TO PLACE

PROBLEM

When you first encountered Joubert Park, how did you react to the complexity of challenges there? HIV/AIDS, poverty, homelessness, immigration, safety, illiteracy. Faced with so many problems, some of us feel overwhelmed, even depressed. Others start to think about what solutions they'd offer from their field of expertise. However you respond, Joubert Park is an encounter with complexity.

We live in a world of never-ending complexity, but complexity isn't the problem. Complex systems are filled with challenges and conflicts that are unavoidable, but these aren't the problem, either. The central problem is how we *work with* complexity. We do everything to avoid it. Either we deny its existence, or we partition problems into separate compartments.

Problems don't exist in isolation, given the nature of our interdependent, interconnected world. But we still rely on reductionism, creating government agencies, institutions and specialists to deal with problems one by one. Experts are trained to drill down into a problem; unfortunately, the deeper they dig, the more they lose sight of everything else that's connected to the problem.

Specialists are skilled, talented, and motivated, but these days, many of them are exhausted and demoralized. Because problems are never solved by ignoring interconnections, disappointment and fatigue are built into our current problem-solving approaches. Not only do we fail to find solutions, we end up generating more problems.

Many experts respond to frustration and failed projects by just working harder. They bargain for more resources, they attempt to influence more decision makers, they spend longer hours at work. They've spent years developing their expertise, feel confident they know what they're doing, and are anxious to make a difference.

What if we experts could acknowledge our frustration and become curious? What if we got interested in the interconnectedness of a problem rather than trying to hold it all within our one specialty? What if we noticed all the others who are connected to this problem, who also are motivated to solve it? What if we set out to explore these interconnections and develop new relationships as a result?

Anytime experts emerge from the deep tunnel of specialization, many good things bloom in the light of day. We discover more is possible with curiosity than with certainty. We discover that *not* being right opens the space for other people's good ideas. We discover there are many people just like us, deeply committed to finding a solution. New ideas and new relationships give us all more energy and inspiration. Frustration and exhaustion transform into enthusiasm and delight as we discover, with others, solutions to complex problems that really work.

If you're an expert (in anything), do any of
these dynamics describe your experience?
Which ones feel important to notice?

PLACE

Joubert Park is a small plot of land that holds centuries of human triumph and struggle. Yet we didn't take you there to be amazed. We took you there because this one tiny park illuminates what's true in many places. When people use a place-based approach to solving problems, when we value the rich resources all around us, when we honestly face our challenges as community, change happens.

This is how we're able to mobilize complexity on our behalf. We recognize that we live in a bundle of life, a network of interdependent relationships. We acknowledge that we're all in this together. We develop faith that we can find what we need by turning to one another. We recognize that we don't solve problems one by one. And we relax because we don't have to solve them all at once. We start, anywhere, and see where the work takes us next.

Place-based change requires us to be present, available, willing. Systems can't be understood from the outside. No matter how intricate a network map we draw, or how many interactions and loops we name, these are static depictions. Beneath their neatness on paper lives the volatile world of human dynamics, emotional energy only visible in real life. This is why we can't know a system until we're inside it, living in its messiness, engaged in relationships, noticing possibilities.

We can't see systems all at once and, fortunately, we don't have to. We start anywhere. We begin with whatever problem grabs our attention, whatever issue opens the door. It's as if we stepped into a tree's root system and, once inside, can see the density of interconnections, how everything is linked to everything else, how cutting out any one thing would create many destructive consequences.

Inside, we also discover who cares about an issue, who's willing to take action, who's willing to step forward as a leader, who needs care, who needs encouragement. None of this is visible if we stay outside in the comfort of objective expertise.

Once we start anywhere, we have to stay alert to where we are, what we're learning and what's next. It's not about how well our plan is working, but whether we notice the signals swirling around us. What are present-moment opportunities, who's shown up willing to work with us? We can't fall asleep or rest on our accomplishments. Yet as we listen to the call of the system, as we follow it wherever it beckons us, things start to change. People become confident. Community strengthens. Problems get solved.

Go inside. Start anywhere. Follow it everywhere.

Have you ever begun without plans or strategies?
What did you learn by starting anywhere?

"WE DIDN'T DREAM OF MANDELA"

Many years ago, shortly after Nelson Mandela became president, a South African CEO spoke to a group at a seminar on self-organizing systems (which Meg was co-teaching). At one point, he looked around the room and said, "You must all come to South Africa. We didn't dream of Mandela. We never expected forgiveness. What we are doing is not just for us, but for the world. Come prepared to listen to our stories (everyone has a story), and learn from us. Return home willing to share what you've learned and to keep our stories alive."

The millions of stories that come from the New South Africa and its troubling history are a gift. This history (and why we took time to briefly chronicle it) is a story of the human spirit in all its paradoxical complexity—our capacity for violence and dehumanization, our capacity for survival and triumph, for hatred and compassion, for abuse and forgiveness. South Africa's story is humanity's story.

Their story continues, a refiner's fire where every day people choose between violence and patience, between forgiveness and revenge, between the ways of modern life and the traditions of community. South Africa's future is unknown, but it remains a powerful teacher. Here, we are confronted with everything that's possible, everything that's wrong, nearly fifty million diverse people bound together in hope and fear trying to find the future.

History plays a critical role in how we shape the future. What we tell ourselves about the past gives us ground (even though these stories change). People who persevere know where they come from. They stand on the firm shoulders of their ancestors and draw sustenance from the old stories. We humans need to know that we participate in something bigger, that traditions will outlast us, that history will continue to unfold beyond this moment.

Present culture misleads us to believe that we make it on our own, that we need vision and determination but not ancestors. Yet the future takes form not only from our dreams, but from our roots. We're never alone in our work. Not only do we have the company of those around us now, we also have the strength of those who labored long before us.

KUFUNDA LEARNING VILLAGE, ZIMBABWE
FROM EFFICIENCY TO RESILIENCE

I have read that Africans all over the world are linked by slavery, but it's not true. We are linked by our resilience, that inbred evolutionary ability to live and grow and love against all odds.

—*J. Nozipo Maraire,*
    Zimbabwean author and physician

Mangwanani. Good morning. I slept well if you slept well.

Forty people are sitting around the perimeter of the open-sided *dare*. The thatched roof soars twenty feet overhead, a majestic acorn cap topping what Marianne Knuth calls our "container," the circle that hosts the community at Kufunda Learning Village. Like the glass that surrounds and protects the flame of a lamp so it can burn more brightly, Marianne says, so, too, does our circle create the space in which each of us can tremble and shine with our own radiance.

My name is Virginia Tizora. I come from Zvimba. This is my fourth time at Kufunda. The first time when I came, I was very excited to learn how to make the arborloos. That's what I came for. But when I was here, I was very interested in everything I learned. I wanted to come again. I'm very pleased to see you!

Virginia beams, regal in her red and gold wrap dress and matching headscarf. She leans in toward the circle, her eyes flashing with joy and a youthful mischief that belies her fifty-plus years of laborious rural life. She holds a glass globe in both hands, the talking piece that will travel around the circle until every voice has been heard, even those that for reasons of age or gender or politics have been silenced in this troubled country. You, too, will have a chance to speak your heart's wisdom when the talking piece makes its way to you. Trust yourself: The right words will come at the right time. For now, just listen.

My name is Allan Mahachi. I stay at Kufunda. I live at Kufunda. I work at Kufunda. Everything about me is Kufunda. I'm happy to meet you guys.

Allan roars with laughter. He is Kufunda's class clown, a dreadlocked young man with a booming James Earl Jones voice. He moved to Kufunda

The open-sided *dare* that hosts the circle of community at Kufunda is surrounded by massive granite boulders.

FROM EFFICIENCY TO RESILIENCE

from nearby Ruwa when he was only twenty-three, becoming a Kufundee, one of nearly twenty people plus their families who live and work at this learning and demonstration center just a half hour's drive from Harare, Zimbabwe's capital. He's the on-site IT guy who maintains Kufunda's connection to the outside world through its solar-panel-powered computer and Internet network. He's also the go-to guy if you're looking for a late-night party.

I heard someone once say, "Don't tell people what to do, but show them where you want to go." This is what I've learned in this place.

This is Silas speaking, one of the first Kufundees who came to practice and teach permaculture, an approach to agriculture that mimics, rather than tries to subdue, nature. He, too, has long dreadlocks that he keeps tied up under a wool hat. But Silas's nature is the counterpoint to Allan: He is quiet, reflective, a devoted practitioner of meditation and an old soul in a thirty-eight-year-old's skin.

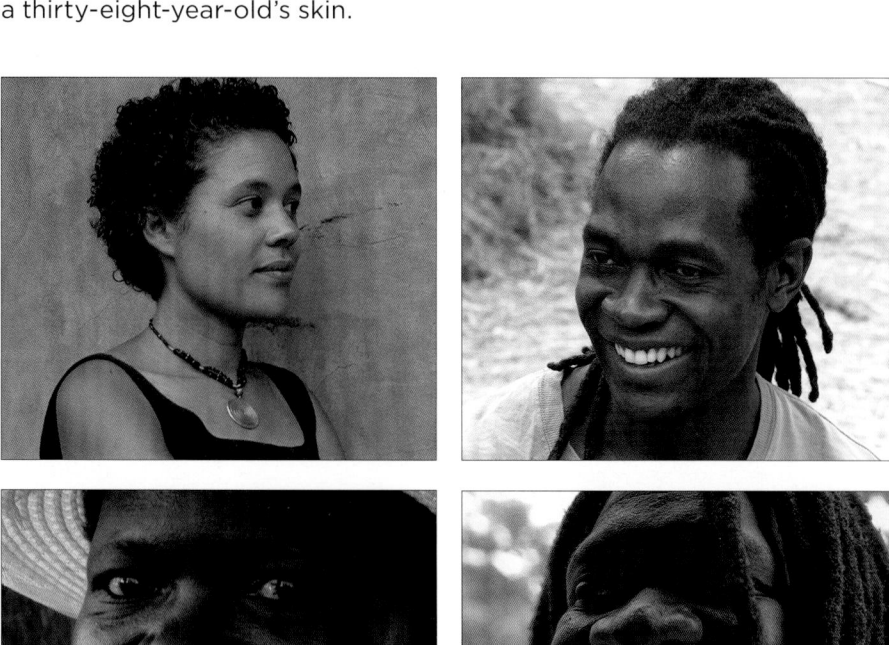

Kufundees (clockwise from top left): Marianne Knuth, Silas Lusias, Allan Mahachi, and Sophia Nekati.

Being at Kufunda has taught me a lot about who I am and how I can help others. I've come to realize that what we must do is share. We know that we have everything we need; we just have to take the time to discover it.

He pauses, sits perfectly still, cradling the glass ball in both hands and gazing gently into each face in the circle. Tranquility descends on us. The moment is timeless and familiar: People have been gathering in circle like this ever since community began. We have entered a different quality of time, of connection, of communion. The talking piece resumes its journey around the circle, eventually tumbling into the lap of Sophia, a tiny woman with fierce eyes and a deep, soft voice.

Mangwanani. I slept well if you slept well. My name is Sophia. At Kufunda, I learned about my life again. Before, I did not take HIV/AIDS very seriously. But I came here and said, now is time. I went for the testing. My results came back positive. I have had very big pain. Now I am on the herbal team, making medicines. Kufunda is now my life.

A bell rings, piercing the heavy air and reverberating off the massive granite boulders that perch inexplicably on the land, like gods and guardians protecting the circle. It is a call for silence, which the Kufundees say is also part of the conversation. There is no need for action now; you are not meant to do anything. You are invited to bear witness to another's suffering, to listen deeply with your heart wide open—without leaping up to fix, heal, soothe, or respond. This, perhaps, is the essence of what it means to be in Zimbabwe in these times: to engage in the excruciatingly difficult practice of simply bearing witness. (On June 12, 2010, Sophia passed away from tuberculosis. She was a fighter, the Kufundees said, who knew it was time to let go of the fight.)

Once again, stillness descends on the circle. You can hear the breeze ruffling the leaves of the msasa tree and the lucky bean tree. Jack, a rangy mutt beloved by the community, roams the circle, eventually settling in at Marianne's feet. Kudzi, Sikhethiwe's (pronounced *Skit-too-wey)* infant son, squirms and murmurs on his mother's lap. Minutes pass. A plaintive voice arises, offering a few thin notes of a song in Shona. It is Anna Marunda, a magnetically graceful woman from Rusape who sits across from you. As she rises to her feet, her voice billows out, gaining strength and power, slowly enveloping the circle. Other voices stretch into harmonies to fill the space beneath her. Suddenly, the song has picked up pace, or maybe it has ended and a new one seamlessly begins, for people are now on their feet, clapping their hands and stomping their feet as the song continues to rise and rise and rise in speed and volume and spirit.

FROM EFFICIENCY TO RESILIENCE

We are marching o-ver to Jer-u-sa-lem. We are marching o-ver to Jer-u-sa-lem. The song bounces from Shona to English and back to Shona. You are being pulled from your seat to travel around the circle in that same rhythmic step, mimicking the African women by thrusting your butt back as your feet travel forward, clapping your hands and joining the throng of voices rising and falling. *Jer-u-sa-lem! Jer-u-sa-lem! Jer-u-sa-lem! Jer-u-sa-lem!* Over and over again, faster and louder. Then young Stephen, who works on the building team, shouts out in a voice that penetrates the clamor, *"MO' FIRE!"* and the song shifts again. The men pound out a base line, leaping and skipping faster around the circle while Stephen rips out a series of unrestrained hip shimmies, popping and locking in his own hip-hop creations, grinning wildly. The singing and the shouting and the stomping go on and on until you think you can't dance anymore and everyone collapses in giggles back in the circle.

This is how Kufundees metabolize grief. This is how they endure the pervasive and relentless suffering that today plagues their once magnificent country.

89.7 SEXTILLION PERCENT INFLATION

Want to know what 89.7 sextillion percent inflation[42] feels like? Then accept Sikhethiwe's invitation to join her on the weekly trip to Harare to buy food. While Kufunda has its own extensive gardens, it doesn't yet produce enough to feed participants when it hosts a program, such as this Learning Journey.

The best way to prepare yourself for this all-day adventure is to think of it as a game, a scavenger hunt designed for currency traders who get off on incomprehensible calculations and split-second decision making. Today, the Zimbabwean dollar is trading 5,000-to-1 against the U.S. dollar, but this is October 2008, which means the government has already chopped ten zeroes off the currency a few months prior (and will lop off an additional twelve zeroes in February 2009 in a futile attempt to control hyperinflation). Sikhethiwe is acutely aware that you'll need to spend what you've got as quickly as possible, because by this time tomorrow, the exchange rate will have doubled to 10,000-to-1. She's starting out with US$400 in her pocket, a list of the prices she paid last week and a spot for you in the truck between her and Simba, the driver. Let the games begin.

The first stop is in a warehouse district somewhere outside the downtown area. You climb the stairs up to an office, where a small blackboard

Many years ago, I asked my friend Tim Merry, who at the time was running a learning center in Nova Scotia, what motivated him to do his work. He said he wanted to learn and teach the skills necessary for communities to be sustainable—and that he wanted to be ready for the day no food showed up on the grocery store shelves. I remember teasing him about his apocalyptic concern. This was Canada, after all, and of course there would always be food on the grocery store shelves!

Then I got to know Zimbabwe, traveling there once or twice yearly from 2003 on, watching this once splendid country spiral into catastrophe. For many of us in the West, it's impossible to imagine a fate for ourselves like Zimbabwe's. We can point our finger at the uniquely disastrous regime of Robert Mugabe's government and feel secure in the arms of our democratic institutions.

But as I observed Zimbabwe's decline, it became clear to me that blaming Mugabe was an oversimplification. Zimbabwe's agricultural sector, for example, relied heavily on oil and subsidies to fuel its food production. When those were withdrawn, the food system collapsed.

Our food system here in the United States isn't designed any differently—it, too, depends on oil and subsidies. It, too, is a brittle system, one that leaves us vulnerable to shocks and disturbances (as we're witnessing in the skyrocketing outbreaks of salmonella, *E. coli*, and other contaminations). Our food system was designed to be maximally efficient, rather than resilient—that is, capable of adapting to and recovering from life's surprises.

Unlike Tim, I haven't been training for the day when our grocery stores are empty. But I do believe there are lessons to learn from Zimbabwe about how dependence on maximally efficient systems exposes us to the risk of collapse.

Deborah

lists prices for chicken parts—heart, neck, feet, liver. Eight ounces of feta cheese is selling for the remarkable price of US$8. Today, the seller is willing to accept U.S. dollars, which she can exchange on the black market. (It won't be until January 2009 that the government finally legalizes trade in U.S. dollars, the South African rand and the euro to supplement the embattled Zimbabwean currency.) Sikhethiwe forgoes the feta and purchases sugar and ten jars of peanut butter—all of which appear to be only about three-quarters full.

Next stop is a small convenience shop downtown with a queue of about twenty-five people standing outside the window. Upon her approach,

Sikhethiwe is waved in the door, pulling you along. The narrow corridor has just enough space for the two of you and the Southeast Asian family reigning over the meager stash of chips, crackers, cigarettes, juice boxes, yarn, and other corner store goodies. Here, people are paying in Zim dollars. Beneath the counter is a makeshift cash register of five cardboard boxes with the tops cut off that can accommodate and sort the volume of bills they'll receive today. Sikhethiwe has called ahead to arrange for the purchase of some bulk items stored in a separate room—rice, flour, the ubiquitous orange drink. She sits down with a young man to negotiate prices and a black-market exchange rate for our U.S. dollars. You interrupt them to point out that there appear to be mouse turds in the rice and need a fresh bag, but they both laugh uproariously at your naive notion that there would even be another bag!

Third stop: the outdoor marketplace at Mbare township, a shantytown filled with immigrants and people from the rural areas who come to Harare seeking work. The open field is a jumble of bedraggled tents and rusted tables piled high with tomatoes, cucumbers, squash, melons, beans, onions and grains. It looks like any other informal marketplace the world over, except that here, the earth beneath your feet is a decadent carpet of ripped and whole bills that have been ground into the dirt—remnants of the useless currency that is hyperinflating itself into oblivion. This marketplace is also a remake of itself: Just a few years ago, the entire neighborhood was looted and razed in Operation Murambatsvina (Remove the Rubbish), a government effort to crack down on black-market trading. But people are resilient, and in the absence of a viable alternative, the ramshackle tables and tents and shacks went right back up in the same spot.

Sikhethiwe (with Kudzi on her back) will spend all day negotiating Zimbabwe's black market to secure food, including jars of peanut butter only three-quarters full.

There are no prices listed anywhere; everything is a long conversation, a social call, a negotiation, and finally an exchange of a fat stack of bills for a sack of potatoes. Sikhethiwe asks you to step out of sight: Your presence as a foreigner is driving up prices for her, so you head back to the truck to wait. Two hours later, she and Simba reappear hauling bags of onions, peppers, avocados, tomatoes, bananas, melons, apples, garlic, and ginger. By now it's late afternoon, and you still have three more stops to make before the game ends.

Sextillion percent inflation means paying 100 billion dollars for three eggs, owing the phone company $2,654,287,527,899 on your latest monthly bill, and always buying two beers at once because by the time you finish the first, the second would otherwise cost you double. It means having the schools shut down because no one is paying the teachers—and those who are willing to teach without pay don't have the bus fare to get to the schools. It means having the hospital shelves empty of supplies—including fresh water for washing since the neglected water supply became contaminated with cholera.

Sextillion percent inflation is a marker of total systems collapse, and Zimbabwe is one of our most accelerated present-day stories of the implosion of a nation. It took less than ten years for Zimbabwe to go from being the breadbasket of Africa—a modernized nation funded by tourism, diamonds, and agriculture—to a nation in which well over half the population is facing severe food shortages, more than 80 percent are unemployed,[43] 3,500 people die each week of HIV/AIDS,[44] and everyone is subjugated to a government that long ago substituted corruption, cronyism, and cruelty for serving its people. Can foreign aid help solve this crisis? Hardly. Between broad-based sanctions against Robert Mugabe's reprehensible government and Zimbabwe's own intermittent suspension of foreign aid workers, there is little hope for outside intervention.

Like Paquetá in Brazil, this is another place where no one is coming to help.

I HAVE A DREAM

Born in 1971 to a Zimbabwean mother and Danish father, Marianne Knuth spent her childhood bouncing back and forth between Copenhagen and Zimbabwe, where she'd stay at her grandparents' rural homestead. She completed a master's at the Business School of Copenhagen (during which time she served as president of AIESEC International, a global organization of fifty thousand students from eighty-seven countries). Soon after, Marianne co-founded Pioneers of Change, a global learning community that supports younger leaders in creating the change they want to see in the world. She was already well established on an international stage when she began to feel the tug of Zimbabwe calling her home. In 2001, she wrote a letter to her friends in Harare, saying:

I have a dream . . .

We have a small farm of 327 acres, 23 kilometers south of Harare, which we bought in 1984 when our family moved to Zimbabwe (my mother returning after over 15 years abroad). On it we grow maize and groundnuts, cabbages and seedlings for sale, and milk for ourselves and the people in the surrounding area. My mother, sister and I hold a vision of something more—for this to be a place where we do things with and for the people of Zimbabwe. Our dreams intertwine, and I hope to see them co-exist on the farm. For now I have decided to get started. While I do not come with solutions or the way forward for sustainable community, I do come with the belief that together we can figure it out. The answers that people need are in their midst, and if we come together we can discover them.

It was a bold move, this walking out, by a bold and visionary young woman. Marianne walked out of a world that had been working well for her and walked on to the dirt beneath her feet, and the gifts of her traditions and relationships. After negotiating with her mother, Marianne carved off about thirty acres of land that would become Kufunda Village, which means "learning" in Shona. Here, communities from nearby townships and farther-off villages would gather to learn how to be healthy, vibrant, and largely self-reliant in a world that was totally collapsing around them. They would return to the old ways of erecting thatched homes with mud-brick walls that would keep them cool in the summer and warm in the winter. They would plant permaculture gardens that dance across the landscape in spirals and swirls, eschewing conventional agriculture's uniform, single-crop rows and chemical fertilizers. In the absence of antiretroviral drugs (which were both scarce and unaffordable), they would discover how to concoct herbal remedies to stave off HIV's lethal advance. They would keep bees, grow mushrooms, harvest rainwater, and plant trees. They would make shoes, carve sculptures and open a preschool.

And they would build toilets.

WASTE EQUALS FOOD

Ticha Murungweni is practically tugging at your sleeve, impatient for the opportunity to show you why arborloo toilets have become the pride of Kufunda. Thin, gangly and devout on the topic, Ticha drags you over to a little thatched house, about the size of one person. Inside is an ordinary toilet seat perched atop a concrete-and-mud stand that covers the open pit below. It is an outhouse, a privy, a thunderbox, a dunny, a biffy, a crapper, a long-drop. Whatever slang it may go by, the outhouse has long been the butt of many a sour joke—certainly not a community's treasure. It is maligned for its heavy, malodorous air of decomposition, the buzz of mosquitoes and houseflies, the careless scum left behind by those who pass through hastily.

Not this one. Inside, a gentle breeze wafts through the side walls, supplementing the built-in ventilation. The little room is spotless, cool, and odorless. A roll of toilet paper hangs neatly on a nail; a watering can and soap are affixed just outside to a tree. But the accoutrements are not what make this toilet design unique, Ticha explains. He leads you several feet away to a small mulberry tree. "Here is where the last toilet stood," he says. "Once the pit is full, we plant a young tree in the soil and move the entire toilet structure to a new location." Look around and you'll observe several fruit trees in the otherwise nutrient-poor and drought-plagued soil. "We call this toilet an 'arborloo' because it allows us to plant many trees— lemon, orange, mulberry, guava."

In the United States, we likely pump as much as four billion gallons of water each *day* to flush away our waste.[45] In Zimbabwe, they don't have

Ticha Murungweni is passionate about Kufunda's arborloos, a sanitation solution that harnesses the nutrients in human waste to grow fruit trees.

FROM EFFICIENCY TO RESILIENCE

the luxury of all that water to spare—nor do they have the excess capital to invest in constructing a sewage system. Instead, years ago most rural homesteads were given the Blair toilet handed out by development agencies. Built over a massive underground room, this toilet fills up over ten to twenty years (years that have by now come and gone) and cannot be used for anything else. It's expensive to build, which leaves rural families with no other option than to defecate out in the open—making them vulnerable to diarrhea, worm infestations, hepatitis, and cholera, the latter of which swept through Zimbabwe from November 2008 to March 2009.

The irony is that organic waste—even human waste—is part of the solution to Zimbabwe's long-term food security. In the past decade, Zimbabwe has experienced widespread soil erosion as a result of deforestation, aggressive agricultural techniques, and drought, making subsistence agriculture increasingly difficult for the 80 percent of the population that relies on it for food and livelihood. Ecological sanitation, Ticha says, is the idea that we can simultaneously solve sanitation problems and support our efforts to grow food by recovering and reusing our waste.

This is the kind of thinking that arises when you know you must work with what you have, when you know that no one is coming to help. Marianne, who has joined you by the arborloo, recalls a story from Kufunda's early years when she traveled to one of the five communities Kufunda partners with and noticed the absence of agriculture on their lands.

"'Where are your crops?' I asked them," she says. "They said they were waiting to receive their fertilizer and seeds from the government. I had to tell them that wouldn't be happening this year." In 2000, after two decades of assistance, particularly in agriculture, the World Bank suspended its lending program to Zimbabwe when the country went into arrears. There would be no more handouts of fertilizer, no more seeds.

"I asked them what they used to do *before* they got handouts of fertilizer and seeds," Marianne continues. "They said they didn't remember! So we agreed to ask the elders."

Marianne and several of the villagers called a circle with the elders and asked them to describe their agricultural practices prior to the 1980s, when the Green Revolution arrived in their home. The Green Revolution—which found its stride in the 1960s, particularly in countries like India and Pakistan that were wrestling with famine—was a technology-intensive form of agriculture that increased crop yields by relying on hybrid seeds, chemical fertilizers, pesticides and herbicides, improved irrigation, and mechanized harvesting. The idea was to maximize the efficiency of the land by taking control of nature and wringing out of her every last drop of productivity—last drops that would be heavily dependent on expensive inputs of oil and water.[46]

Indian environmental activist Vandana Shiva, one of the most respected and informed critics of the Green Revolution, points out the irony of the Green Revolution's impact on agricultural systems. "The Green Revolution was based on the assumption that technology is a superior substitute for nature, and hence a means of producing growth, unconstrained by nature's limits," she writes in her book, *The Violence of the Green Revolution*. "The reduction in availability of fertile land and genetic diversity of crops as a result of the Green Revolution practices indicates that at the ecological level, the Green Revolution produced scarcity, not abundance."[47] Sure enough, she explains, yields improved in the short term. But the new practices also brought in a host of unintended consequences that fundamentally altered people's capacity to feed themselves. Biodiversity was reduced as a range of indigenous crops were replaced with a single hybrid strain. Malnutrition resulted as local diets were replaced by a single food source that did not provide all essential nutrients, and communities dependent on a single food source could lose their entire harvest to a single disease. Water tables were depleted as water-intensive crops replaced local drought-resistant varieties. Chemical toxins leached into the soil. Farmers became dependent on multinational corporations to supply the tools and resources of industrial agriculture.

In Zimbabwe's case, the results of modernizing agriculture have been disastrous. Known as the breadbasket of Africa until as recently as 2000, Zimbabwe was a net exporter of maize, beef, sugar cane, cotton and

Kufunda's permaculture gardens are designed to mimic natural ecologies, requiring as little human intervention as possible. The herb garden spirals right next to the kitchen.

FROM EFFICIENCY TO RESILIENCE

tobacco. Ten years later, 70 percent of Zimbabweans are in need of food aid, and life expectancy has shrunk to a mere forty-four years.[48] Who would you like to blame for this disaster? It's far too easy to point the finger at the government of Robert Mugabe, which evicted and terrorized white commercial farmers and turned their land over to agriculturally illiterate cronies. In reality, there has been a perfect storm of pressures: an ongoing drought that leaves maize withering in parched fields; an HIV/AIDS scourge that ravages the labor force; vast migrations of the population fleeing economic and political oppression; fiscal and monetary policy that obliterated the national currency—and an underlying approach to food production that has optimized efficiency over resilience.

Not so long ago, the elders in Marianne's village knew how to maintain a resilient food system—that is, one that could absorb the disturbances of drought, war and change, and continue to feed the local population. As they sat in circle together, they described age-old agricultural practices that sustained their communities prior to the onset of the Green Revolution and Mugabe's disastrous policies. In some of their ideas, you might hear the language of today's so-called progressive sustainable agricultural practices. *Place elements where they are best positioned to interact with each other*—like planting marigolds with tomatoes to repel nematodes. *One species' waste is another species' food*—a closed-loop system goes from the garden to the kitchen to the human and back to the garden. *Save seeds and safeguard soil*—use nature's abundance and respect her limitations.

These are some of the principles attributed to *permaculture*, an approach to designing agricultural systems that takes its lessons from natural ecologies and strives to make human communities self-sufficient, forgoing industrial agriculture's chemical inputs. Like the traditional agricultural societies who sought to work with rather than control nature, permaculture practitioners assume that we have much to learn from nature's success in creating resilient systems that adapt to and recover from life's inevitable disruptions.

The permaculture gardens at Kufunda twist and whirl through the open field between the kitchen and dormitories, a sprawling mass of sustenance that exudes the possibility of self-reliance. A papaya tree shoots up amid the kale while the herb garden curls around itself in a spiral. The spaces between plants are filled in with straw, which Kufunda has in abundance and uses as mulching to reduce evaporation, control weeds, and enrich the soil. Discarded wine bottles filled with water pitch headfirst at the base of plants to direct water toward their roots. Water-hungry plants are positioned near the edges of thatched roofs to catch the runoff rainwater, and there's a dense jungle of green life back behind the kitchen that receives graywater from the daily cooking and washing up.

There will be no waiting for handouts here. Kufunda has walked out of dependence on fertilizer and seeds, on aid and assistance, on the belief that we don't have what we need and that we can't find a way. They are experimenting with how to respond and adapt to the reality of their circumstances, and passing that learning on to hundreds of people who similarly struggle to free themselves from limiting beliefs.

In 2004, I led fourteen people on a Learning Journey to Kufunda. The group was made up of Americans, Canadians, and Brits. We spent five days at Kufunda, building arborloos, gardening, beekeeping, cooking, and, of course, having rich conversations that usually ended up in song, dance, and laughter. On the last day of the journey, the group expressed their desire to make a gift to Kufunda in gratitude for what they had learned. They proposed to buy Kufunda an irrigation system that would save the Kufundees hours spent every day hauling water bucket by bucket from the well to the garden.

Marianne listened thoughtfully to their proposal. Then she said, "The only way I could accept your gracious offering is if you were willing to purchase an irrigation system for all villages in Zimbabwe. For we are a demonstration center, and how could we demonstrate ways of cultivating resilient food systems if we relied on a technology to which others had no access?"

It was a powerful learning moment for all of us. The Kufundees had an opportunity to increase their efficiency, utilize technology, save time, and reduce manual labor—and they declined the offer. This was not an act of idealism, romanticizing the simple, bucolic life—any more than it was an act of idealism to ask the elders how they used to grow their food. In both cases, Marianne was entirely pragmatic, more concerned with the opportunities and constraints of local conditions than with utilizing time-saving technology. Yes, gardening at Kufunda can be inefficient. But sometimes efficiency just isn't the point.[49]

Deborah

GOD'S POWER KNITTING GROUP, RUSAPE

The excitement at Kufunda has been building for days in anticipation of the journey to Rusape, home to Anna Marunda and nearly thirty thousand people distributed across sparse rural settlements and dense townships. The Kufundees love journeying together to their five partner communities, where the fruits of their efforts become visible. This visit in particular will be a celebration, as the Kufundees are bringing you along, and any occasion to fête a foreigner is good enough reason to throw a *pungwe*, an all-night party where even the grannies dance 'til dawn.

The two-hour bus ride southeast along Mutare Road beats a straight path past *kopjes*, the rocky outcroppings of balancing boulders in magical shapes, past the mupangara and the murumanyama trees, past clusters of thatched homes and a tobacco field or two. The driver turns off the road to follow a two-tire track that bounces through the grassland. And then in what appears to be the middle of nowhere, he stops.

As you clamber out of the bus, you can hear the whooping, hollering, and ululating before you see its source, which materializes as a wave of children dancing toward you along the tire tracks, parting around the bus and beckoning you to follow them down the road. The girls are arrayed in colorful skirts of red, black, and white with matching bandeaus. They are clapping and singing in a three-step shuffle that bursts into the air on the fourth beat as they reach up to gather the sky to their chests. The boys, clad in red or yellow shorts, leap and prance around, their skinny legs flying up into the air as if gravity was something that burdened only older people.

Rusape children dance a welcome to their village. "I have learned that I am a strong woman," Anna Marunda.

WALK OUT WALK ON

You are sucked into the current, dancing and stomping along the dusty path until you arrive at an ocean of wild color, the yellow, pink, and red head scarves of the women bobbing up and down in jubilation, African prints of blue and gold, solid wraps of purple, burgundy, and pink. A baby swaddled in a green blanket sleeps contentedly on its mother's back as she bounces, struts, and chants. The whole village of Tande has arrived, at least a hundred mothers and fathers, teachers and orphans, councilmen, babies, and *mbuyas*, the grandmothers. There will be a formal welcome to the village by the chief; a washing ritual where women on bended knee deliver a basin of water to the headman; a dance and drumming performance by the children; and a song from the preschool-aged orphans. The women will feed you lunch, a morsel of roast chicken for this special occasion alongside bubbling hot *sadza*, the country's maize-meal staple that you'll roll into blistering balls with your fingers and scoop into your mouth. The women have spent hours muscling the stiff porridge around in thick iron pots over the open fire, a laborious task that often occurs more than once a day, as sadza may be the only dish available.

Anna Marunda steps forward with a band of women dressed in white shirts festooned with ribbons that identify themselves as *Kufundees*. She will lead the way nimbly uphill, scrambling over loose rocks and boulders that have you panting and breathless until you reach her homestead, where more women are waiting to greet you—singing, dancing, and drumming once more. Beneath a table laden with crocheted handbags, hats, baby clothes, and blankets, a sign reads, *"It's good to be here! Zvakanaka Kuwe Pano! God's Power Knitting Group, Rusape."* These women have formed a sewing cooperative founded by Anna after her first visit to Kufunda in 2003. She is a widow who had been living on a four-dollar monthly pension from her late husband but required five dollars a month in school fees alone. Since then, in addition to the sewing cooperative, she has started a knitting school, built her own arborloos and is teaching others to do the same (you may notice the evidence of her success in the many fruit trees that now populate the landscape), has a permaculture garden, and is hosting an AIDS dialogue group and providing home care to villagers weakened by the disease.

Anna interrupts the celebrating to invite everyone to sit on the blankets she has laid out on the earth. She introduces the God's Power Knitting Group and then tells her story. "I thought that because I was one of the poorest people in my community, I had no role to play," she explains. "At Kufunda, I learned that each one of us has something special to give.

I have learned that I have been an example in my community for being a widowed woman who overcame severe hardship. I have learned that I am a strong woman. I have learned that I can find peace of mind within myself. I have learned that I am a good listener, and I am trustworthy, so people are coming to me, inviting me to join them."[50]

Since Anna first started coming to Kufunda, the Tande community has opened three preschools. A tree nursery project boasts more than five thousand trees—a mix of exotic fruit trees for sale and indigenous trees for reforestation. More than fifty families have built arborloos and permaculture gardens, which have supplemented their food supply through these baleful last years. Word is spreading, reaching more than 250 people throughout Rusape who also yearn to walk on to self-reliance.

Imagine what Zimbabwe might look like today if there were places like Rusape all over the country utilizing local resources and exchanging innovative practices with others. It would be a land filled with resilient communities.

FROM EFFICIENCY TO RESILIENCE

Zimbabwe is hardly the first country in recent history to endure a sudden, sweeping food system collapse. Cuba had been touted as another miracle of the Green Revolution—until the Soviet Union fell apart. Almost overnight, Cuba lost its supply of oil, the essential resource that fuels industrial agriculture. Within a year, over 80 percent of Cuba's foreign trade disappeared. Suddenly, there were no chemical fertilizers, no seeds, no fuel for tractors and irrigation systems, no way to obtain spare parts. Between 1989 and 1993, the average Cuban lost twenty pounds.[51]

So Cubans started to work with what they had. In the absence of fertilizer and pesticides, they began farming organically. The older folks who used to plough their fields with oxen were invited to offer their wisdom while fuel-dependent machinery sat idly by. Industrial-scale state farms were broken up into small farms and thousands of gardens. In the cities, vacant lots, schoolyards, and patios were transformed into urban gardens where families could grow their own food and sell their surplus locally. By 1999, Cuba had become agriculturally self-sufficient once again—and demonstrated a historic transformation to local and sustainable agriculture.

Resilience is the ability of a system to absorb disturbance and still retain its basic function and structure.[52] In 1989, Cuba did not have a resilient food system. When oil was withdrawn from the structure, the entire system collapsed like a Jenga tower. That is because the Cuban food system wasn't designed for resilience; rather, it was designed to be maximally efficient.

Efficiency has long been the holy grail of the industrial age. Ever since Adam Smith advised us to break down our labor into its component parts, we have doggedly pursued growth through ever-smarter strategies of specialization, optimization, and maximization. We streamline processes, eliminate redundancies, standardize products, automate labor, wring out higher yields, and manage inventories just-in-time—both inside and outside the factory. The Green Revolution, in fact, was an exercise in bringing industrial thinking to the food system. Nobel Prize–winning scientists bred new varieties of nitrogen-gobbling wheat, rice, and maize that resulted in increased crop yields. Vast commercial fields of monoculture that could be rapidly harvested by machine replaced the slow family-farm-scale cultivation of a variety of crops. All this was done in the name of good intentions: the desire to defeat hunger. In fact, the Green Revolution is often credited with having averted a global famine in the second half of the twentieth century that might otherwise have taken millions of lives.

Imagine the faith in technology the world must have had when that Nobel Prize was awarded—a faith so strong that we would be blinded to its unintended consequences. The Green Revolution did save lives—in the short term. It is only now that the long-term effects are becoming visible, and they're causing increasing harm. For as the agricultural output of the Green Revolution rose, so, too, did the cost of its energy inputs—and these rose even faster, resulting in what is today a highly brittle system, one that is likely to fracture when subjected to stress. As in Cuba. As in Zimbabwe.

Born and raised in Zimbabwe, Brian Walker is an ecologist who has studied the relationship between efficiency and resilience. In his book *Resilience Thinking,* co-authored with David Salt, Walker reflects on the risks of our efficiency addiction. "The more you optimize elements of a complex system of humans and nature for some specific goal," he writes, "the more you diminish that system's resilience. A drive for an efficient optimal state outcome has the effect of making the total system more vulnerable to shocks and disturbances."[53] The goal of optimization, he argues, is based on the illusion that there exists in a system some sustainable "optimal" state around which we can model the world.

This illusion has some powerful and compelling champions. One of the world's most revered economists is Jeffrey Sachs, father of the United

Nations Millennium Development Goals (MDGs). Sachs is a staunch advocate of the belief that with the right amount of foreign aid, poor countries can climb up the ladder of economic development rung by rung. It's a virtuous cycle: Throw in the foreign aid, and the rest will take care of itself. This will happen, he describes in his book *The End of Poverty*, as poor countries leverage technology and specialize in the production of goods and services that can be traded in the global marketplace. This trade will increase household savings and public investment—at which point the economic development engine will kick back into gear. But this whole process can *only* happen if the rich countries relieve the poor countries of their debt burdens and throw in sufficient capital to get the machine under way.

In 2002, the United Nations commissioned Sachs and an independent advisory group to develop an action plan for rolling back extreme poverty, hunger, and disease. The eight Millennium Development Goals set poverty reduction targets for countries around the world to achieve by 2015. In his book, Sachs recalls that despite persistent failures among the international community to eradicate disease and debt over decades of foreign aid, when it came to the MDGs, "there was a palpable sense that this time—yes, this time—they just might be fulfilled."[54] But then, he explains, a series of events occurred—the paralyzing George W. Bush-Al Gore presidential election, corporate scandals, the end of the stock market boom, and September 11th—resulting in a string of broken promises.

Sachs's explanation seems to imply that the MDGs would be on track, if only these disruptions hadn't occurred. That's the illusion of the "optimal state"—a future in which things like oil shocks, failed governments, and terrorist attacks don't happen. The illusion may work well in the short term, but in the long term, life unfolds unpredictably and chaotically. And yet we persist in making plans and setting targets as if we were able to control their outcomes. When we aim to produce the efficient optimal state, we are designing systems whose fate may hang in the balance of a single variable. Cuba's food system depended on oil. The Millennium Development Goals—and every participating poor country—depend on foreign aid. When those variables are withdrawn, these systems lose the capacity to absorb disruption and maintain their basic function.

Unsurprisingly, things aren't exactly on track for the MDGs.[55] It looks like as many as one billion people will still be living in extreme poverty by 2015. Hunger seems to be working its way back up to pre-1990 levels. The volume of water withdrawn for agricultural purposes has grown rather than decreased (although, fortunately, there have been great strides taken in improving access to drinking water). Nonetheless, in his 2009 midterm report on the MDGs, United Nations Secretary-General Ban Ki-Moon urged world leaders to stay the course. "This report shows that the right policies and actions, backed by adequate funding and strong political commitment, can yield results," he writes. "Rather than retreat, now is the time to accelerate progress towards the MDGs." We must "redouble our efforts."[56]

As with the Green Revolution's intent to eradicate hunger, our efforts to defeat poverty arise out of the most noble and compassionate of human intentions. We want to help, we want to end the suffering of others. But our strong commitment to wanting to help blinds us to the potential destructiveness of our assumptions and practices. We treat failure as a call to redouble our efforts—to do the same, only better and faster. We never stop to question whether these are the right methods, and we fail to notice the negative consequences. Consider Haiti: The United States Agency for International Development (USAID) policy in the 1970s and 1980s encouraged Haiti to replace its agricultural economy with an export-oriented manufacturing sector that would boost GDP.[57] Large numbers of Haitians migrated from the countryside to the city, resulting in dangerous overcrowding in Port-au-Prince. When the earthquake struck in January 2010, overcrowded conditions and hastily constructed homes led to devastating tragedies. A few months later, former President Bill Clinton publicly apologized for policies during his term that destroyed Haiti's rice production, leaving the country unable to feed itself. The consequences of those policies only became visible more than a decade later.

It is time to walk out of the illusion of stability, to walk out of the addiction to the efficient optimal state. Life *always* bursts through the door—why not expect it? A resilience approach knows that uncertainty and surprise are inevitable. Writes Walker, "Resilience thinking is about understanding and engaging with a changing world. By understanding how and why the system as a whole is changing, we are better placed to build a capacity to work with change, as opposed to being a victim of it."[58]

A resilient system that has the capacity to rebound from disturbance does this by increasing its diversity and redundancy, by forgoing growth and speed in favor of sustainability, and by engaging in a wide range of small local actions that connect to one another. Kufundees cultivate resilience when they practice permaculture—by industrial standards, an inefficient and labor-intensive form of agriculture. They cultivate resilience when they harvest rainwater and reuse wine bottles—rather than install water-table–depleting irrigation systems; when they patiently nurture fruit trees in the rich humus that others view as troublesome waste; and when they mash local herbs into pastes and pills that boost immune systems to support them as they seek access to elusive antiretroviral drugs. They cultivate resilience when they hold more concern for a community's capacity to meet its needs for food, water and well-being than to participate in the global marketplace. And they cultivate resilience by building a web of relationships among people throughout Zimbabwe who believe that they have the capacity to solve their own problems.

No one would deny the need for those who have resources to help support Zimbabwe in climbing out of its current morass. The trouble begins when we commit ourselves to a narrow set of beliefs about the optimal path. The Sachs approach would have Zimbabweans waiting on foreign aid to jump-start the economy—just like the villagers who were once found waiting on donated fertilizer and seeds to jump start their crops. Kufundees have walked out of the limiting beliefs that result from kowtowing to efficiency. They have walked on to declare that we have what we need—now let's get our hands in the dirt.

The Kufundees are in good company worldwide. There is a massive movement of people everywhere who are busy doing the small-scale, heavy-lifting, slow, and laborious work of building resilient food systems. This movement goes by many names and identities—local food, slow food, fair food, good food. It includes the permaculture practitioners, urban farmers, and organic gardeners; the locavores, seed savers, and fermenters; the farmers' markets, food co-ops, and community-supported agriculture groups. It is immeasurable in size and boundaryless in reach—best made visible in the United States, perhaps, by the skyrocketing growth of small farms, farmers' markets, and shelf space for local food at conventional grocery stores. For some, such as Cubans and Zimbabweans, this movement emerged in response to the collapse of the dominant food system. For others, it's been a choice to walk out of the tasteless, sometimes toxic, machine-made, resource-depleting food of industrial agriculture—and to walk on to cultivate and consume good, clean, and tasty food grown nearby.

Our resilience as a community depends upon our capacity to look forward, to look backward and to look honestly at our situation today. Resilience isn't a new idea; there is much to learn from the past about how to create resilient systems. We're only here today because our ancestors learned how to deal with disturbances and upheavals. When we ask for the wisdom of those who've come before—as Marianne did when she consulted the village elders—we learn not only valuable ideas and techniques. We also learn that we're part of a long line of people who are skillful and inventive. We can be confident that we have what we need, and in the words of Zimbabwean poet Bev Reeler, we can claim our wealth.

> The planet has turned,
> the thrush has changed her song
> the days grow longer
> hotter
> drier
>
> This is not a comfortable season
> it is what comes before the yet distant rains.
>
> The Kufunda community has traveled a long journey
> from defining themselves from a place of poverty
> they have begun to claim their wealth.
>
> They have made soap, and body lotion
> made compost and permaculture
> painted their rooms
> polished their floors
> welded hangers
> made tables
> cooked
> made fires
> written their stories
> brought water from the well
> sung, danced,
> played drums, and mbiras and marimbas
>
> They have moved from looking at themselves
> to looking at their communities
> to looking at their traditional cultures
> and back to themselves.

EFFICIENCY

It seems difficult to imagine anyone who *hasn't* experienced the impacts of the efficiency mindset, with its endless cycles of shrinking budgets, diminished resources, downsized staff. How many leaders, how many times, exhort us to "do more with less"?

The efficiency mindset mindlessly focuses on simple numeric measures to describe the health of a system, a community or a person. Efficient solutions appear as a formula, a budget, a spreadsheet. Numbers are easy to manipulate, they make the world appear manageable. Yet nowhere do they account for skills, relationships, experience, motivation, or learning—the essential capacities that predict success or failure.

We get so seduced by efficient formulations that we assume our work is done once everything looks good on paper. But then what happens? As these programs or budget cuts go into effect, what are the results? Do we get the outcomes we planned for? Have these been sustained? What else happens as a result of our actions? What are the unintended consequences, and who's dealing with them? What would we learn if we were brave enough to ask such questions about Zimbabwe, Cuba, Haiti, and countless other places and organizations throughout the world?

Efficiency begins with good intentions. We want this organization to survive. We want to solve big problems. We want to end world hunger. On paper, the logic is compelling: We reduce hunger by increasing crop yields; we increase crop yields by using hybrid seeds, chemical fertilizers, and factory farms; we produce more food. Hunger ends.

But then the long-term consequences clamor for attention. If we would look at, for example, the Green Revolution, we'd see that hunger didn't end. That now, in addition to hunger, there are polluted streams and fields, toxic factory farms, and dislocated rural people who've lost their cultures, who are crowded into cities, homeless and hungry. We'd see we're in more trouble now than when we began, that an efficient solution spawned many more problems more difficult to solve than just hunger.

Perhaps the greatest tragedy is that we don't want to look long term. We don't learn from experience, we don't question our methods. If initial attempts to end hunger, or change organizations, don't work, we just do more of the same. We redouble our efforts, assuming all that's needed is more money, drive, determination.

The great challenge of this time is to learn from experience. What becomes visible when we question our methods, when we notice the long-term consequences of our good intentions, when we bravely bear witness to what's happened as a result of our reliance on efficiency?

When have you been affected by the
efficiency mindset, either at work or personally?
What have been some of its impacts?

FROM EFFICIENCY TO RESILIENCE

RESILIENCE

Resilience is learning to dance with life, to flex, adapt, and create as life keeps surprising us. It's a capacity as old as our origins, otherwise we wouldn't be here. Throughout time and culture, humans have learned how to survive, to persevere. Until recently, many of us thought we didn't have to worry about resilience. We believed in continuous progress, that life was always going to get better. Now, perhaps, we understand that systems do fail, that economies do collapse. Yet it's hard to comprehend what that would really be like. We won't know what it feels like until we're in it.

As more people experience hardships and loss, *resilience* has become a popular word. It's often described as a personal capacity, something we need to develop on our own. But like any of life's strengths, resilience grows in relationships, in community. This is what the Kufundees so clearly teach us.

Their journey has been long and complex. They came from ancient traditions, from cultures of community, from ancestors of great artistry and expression; they endured colonialism's dehumanization, modern development's efforts to help, ruthless dictatorship, famine, and pandemic. They journeyed all this way and learned to become resilient, but only after they accepted that no one was coming to help.

Not only did the Kufundees have to overcome centuries of oppression; they had to give up being dependent. Sad to say, dependency is an unintended consequence of helpfulness. Whenever we receive help, it's easy to let that person or group take over. The more they offer, the more we can just sit idly by and wait for rescue. Yet over time, this backfires. We can lose confidence in our abilities, forget what we once knew, and think of ourselves as poor and needy.

As systems collapsed in Zimbabwe, people lost the resources that we think are essential—food, money, safety. But instead of collapsing themselves, the Kufundees turned deprivation into discovery. They discovered abundant resources within themselves, skills and gifts that manifested in the embrace of community. Together, they explored, took risks, succeeded, failed, lost heart, tried again. At times they separated into private struggles and grief; without one another, their lives became harder to bear. And then they'd come back, sit in circle again, and notice their strength returning.

Collapse always causes terrible suffering. Yet we humans have an enduring capacity not only to survive, but to learn and grow. Resilience is in us, if we look for it. Whatever our material circumstances, we can feel confident that we have what we need, no matter what happens. It's right here in us, not alone, but as community.

When have you been given someone else's plans
or practices and told to just implement them?
How did you respond?

GOD'S POWER KNITTING GROUP

The women's knitting circle in Rusape is a beautiful illustration of the spirit of life that seems to thrive in many African communities independent of the tragedies and grief that surround them.

People who first visit Africa often comment on how much they feel at home. Although everything is very different—culture, dance, music, art, animals, people—there's a sense of comfort, of deep familiarity. Perhaps we feel we're home because, anthropologically, we are. We humans all originated in Africa. All the continents originated in Africa. Africa is also our home.

Yet there's something else. In Africa—besieged by grief and loss, endlessly suffering from abuse, hunger, disease—it is still possible to experience what it means to be fully human, fully alive. In moments of grief, people stand up and dance, not to deny the pain, but to use that searing energy and metabolize it into movement, even into joy. In moments of frustration, people convert the red energy of anger into intense physical rhythms— singing, clapping, drumming.

This joy arising from despair can be perplexing. What's going on? Are people in denial or avoidance? Or is it something new in our experience? What we're witnessing is an alchemic transformation, working with the darkest human emotions and turning them into brief moments of gold. The energy shifts from dragging us down to lifting us up. These transformations are always physical, they require movement, they require us to join together in song and dance.

God's Power Knitting Group is another variety of transformation. Women who were told they were worthless, who believed they were poor, helpless, victimized, women who should have given up, instead gathered together and began knitting. This is what women in African communities do. They grow gardens, they sew school uniforms, they design and sell crafts, and they plant trees.

They seem willing to encounter life, all of it. Is there anything more we'd desire for ourselves? We have much to learn from Africans.

WALK OUT WALK ON

SHIKSHANTAR, INDIA
FROM TRANSACTING TO GIFTING

Sarita kare na paan, vriksh na fal chaakhe kadi
Khet na khave dhaan, parhit neepjey sekhra.

The river never drinks its own water.
The tree never tastes its own fruit.
The field never consumes its own harvest.
They selflessly strive for the well-being of all
those around them.

—*Mewari proverb, India*

Here is a dream of India.

Gandhi, Krishnamurti, Tagore, Vandana Shiva, and Arundhati Roy[59] are sitting beneath the shade of a banyan tree, its thick limbs dangling rootlets down toward the cracked earth. The air is thick and wet, a premonsoon heat wave of more than 110 degrees. These great sages of then and now are sipping chai together and discussing their favorite topics—poetry, philosophy, activism. Krishnamurti opens the conversation with a question.[60]

Krishnamurti: Does life have a meaning, a purpose? Is not living in itself its own purpose, its own meaning? Why do we want more?

Tagore: The greed of gain has no time or limit to its capaciousness. Its one object is to produce and consume. It has pity neither for beautiful nature nor for living human beings. It is ruthlessly ready without a moment's hesitation to crush beauty and life out of them, molding them into money.

Gandhi: God forbid that India should ever take to industrialism after the manner of the West . . . keeping the world in chains. If our nation took to similar economic exploitation, it would strip the world bare like locusts.

Roy: The structure of capitalism is flawed. The motor that powers it cannot but vastly increase the disparity between the poor and the rich globally and within countries as well.

Shiva: The ecological economy is an economy of renewal where you have six foot of bamboo growing in a few months, or a new goat in seven months. But we're creating scarcity in an abundant world. Poverty is a human creation—nature doesn't create scarcity—human systems do.

Gandhi: I suggest that we are thieves in a way. If I take anything that I do not need for my own immediate use, and keep it, I thieve it from somebody else. I venture to suggest that it is the fundamental law of Nature, without exception, that nature produces enough for our wants from day to day, and if only everybody took enough for himself and nothing more, there would be no pauperism in this world, there would be no man dying of starvation in this world.

Tagore: Our living society, which should have dance in its steps, music in its voice, beauty in its limbs, which should have its metaphor in stars and flowers, maintaining its harmony with God's creation, becomes, under the tyranny of prolific greed, like an overladen market-cart jolting and creaking on the road that leads from things to the Nothing, tearing ugly ruts across the green life till it breaks down under the burden of its vulgarity, on the wayside, reaching nowhere.

Roy: People are so isolated, and so alone, and so suspicious, and so competitive with each other, and so sure that they are about to be conned by their neighbor, or by their mother, or by their sister, or their grandmother. What's the use of having . . . whatever it is that you have, if you're going to live this pathetic, terrified life?

Gandhi [winking]: No doubt, capital is lifeless, but not the capitalists who are amenable to conversion.

Tagore: The best of us still have our aspirations for the supreme goals of life, which is so often mocked by prosperous people who now control the world. We still believe that the world has a deeper meaning than what is apparent, and that therein the human soul finds its ultimate harmony and peace. We still know that only in spiritual wealth does civilization attain its end, not in a prolific production of materials, and not in the competition of intemperate power with power.

Krishnamurti: Surely a man who is living richly, a man who sees things as they are and is content with what he has, is not confused; he is clear, therefore he does not ask what is the purpose of life. For him the very living is the beginning and the end.

Shiva: In nature's economy the currency is not money, it is life.

Gandhi: Whenever you are in doubt, or when the self becomes too much with you, apply the following test. Recall the face of the poorest and the weakest man whom you may have seen, and ask yourself, if the step you contemplate is going to be of any use to him. Will he gain anything by it? Will it restore him to a control over his own life and destiny? In other words, will it lead to *swaraj* [freedom or self-rule] for the hungry and spiritually starving millions? Then you will find your doubts and your self melt away.

Krishnamurti: In oneself lies the whole world and if you know how to look and learn, the door is there and the key is in your hand. Nobody on earth can give you either the key or the door to open, except yourself.

Tagore: I slept and dreamt that life was joy. I awoke and saw that life was service. I acted and behold, service was joy.

THE CALL FOR *SWARAJ*

You may have already formed an impression of Shikshantar before ever setting foot in India. This is the learning center in Udaipur where Daniel encountered the double edges of frustration and joy in inventing anew the *cycle mixie*. It is the place where *kabaad se jugaad* (the upcycling practice that you first encountered in Mexico) has transcended practice and become a philosophy—a spirituality even—for transmuting garbage into grace through hardy ingenuity. Shikshantar is steeped in philosophy, brewed from a rich mix of poets, sages, scholars, grandmothers, dreamers, writers, storytellers, and artists. Gandhi's concept of *swaraj* is its primary ingredient, the black tea into which all the other spices are infused—Tagore, Krishnamurti, Sri Aurobindo, Vinoba Bhave,[61] as well as the wisdom of common people, everyday life, elders, and *dalits* (untouchables). This is your invitation to taste swaraj, to roll the complexity of India around on your tongue. You don't have to understand it—just put a few of these sentences from Shikshantar in your pocket, carry them around with you, pull them out occasionally for refreshment.

> The call for swaraj represents a genuine attempt to regain control of the "self"—our self-respect, self-responsibility, and capacities for self-realization—from institutionalization; that is, the submission of the human spirit to the will of institutions. As Gandhi states, "It is swaraj when we learn to rule ourselves."
>
> Swaraj requires that we regain our faith in the capacity of human beings and restore agency, the locus of power, back to individual and local communities.
>
> The process of swaraj seeks to create a reflective and participatory context for people to ask who we have been, who we are, and who we want to become.

This feels like heady stuff, doesn't it? What are you expecting to find when you walk into the Shikshantar learning space in Udaipur, the City of Lakes in the state of Rajasthan? What images of India are you carrying around with you? Are they images of poverty—beggar children tugging at you for change, overcrowded streets, rivers polluted with plastic debris? Are they images of technology—call centers and tech support and professional outsourcing? Are they images of Bollywood, Hindu gods and goddesses, men playing sitars and women in saris dancing?

Here is another image of India—one in which people are practicing swaraj by rejecting today's ready-made world, a world in which everything we consume has been processed and prepackaged by someone else: ready-made clothes, ready-made food, ready-made homes, ready-made education, ready-made medicine, ready-made entertainment. Here, instead, is an image of Shikshantar, a place whose purpose is to provoke new thinking about education.

I had heard about Shikshantar for years before I made my first visit in 2005. Through our work together at Berkana, Manish Jain, one of Shikshantar's co-founders, had become a colleague and close friend. But no matter how many long and late-night conversations we would have about Shikshantar's approach to rethinking education, I couldn't wrap my mind around what they actually *did*. Manish talked repeatedly about swaraj, Gandhi's invitation to take responsibility for ourselves. He would patiently explain how Shikshantar's work was to experiment with creating our own learning, weaning ourselves from the ready-made world where all that's expected of us is to be good consumers.

When I arrived at Shikshantar, I observed a hive in action—people everywhere discovering and inventing their own unique ways to grow and prepare food, maintain health, construct household goods, tell stories, create art. At first, there didn't seem to be any rhyme or reason to their activities. Everyone carried on with his or her own vision, forming partnerships and teams as needed. It was only after a full week immersed in this lively environment that I began to see what held the whole together. Shikshantar's coherence is derived from its shared values and beliefs that serve as an underground aquifer nourishing all the activity above the surface. That aquifer runs deep, saturated with India's three-thousand-year-old philosophical and spiritual heritage—which is why it matters to listen to the voices of the wise men and women who have come before. And which is why we began our journey to India the only way we could have—with the insights of the wisdom-keepers who have shaped everything Shikshantar is today.

Deborah

It is 9 A.M. It is 3 P.M. It is 8 P.M. It doesn't matter: The scene is the same. At every time of day, people come and go, following their own personal rhythm of work, play, rest, and surprise. On the left as you walk in, Guddi is sitting at the *charka*, spinning cotton into string which can be made into clothes or bags. Through the doorway, Vishal is practicing kabaad se jugaad by rolling old newspapers into long, thin tubes that will be woven into baskets and bowls. A pile of CDs awaits his attention for becoming a lampshade. Nirmal is sawing away at a piece of coconut shell out of which he will make earrings and necklaces to display at next week's Hamo Desi Mela, the monthly festival where community members exchange locally grown organic food, herbal medicine, and handicrafts. Pannalal wanders in, returning from Sandeep's urban garden carrying a cabbage covered with a fine dust of ash, which has served as a natural insect repellant. He delivers the cabbage to Sunny, a sixteen-year-old who has devoted himself to experiments in oil-free food and healthy cooking. He is preparing the cabbage for today's lunch, which will be chopped, flavored, and delivered in a blackened pot to the roof, where Manoj has set up his upcycled solar cooker. The cooker is made from a rusted trunk, broken mirror, rubber tire tubes, and an old car windshield, all of which were found discarded throughout the neighborhood. Ram is also outdoors tending the herbal nursery that will provide the primary ingredients for homemade medicine, soap, tooth powder, and massage oil.

Everyone here is following their passion, working at their own pace. But this is hardly rugged individualism. This is a hive where each member has his or her unique function to perform in service of the whole. There is order here, but it may feel like chaos. Who is in charge? What are the priorities? Where are decisions being made? This is truly an experiment in self-organization, where each person pursues his or her own work rooted in the same shared beliefs. Very different projects emerge, yet they form a well-coordinated, orderly and effective whole. Here, those beliefs are based on swaraj, the commitment to walk our own path in the world.

That is why you don't always see Manish and Shilpa and Vidhi Jain here—the team that co-created this place. The formal kind of directive leadership is not needed here. These three are out in the community right now. Vidhi, Manish's wife, is organizing a gathering for the Families Learning Together network, a group that is exploring what life would look like if families—rather than schools—were at the center of learning experiences.

Sunny prepares lunch; Manoj then cooks it on the roof in an upcycled solar cooker made from a rusted trunk, broken mirror, rubber tire tubes, and an old car windshield.

FROM TRANSACTING TO GIFTING

Shilpa, Manish's sister, is talking with other bicycle enthusiasts to prepare for the upcoming *cycle yatra*, a weeklong, money-free bicycle journey that will explore what it means to fully engage in gift culture. Manish is visiting one of the elders who is part of "Udaipur as a Learning City," a citywide effort to reclaim informal learning spaces such as recreational areas, neighborhood and cultural associations, arts, and community media. Citizens throughout Udaipur are working together to reweave intergenerational relationships among artists, farmers, workers, healers, craftspeople, educators, storytellers, and politicians, and among children, adults, and elders.

You, too, are being invited to venture out into Udaipur. Rohit, a twelve-year-old apprentice, is asking you to join him on the daily *gobar* run. Don't ask any questions; just say yes and grab a bucket as you walk out the door.

The streets outside Shikshantar are narrow and winding, crowded with cars, rickshaws, scooters, tourists—and quite a few cows. Yes, the rumor is true: Cows are sacred in India. While long revered by Hindus for their production of milk, ghee (clarified butter), and dung, cows were politicized in the late 1800s when protecting them became a movement to mobilize Hindus against British imperialism. Today in Delhi, for instance, more than forty thousand cows share the capital's overcrowded streets with thirteen million residents—that's one free-range cow for every 325 city dwellers![62] The good news about this—if you're practicing swaraj and rejecting the ready-made world—is that fuel, the cow dung kind, is abundant and free.

Rohit leads the way down quieter streets, moving away from the city center until you come to an outdoor crematorium. Here, other gobar collectors hesitate to go, so it is easy to find fresh loads. He points out a heap of day-old dung drying in the sunshine. You are meant to pick this up with

Whether making fuel chips, soap or soil, mixing *gobar* gets you back in touch with the natural world. The Shikshantar team is like family—they eat, play, work and invent together.

your ungloved hands—an opportunity literally to get back in touch with the natural world—and deposit it in your bucket. Do you recoil at this? Take a breath and reflect: You've probably been dousing your body for years in unnatural chemicals; what's so alarming about natural ones? Besides, humans have been harvesting dung for fuel ever since we became co-dependent on cattle. As it is, of today's 840 million Indians who live in rural villages, nearly half of their domestic fuel requirements are met by India's 280 million cows.[63] Making fuel from cow dung is easy. Just grab a handful and shape it into patties, about Frisbee-sized. Lay the patties out to dry. The sun will take care of the rest, and soon you'll have easy-to-use fuel chips.

Today's gobar, however, has a different fate. It will be transformed into *amrit jal*, "the drink of the gods," a fast-track process for creating fertile soil. Here's the recipe: First, you'll collect several bucketfuls of gobar and haul them back to Shikshantar. Next, add some water, cow urine, jaggery (hardened molasses), and stir. No, not with a stick or a ladle. With your *arm*, right up to the elbow, creating cool circles of ooze. This should amplify the redolent bouquet of manure, which will help reconnect you, no doubt, to organic living. Be sure to use your left hand; this is the practice in India, since people eat with their right. Mix it all up until the texture feels like a thick, goopy sludge. Wait three days, stirring occasionally, and then add water. On the fourth day, add brown biomass (leaves, grass, and straw) and soak the mixture overnight. When it's ready, you can alternate layers of amrit jal with sand and topsoil, forty layers deep, and wait another hundred days. This will produce *amrit mitti*, "the soil of the gods," rich organic soil that can be used for raised beds or poured on top of chemically compromised soil, which ordinarily can take up to three years to convert.[64]

Whether making fuel chips or accelerating soil conversion, there is wisdom in this process. It harnesses a resource that is freely available to ease the burden of daily energy consumption—and enables self-reliance. Traditional wisdom has it that burning gobar to fuel kitchen fires maintains the perfect temperature to ensure that nutrients in food are not destroyed by overheating. When burned in combination with neem leaves, gobar smoke serves as mosquito repellent. Gobar soap, made with neem and aloe vera, clears rashes and pimples. When mixed with clay to form floor tiles and adobe walls, gobar helps houses breathe and regulate temperature. And gobar can be converted as bio-gas into electricity.

For Shikshantar, collecting gobar is part of its challenge to the patterns and practices of the ready-made world. In modern culture, most of us have become blind to the resources that nature so abundantly provides, and we've become ashamed of manual labor. Gobar, collected and transformed with our hands, is just one means of reconnecting us to Earth's unending riches.

Just as you finish washing up in time for lunch, Manish returns, bringing his little daughter Kanku with him. She, too, is part of the Shikshantar family, a full-time learner and mischievous sprite who immediately wants to know, in bits of English sprinkled with Hindi, who you are and why you're here. She grabs your hand and runs you around the room, pointing out the drawings and collages and posters that plaster the walls, the giant puppets and handmade masks that hang from the ceiling, the rows and rows of books and DVDs, many of which have been produced and published by Shikshantar and its friends. People are coming into this room from every direction to sit cross-legged on the floor and share the community lunch. After all, this is a family, just not one created entirely by blood, and like nearly all families everywhere, they break bread together—in this case, corn *rotis*—as a means of reconnecting. Be careful how much you accept this first time around. Ram is going to spoon steaming heaps of rice, *patta gobhi,* and *dal* on your plate. Before you've finished, he'll come around again. And he'll keep coming around to give you more than you could possibly eat until you learn how to play this game that pits Indian hospitality against Western resolve. Just know that you will likely lose as you work your way through every last morsel on your plate, which must be wiped clean before Ram himself will finally sit down to eat his meal of whatever remains in the pot.

There is a saying in India: *Atithi Devo Bhava*, a Sanskrit phrase meaning "The guest is god." The phrase has been co-opted by the tourism industry,

Manish Jain, co-founder of Shikshantar, invites friends and colleagues into an exploration of gift culture. Children and Shikshantar volunteers make giant puppets and perform free shows for the community.

but it originated in the Upanishads, ancient Hindu texts that proclaimed feeding the guest—including the stranger—to be the noblest of all acts. Thus is hospitality gifted, not earned. No equal exchange of value must first be agreed upon. Perhaps Ram's generosity offers you a glimpse into one of Shikshantar's most essential, most heartfelt explorations: a journey into *gift culture*, the antidote to our ubiquitous transactional culture that has turned the accumulation of material resources into a near-sacred pursuit the world over. What if, just what if, in Manish's words, we were invited back into our sacred role as active gift givers—from *Homo economicus* to *Homo giftus*?

HOMO ECONOMICUS VERSUS *HOMO GIFTUS*

Manish Jain has been exploring the dynamics of gift culture since he began his work at Shikshantar in 1999. Born in India and raised in the United States, Manish returned to India to "unlearn" his master's degree in education from Harvard and his training as an investment banker at Morgan Stanley. He holds this paradox with grace, his tall frame draped in *kurtas* one day and Western shirts the next, digging in the dirt today and flying off to keynote an international conference tomorrow. But little makes him happier than spending the afternoon at Shikshantar engaged in long, intoxicating conversations that challenge our assumptions about the world. Today will be no exception as Manish invites you into an inquiry about gift culture, which he begins by quoting Indian activist and former Jain monk Satish Kumar: [65]

> We have learned much from the native Americans, the Australian Aboriginals, the indigenous peoples of India (*adivasis*) and the Bushmen of Africa. We have been guided by Jesus Christ, the Buddha, Mohammed and Mahavir. We have been inspired by Valmiki, Shakespeare, Tolstoy, Jane Austen and many other writers. We have benefited from the lives of Mahatma Gandhi, Mother Teresa and Martin Luther King. They were not motivated by fame, fortune or power. Buddha claimed no copyright on his teachings, and Shakespeare received no royalty cheques. We have been enchanted by music, paintings, architecture and crafts of many cultures, from time immemorial. We have received a treasure house of traditions as a free gift.
>
> In return, we offer our work, our creativity, our arts and crafts, our agriculture and architecture as gifts to society—to present and future generations. When we are motivated by this spirit, then work is not a burden. It is not a duty. It is not a responsibility. We are not even the doers of our work. Work flows through us and not from us. We do not own our intellect,

our creativity, or our skills. We have received them as a gift and grace. We pass them on as a gift and grace; it is like a river which keeps flowing. All the tributaries make the river great. We are the tributaries adding to the great river of time and culture; the river of humanity. If tributaries stop flowing into the river, if they become individualistic and egotistical, if they put terms and conditions before they join the rivers, they will dry and the rivers will dry, too. To keep the rivers flowing, all tributaries have to join in with joy and without conditions. In the same way, all individual arts, crafts and other creative activities make up the river of humanity. We need not hold back, we need not block the flow. This is unconditional union. This is the great principle of *dana*. This is how society and civilizations are replenished.

Dana is a Sanskrit term meaning "generosity" or "giving" without any expectation of return. It is a way of being in the world that flips self-interest on its head. A life well lived is one in which we each find an opportunity to *give our gifts* rather than to *have our needs met*. Our purpose is defined by what we offer, rather than what we can secure for ourselves and our families.

Contrast this with the values of transactional culture—the one that prevails throughout the global marketplace—in which everything we need to live comes to us through a process of exchange based on money. Over time, what has emerged and solidified the world over is a global culture that invites us to consume as much as we can and hoard money and material possessions.

Here are a few more beliefs by which *Homo economicus* chooses to live: Value can be quantified and measured; my sense of security is derived from the quantity of resources I have rather than the quality of relationships I'm in. I have a right to acquire as many resources as I can; I have a right to extract natural resources from the earth. The surpluses I generate belong to me; I should store them to produce future wealth. Since price goes up when supply is constrained, inducing scarcity can generate wealth.

What are the consequences of *Homo economicus's* way of life? We buy and sell our homes and our land, our labor and our ideas—even our bodies and organs are for sale. Nothing is beyond the reach of this transactional culture.

But wait. Before getting all worked up about how *bad* this system is—or how *good* it is—it might be worth pausing for a moment to look at it as just, well, a system.

In *Reinventing the Sacred*, biologist Stuart Kauffman writes, "The industrialized world is seen to be, and is, largely consumer oriented, materialistic, and commodified. How strange this world would seem to medieval Europe. . . . We of the industrialized world forget that our current value system is only one of a range of choices. We desperately need a global ethic that is richer than our mere concern about ourselves as consumers."[66]

Transactional culture was not inevitable. It is not human nature. It's just our culture. But we each have a story about why it is so. Perhaps it is a Darwinian tale that says he who can secure resources for himself and his family is most fit to survive. Or maybe it's an economic and political tale that heralds the triumph of capitalism over communism, socialism, and fascism. Or even a pragmatic story about accepting *the way it is* because it feels unimaginable to challenge a system that has created the global marketplace.

There is an ancient Jewish folktale that depicts a man who visits hell, amazed to find its inhabitants all seated at long tables, with fancy tablecloths, beautiful silverware, and bountiful food in front of them. Yet no one was eating, and all of them were wailing. When he looked closely, he saw that none of them could bend their elbows; thus, although they could touch the food, no one could bring it to his mouth. The visitor then goes to heaven, where the scene is identical: long tables, fancy tablecloths, beautiful silverware, and bountiful food. And here as well, people cannot bend their elbows, yet no one is wailing—because each person is serving his neighbor.[67]

Alternatives to transactional culture abound throughout the world, in both traditional and modern cultures. The indigenous peoples of Mexico practice *tequío*, the voluntary gifting of work and time—such as cleaning up a road or planting a garden—offered for the sake of the collective good. In Mali, *dama* is a pay-it-forward practice of keeping gifts on the move, circulating continually through the community. Students of Buddhism offer *dana* to their teachers, a formal spiritual act of giving that arises from the purity of heart in the giver and leads to greater spiritual wealth. Among Native American communities of the Pacific Northwest, the potlatch is a festival in which wealth is redistributed through reciprocity; the status of a family is determined not by how much is owned but by how much has been gifted to others. In India, *sewa* is a spirit of selfless service, performed without any expectation of reward or gain.

And the list goes on. *Butsu Butsu Kokan* in Japan. *Susu* in Trinidad and Tobago. The *Kula ring* in Papua New Guinea. *Aropa* among some Pacific Islanders. *Barn raising* among the Amish.

Homo giftus offers goods and services freely, without any expectation of return. Its value is measured by the quality of our relationships rather than the quantity of our profit. Our capacity to give is infinite, unconstrained by shortages and fear of scarcity. Perhaps what's most incredible about the culture of *Homo giftus* is that it shows up every time our transactional culture breaks down—in times of human-made and natural disasters, grief and illness, celebration and joy.

What if *this* is human nature? How would we explore this dimension of ourselves? How could we rediscover our capacity to act with generosity and to receive gifts offered by others' generous impulses?

The folks at Shikshantar have an invitation for you, one that will immerse you in gift culture. It's called a *cycle yatra*.

CYCLE YATRA

Bin Paise Cycle Yatra, Chale, Chalo! Chale, Chalo! Cyclewalleh zindabad! **Money-Free Bicycle Journey, Let's Go! C'mon, Let's Go! Long Live the Bicycle Riders!**

—*Shilpa Jain*

Twenty-five bicycles are parked outside Shikshantar, bedecked with ribbons and balloons, papier-mâché masks and puppetry, hand-held drums and flutes and whistles. Twenty-five riders are bustling around, strapping sleeping bags to rear racks and affixing signs to the handlebars: *Dosti* (Friendship), *Ram Bharose* (We're in God's hands), *Jaiso an vaiso man* (So we eat, so we are), *Apne seekh apne hath* (Our learning is in our hands). The riders themselves are adorned in garlands, head scarves, and bandanas. They are preparing for a weeklong *cycle yatra*, a journey out of the city and into the arms of whomever they might meet along the way.

Would you like to join this adventure? All you have to do is leave behind your money, credit cards, cell phone, iPod, snack food, and all things plastic. For you are entering Gift Culture, and there will be no monetary transactions this week. Over the next two hundred kilometers, you will secure your food and shelter with the gifts of your labor, your creativity, and your capacity to build relationships with strangers. You will practice surrender. Surrender to the tires that will burst on the unkempt dirt roads, surrender to the single gear that has the hills claim victory over your legs and your lungs, surrender to the brakes that may fail as you soar downhill—and to the wisdom of the veteran rider who advises under such circumstance that you wait for a curve in the road and then *jump!*

And you will receive the refreshment of floating in a cool lake, the soothing touch of fellow riders massaging your feet and walking on your tired back, the ambrosial rush that comes from sucking on bits of sugar cane from a passing field.

You may find yourself hauling stones and being offered a place to sleep, painting murals and receiving fresh buttermilk, singing songs and entertaining children and performing short plays just for the sheer delight. This is a world of reciprocity, the antithesis of the market, and there's no guarantee that what is exchanged will balance out. Here, you throw yourself into the hands of the universe and say, *I offer my gifts to you, and so shall others to me, strangers and friends alike.*

Can you trust this? Listen to Shilpa tell a story from her first *cycle yatra*:

We had reached our "destination" (the point on the other end of our loop, from which we were going to start heading back to Udaipur): Jaisamand Lake. It was beautiful, and several people got in for a swim. The sun was hot, so we decided we would stay there 'til it dropped a bit and then make our way to a village for the night. In the meantime, we started chatting with all the different vendors there, who were curious about us and our bicycles. In a short time, we found ourselves painting a mural on the side of one of their stalls, chopping vegetables for the *chaat*, and soon performing the short plays, juggling and music we had prepared as offerings for the villages we visited. In return, we accepted tea, fruits and even camel rides!

Then, the boatmen, who take tourists as well as locals on the lake, asked if we would come to their island for the night. Their family had been living on the island for 400 years, and 65 family members lived there now. They helped us find a place to keep our bicycles for the night, and we

Adventurers head out on a *cycle yatra*, a money-free bicycle journey into the arms of gift culture, trusting that someone, somewhere, will provide food and shelter.

FROM TRANSACTING TO GIFTING

accompanied them at sunset to their homes on the island. Two by two, we each entered a home and chatted and cooked food with them and ate together. All the children gathered around us at night and we shared our tent and musical instruments with them and played games together. The stars that night, from an island floating in Asia's largest man-made lake, were astounding.

In the morning, we woke early and helped clean the cow and buffalo sheds. We pounded corn to release its kernels and helped collect it into bags. Some of the friends exchanged their knowledge of macramé, and we played some more games together. Then, the boatmen took us back to the shore, where we found our bicycles safe and sound. Pedaling away, we were all overwhelmed and delighted by the generosity and beauty of the entire experience. It had been magical.[68]

Are you willing to make yourself this vulnerable? To trust that someone, somewhere will provide? Can you give yourself over to a rhythm that is determined by the people you meet, the places you journey, and the experiences you participate in? Can you be this trusting of life?

When you return from the *yatra*, be gentle with yourself. It may seem strange to notice how much of our lives is devoted to consuming the ready-made world. It may be unsettling to discover how little is required to feel joyful and secure—and how freely those who have less than we do share what they have. We put so much effort into seeking security—accumulating wealth, advancing our career, acquiring things, planning for the future. How much of that security is real and how much illusion?

Of course we can't live in gift culture all the time. But we can taste it and we can begin to explore the edge between seeking security and trusting that we'll find what we need. We can experiment with what it would be like to participate in the transactional economy *just enough* to have what we need—and to gift out everything else. Instead of seeking always to acquire more, we might experiment with sufficiency.

This is exactly the experiment in which Mukesh Jat finds himself.

THE STORY OF MUKESH JAT

Here is the choice confronting Mukesh Jat: move to Indore, the commercial capital of central India's Madhya Pradesh, to find a job, or stay with his family in the village of Anjad to cobble together a livelihood. He's done it before—he worked for a water company in Indore earning 800 rupees ($17) per day. Quite a good income, actually. But his heart wasn't in it, and

As I've shared the story of Shikshantar's cycle yatras with friends and colleagues in the United States, I've been amazed by the emotion it provokes. Some people just light up, delighted by the idea of leaving their material possessions behind, envisioning that leap of faith as joyful, inspiring. Others are aghast—"At least take a cell phone!" they say. We all have different needs for safety and security. But security can also come from relationships rather than stuff, and gift culture is an invitation to deepen our relationships.

I've never been on a cycle yatra (though Manish says he's planning to correct that on my next trip to India). But I've witnessed the gift culture arise time and again here at home, especially when it's most needed. When I broke my leg, friends appeared to offer rides and run errands. When someone dies, we surround the mourners with food, love, and support. After Hurricane Katrina in New Orleans, strangers opened their homes to each other. We offer our gifts in ordinary times as well, when we volunteer, lend an ear to a friend, do a favor for a neighbor. The gift culture is not extraordinary; it's alive and well, always.

Whether or not I do go on a cycle yatra, these stories have inspired me to believe that people are innately generous—that we *want* to give our time and talent to one another. It's in our nature to offer support to each other spontaneously, when we see a need or opportunity. Perhaps we really are best described as *Homo giftus*.

Deborah

he yearned for village life. Besides, things are different now. He is a newlywed and a new father, and with his mother also under his roof, he has a household of four to come home to. Which means he also has a household of four to support—and therein lies the dilemma.

So far, he has been trying to make it in the milk business. But no matter how productive Kali the cow might be, one cow is hardly enough to sustain a family of four. Besides, this particular cow is a troublemaker. Like her namesake, the goddess Kali the destroyer, this Kali has an aggressive side—kicking people, charging at women. Mukesh's mother has had enough and wants Mukesh to sell the cow.

This is when Lakshmi intervenes, the goddess of wealth, she who has a fondness for cows.

Like many villages throughout India, Anjad has been victim to the Green Revolution that transformed subsistence agriculture into industrial processes, dousing the land in chemical fertilizers and pesticides that are costly and toxic. Mukesh had witnessed the destructive impact of industrially farmed wheat on his own land, compromising the vitality of the soil and rendering its farmers' livelihoods dependent on a single crop.

Lakshmi must have been whispering into Mukesh's ear at night when he dreamed up the idea of building a bio-gas plant and producing organic fertilizer. It was all right there. In the corner of the small courtyard at Mukesh's home, Kali deposited all the gobar Mukesh would need to get started.

When you visit that courtyard today, you'll see the bio-gas pit into which Mukesh dumps dung and water in a one-to-one ratio. That feeds the digester, where methane is extracted and piped through to Mukesh's kitchen, supplanting the liquefied petroleum gas cylinders that Mukesh used to stand in line monthly to collect. In fact, Kali's gobar produces more gas than Mukesh's household needs, so he runs a second line to his uncle's

Clockwise from left: Mukesh Jat, Kali the cow, cleaning manure with the spinning wheel, composting in vermi-beds.

home nearby. It cost him 8,000 rupees (about $175) to build the system (funding that he accessed as a Berkana Fellow, one of the programs of The Berkana Institute that supports younger leaders in discovering right livelihood[69]). It took less than sixteen months to recoup his investment.

Next, Mukesh gathers up the sludge left over after the methane is extracted and deposits it into the vermi-beds. Vermi-composting is the use of earthworms to accelerate the breakdown of organic matter into nutrient-rich, organic fertilizer. With an additional investment of 12,000 rupees (about $265), Mukesh constructed ten rectangular concrete beds where worms, water, and gobar perform their miraculous alchemy into the luscious compost that nourishes organic agriculture. Stick your hand into this earth. It is cool and alive, soft against the skin. It is the kind of earth you'd want your food to bathe in.

Every step of the way, Mukesh labors in the spirit of jugaad—that improvisational problem solving that keeps cropping up everywhere you go in India. He erects a shed and vermi-wash unit out of a broken pot and leaky tank. He designs a spinning wheel from scrap metal and a net to clean the manure of pebbles. He tries out his first batch of organic manure on his own fields before sharing his story with local farmers. Word begins to spread, and other farmers ask to use the fertilizer on their own crops. Mukesh happily sells them his product and buys a second cow.

A year after starting, Mukesh is on a roll. Three more big cows stand next to Kali, and they now have given birth to four young ones. The biogas plant is feeding a third kitchen and a new toilet. A cousin has leased him additional land, where he has constructed ninety more vermi-beds. The demand for Mukesh's organic manure has risen among local farmers. All in all, he is earning a *lakh* in profit—that's 100,000 rupees (more than $2,000). Growth, security, and a promising future are assured.

This is the microenterprise dream come true, isn't it? A small investment sets a family on its path toward self-sufficiency; over time, those small investments become larger and the family's future increasingly secure. Better still that Mukesh's small business yields a greater good for his local community—helping convert fellow farmers to a more sustainable form of agriculture.

Why, then, is Mukesh expressing doubt about that path? It's because his experiment has cast him onto that uncomfortable edge between transacting and gifting, between growth and sufficiency. "When the farmers started showing interest in the product, thoughts of big business and prosperity started circulating in my head," Mukesh tells you. "But later, I had a different perspective about helping other farmers start their own production units, and I realized where my priorities lay. Instead of starting a business enterprise out of self-interest, I understood the advantage for our community if more farmers began production themselves—and what role I could play."

Mukesh is now cultivating a network of relationships among local farmers, many of whom are starting similar projects of their own. He is gifting his knowledge, his time, his assistance—while still selling his fertilizer. This is the path of *right livelihood*, a mindful way of living that balances service with self-interest, community vitality with economic security. This is what it might look like to transact in the market as little as necessary to sustain our health and well-being—while giving as much of ourselves as we can to our community.

But we live in a world that demands we participate in the marketplace. Once we get a taste of success, it can be exceedingly difficult to turn our back on it. Why is growth so seductive, anyway? This is a topic Manish has thought about a great deal. So let's return to Udaipur and end our journey in India the way we began, by reclining in the shade of the banyan tree, sipping a cup of chai and reflecting—this time with Manish—on the fundamental operating assumptions that drive our global transactional culture.

FROM GROWTH TO SUFFICIENCY

"For thousands of years, we've known that having more stuff doesn't give you happiness and fulfillment," Manish begins. "But that basic wisdom has slowly been eroded within the span of a couple of generations. Growth promises some illusion of greater freedom and security—if I accumulate more stuff, I don't have to depend on others, I don't have to negotiate with others, I have a new kind of power. The accumulation of stuff becomes our primary spiritual and psychological purpose and dominant social identity—rather than the quality of our relationships, our creativity, or our consciousness." Our transactional culture, he adds, assumes that there is some unlimited nature to this growth, that we can accumulate infinitely. And this may have something to do with our money system.

"What's different about money is its accumulative power," Manish continues. "Natural goods have a limited time to be consumed before they perish. Money is nonperishable, therefore seemingly infinite and immortal. It is an abstraction that defies both life and the limits of our mind, but defines our culture. And we are trapped in it."

In his book *The Future of Money*, Belgian economist Bernard Lietaer illuminates the absurdity of our transactional culture in which everyone seems to be "waiting for money." He writes:

> Imagine a Martian landing in a poor neighbourhood and seeing rundown communities, people sleeping in the streets, children without mentors or going hungry, trees and rivers dying from lack of care, ecological break-downs and all of the other problems we face. He would also discover that we know exactly what to do about all these things. Finally, he would see that many people willing to work are either unemployed, or use only a part of their skills. He would see that many have jobs but are not doing the work they are passionate about. And that they are all waiting for money. Imagine the Martian asking us to explain what is that strange "money" thing we seem to be waiting for. Could you tell him with a straight face that we are waiting for an "agreement within a community to use some-thing—really almost anything—as a medium of exchange"?
> And keep waiting?
> Our Martian might leave wondering whether there is intelligent life on this planet.[70]

Many people have analyzed how our global financial system arose from our shared agreements about money (you can learn more about this at the *Walk Out Walk On* website). But for now, let's consider just what we need to know about the relationship between money and growth to better understand Manish's point of view.

In his book *The End of Money and the Future of Civilization*, American economist Thomas Greco describes how banks create money out of thin air when they make loans against their reserves.[71] They then charge interest to account for risk and the passage of time. But when the bank issues the loan, it only creates enough money to account for the principal. It does not create the money that will be needed to pay for interest. Because there isn't enough money in the money system to pay for both the principal and the interest on a loan, the economy must grow so that more debt can be created to pay for the interest due. Otherwise, existing debts go into default, and people—or ultimately, the economy—collapse.

It's like a game of financial musical chairs where there just aren't enough seats to go around, and someone's got to get kicked out of the game.[72] We are stuck in a positive feedback loop, Greco says, where debt begets interest, and interest begets more debt. After a point, none of this has anything to do with the actual production of goods and services. We just need to keep growing fast enough to stay ahead of ourselves—and everyone else. So we run around in a frenzy, hoping we won't be the one left standing without a chair.

A growth imperative has been designed into the very DNA of our dominant economic system. Everywhere we look, we find people seeking to produce more and more, faster and faster. We measure businesses by their ability to increase year-over-year earnings. We expect farms to generate consistently higher crop yields. Doctors are meant to serve larger numbers of patients more rapidly. Even nonprofit organizations are frequently evaluated by how much their budget has grown. (How counterintuitive it must be for some, then, that Shikshantar declared its intention to shrink its budget from year to year. In 2003, its budget was about $22,000. By 2009, it had gone down to $13,000 while the organization's reach had tripled. This was accomplished by transitioning many expenses into gift culture, such as workshop space, food for events, and housing for guests; by deepening their practice of jugaad, thereby reducing their need to purchase items; and by strengthening their network of partnerships through which they created learning opportunities.)

Growth is one of our transactional culture's highest values. Greater production and greater consumption of stuff is a fundamental social value—so pervasive that we can't even see it, so pervasive that when a crisis hits, we're invited to go shopping. We trust in progress, confident that things will always get better; we're riding a trajectory of ingenuity and technological advance that has no end.

But as Manish points out, as a consequence of believing in unlimited growth, we're now living in a culture of destruction. "In transactional

Shikshantar's intergenerational experiments in gift culture invite learners to labor with their hands, including spinning cloth with the *charka* and working with clay.

WALK OUT WALK ON

culture, we use and throw away people, resources and ideas," he says. "Everything can be converted into a commodity until there's nothing sacred left. Land, water, air, seeds, even grandmother's cookies—our most intimate and profound aspects of life—are subject to this commodification. Gandhi talked about the notion of *trusteeship*: We are not really owners of anything. Nature doesn't work with ownership. We are guardians or trustees, stewarding resources that are part of a commons of human beings and life on the planet. We don't have a right to hoard things—or to mindlessly throw them away."

Gandhi saw trusteeship as a means of rebuilding an egalitarian society. It would be a pathway back toward right livelihood and sufficiency. He wrote, "Supposing I have come by a fair amount of wealth—either by way of legacy, or by means of trade and industry—I must know that all that wealth does not belong to me; what belongs to me is the right to an honourable livelihood, no better than that enjoyed by millions of others. The rest of my wealth belongs to the community and must be used for the welfare of the community."[73]

When Mukesh walked out of the growth imperative, recognizing that he had enough and that everything else might be gifted to his community, he embodied trusteeship. There are movements of people everywhere, like Mukesh, who recognize what they already have and are working with it differently. They are the kabaad se jugaad practitioners throughout India and the upcyclers around the world who reconstitute their waste. They are the zero-waste movement members who aspire to use only those resources they can put back into circulation; the do-it-yourselfers who labor with their hands and their creativity to meet their most basic food and shelter needs; the developers in the open source software movement who give away their code so it can evolve collectively; and the community currency pioneers who are creating local living economies by experimenting with new forms of money—such as mutual credit systems and time-based currencies—that strengthen local relationships and rebuild the commons. (As recently as the 1980s, there were fewer than a hundred such currency systems in the world; today, some estimates put that figure as high as five thousand.[74]) Each of these groups has walked out of growth and walked on to sufficiency.

Gift culture is about trusteeship, about stewarding the commons rather than ourselves. It's about taking care of the whole so that everyone has enough. We offer what we can, and we value gifts on our own terms—rather than those dictated by the marketplace. We turn to one another for our needs—to local businesses, teachers, artists, gardeners, craftspeople—rather than to the anonymity of the global marketplace. We walk out of our identity as *Homo economicus,* and we walk on to discover the patterns and practices of *Homo giftus.*

·· • ··

The sun is setting over the streets of Udaipur as you drain the last drops of your chai. The city begins to soften as people make their way home to prepare dinner with their families. It is quiet, perhaps for the first time in what has been a very long, hot day. A garlanded cyclist rolls past hauling heavy bags in exchange for his dinner. A cow ambles by, pausing across the road to offer her gift of gobar to the commons. How gifts appear in the most surprising ways! As you doze off under the banyan tree, Tagore returns to your dreams, offering a parting poem asking us to notice how we've imprisoned ourselves in our transactional ways.

"Prisoner, tell me, who was it that bound you?"

"It was my master," said the prisoner.
"I thought I could outdo everybody in the world
in wealth and power,
and I amassed in my own treasure-house
the money due to my king.
When sleep overcame me I lay upon the bed
that was for my lord,
and on waking up I found I was a prisoner
in my own treasure-house."

"Prisoner, tell me, who was it that wrought
this unbreakable chain?"

"It was I," said the prisoner,
"who forged this chain very carefully.
I thought my invincible power
would hold the world captive
leaving me in a freedom undisturbed.
Thus night and day I worked at the chain
with huge fires and cruel hard strokes.
When at last the work was done
and the links were complete and unbreakable,
I found that it held me in its grip."[75]

TRANSACTING

In Western culture, it's easy to hear these expressions in everyday conversations: "What's in it for me?" "What will I get out of this?" "I owe you one." Do you ever hear yourself saying any of these? When you're home, do you ever bargain with your children, bribing them to be quiet, using candy to get them to do what you want, or threatening them with what you'll take away if their bad behavior continues?

If any of these behaviors are familiar, welcome to the culture of *Homo economicus.* Even if we don't want to participate in this way of living, even if we know how destructive it is to be constantly bargaining and negotiating, it's very difficult to escape its grasp.

Consumer culture needs us to be mindless and hungry. It constantly tells us that we need more and more, that whatever we have isn't enough. We're urged to consume as much as we can as the means to keep our current way of life flourishing. If we cease to consume, we'll need fewer things, and fewer people will be employed. This is the tragic dilemma of our time—we can't stop consuming without causing more suffering even when we realize that we can't alleviate our real suffering by consuming.

This is the world that Tagore foresaw: "The greed of gain has no time or limit to its capaciousness. Its one object is to produce and consume." We're urged to accumulate as much as we can so we'll feel safe and secure. We're taught how to compute and negotiate so that we get the best deal, so no one takes advantage of us. These dynamics are very compelling; better to get the upper hand, better to drive the hard bargain, better to win. It's easy to get caught up in the game—and you get a lot of nice stuff.

These messages are so powerful in modern global culture that it takes a great deal of awareness and discipline to silence their seductive lures. If we don't like what's happening to ourselves, our children, our colleagues, and our communities as we continue down the path of endless accumulation, then we need to reclaim the life we want. As at Shikshantar, we can practice swaraj, self-rule. We can practice swaraj by turning off the insistent cries of consumerism. We can think about what we really need, when enough's enough. We can consider how we want to feel at the end of our lives, what achievements will have enduring value.

Swaraj recalls us to who we want to be as human beings, past the glitter and junk of consumerism, past the superficial and meaningless transactions. Swaraj restores us to a healthy self-interest, where we exercise our freedom, self-confidence and creativity for the benefit of many, where we focus on who we want to become and what we want to contribute—not for gain, but as gift.

How are the demands of consumer culture impacting
you, your family, your community?

GIFTING

At Shikshantar, we witnessed the same creativity, inventiveness, love, and joy that were evident at Unitierra in Mexico, among the warriors in Brazil, at the GreenHouse in Joubert Park, in the circles at Kufunda. How do people without material things, with very few resources except themselves and each other, create such happiness?

These are all gifting communities. You may have noted how much support they gave each other, how when they learned a new skill or created an invention, they were quick to share this with friends and neighbors. We didn't see them hesitating or holding things back for themselves. They weren't asking "What can I get for this?" They wanted to know, "How can this serve?" And they trusted that others would want to serve them.

Gift culture nourishes us in deeply satisfying ways. As we share our skills and discoveries, and then have our gifts greeted with enthusiasm, we feel inspired to keep creating. We discover our own capacity for creativity and for generosity. It's hard to retreat into self-interest when your neighbors are so delighted by what you've just given them.

Gifting sets in motion a cycle of generosity where one gift prompts another. As generosity grows, emotions that destroy relationships, especially jealousy and competition, recede. These strong emotions place blinders on us, we don't want to see people's talents or acknowledge their skills. We think that by shrinking them, we'll feel better about ourselves. In a generous society, we don't need to reduce others in order to feel superior. We start to enjoy each other, even encourage each other. Once we experience this quality of community, it's hard to go back to pettiness and jealousy. We're so much more gifted, all of us, in a generous society.

Most of us already know this, even as we're struggling with transactional culture. We've had experiences of working together without thought of personal gain; we've shared moments of hard yet purposeful work that gave us more satisfaction than any object or paycheck ever could. These experiences, wherever they've occurred, give us a glimpse of how humans are meant to live together.

What creates lasting happiness in life? What few things become most important as we approach the end of life? Isn't it about family and relationships? Isn't it that we've contributed, that in some small way we've made life better for our children, for others, for the future?

We can reclaim our own wisdom. Wouldn't we all rather live together as *Homo giftus?*

Where might you next offer your talents,
ideas, and skills as gifts?

AN INVITATION TO EXPERIMENT

Work flows through us and not from us. We do not own our intellect, our creativity, or our skills. We have received them as a gift and grace. We pass them on as a gift and grace; it is like a river which keeps flowing. All the tributaries make the river great.

—Satish Kumar

What would it feel like to experience our work as gift and grace, streaming through us, one small tributary in a great river flowing to the future?

When we speak of offering work as a gift, it doesn't mean that we stop charging money for our services. We have to be realistic about the world we live in. But we can change *how we offer* our work at more subtle levels. We can notice all the strings we attach to our efforts—our need for approval, recognition, status, appreciation—and think about whether we want to cut them.

If you'd like to experiment with exploring your work as gift, here are some things to consider about gifts and gifting. A gift is a gift when:

> I offer it freely. There are no conditions. I give it because I want people to have it. I do not need to gain from it personally.

> I let go of needing the gift to be appreciated. I don't call attention to how hard I've worked, what it's taken me to get here, how dedicated and committed I am, what a good generous person I am.

> I don't look for approval, recognition, or thanks. I offer my work, then turn away. I don't stand and wait for compliments. I don't expect any kind of gratitude. I don't resent the people who didn't thank me.

> I let go of what I just offered. I move on, looking for the next place I might contribute.

It's not easy to change from our transactional mindset to these high standards of gifting. But it's worth a try. As we notice the emotional price tags we place on our work, we can choose to let go of them. Little by little, we can snip the strings that keep us from knowing the free and open space of generosity. As we discover the delights of gifting, we also begin to recognize the gifts that others are offering to us. In this way, generosity grows, creating relationships of immeasurable value.

AXLADITSA-AVATAKIA, GREECE
FROM INTERVENTION TO FRIENDSHIP

If I knew for certainty that a man was coming to my house with the conscious design of doing me good, I should run for my life . . . for fear that I should get some of his good done to me.

—*Henry David Thoreau*

Καλωσόρισμα, *Welcome!*

As hosts of the Art of Learning Centering, we would like to welcome you to this remarkable gathering at one of our own communities, Axladitsa-Avatakia. The theme of this year's gathering is "living the worlds we want today." During the next ten days, we will practice this by feeding one another, working on the land together, playing games and engaging in the questions that matter most.

In some ways, our time is like a family reunion, gathering together the diverse threads of our tribe. Imagine 60 family members creating a meal together, each community offering its unique flavors to create a sumptuous banquet. This is how we will organize our time together: preparing the space, bringing forth our gifts, enjoying and digesting the meal, and preparing to go back home.

We will have an opportunity to host one another, and to make visible what draws us together and what makes us unique. There is incredible richness in our community. Together, we will uncover this abundance, name it, and determine how next we intend to offer it to the world.

Thank you all for making the effort to be here.

Bon appétit!

An invitation from the Art of Learning Centering Design Team: Rodrigo (Brazil), Vanessa (Canada), Maria and Sarah (Greece), Manish and Nitin (India), Sergio (Mexico), Mabule (South Africa), Deborah, Bob, and Aerin (United States).

GREETING EACH OTHER AND THE LAND

The gods are having a party up on Mount Olympus, feasting on ambrosia and nectar and lazing about on thrones forged by Hephaestus. Apollo entertains them with his enchanting lyre, while the gods converse about the affairs of heaven and earth, working their way into your dreams as you fly in to the northern city of Thessaloniki. This image is a portent of things to come during your time in Greece, home to Zeus, Hermes, Aphrodite, Athena. You are in the birthplace of Western civilization, a land whose heroes and legends have impregnated many of the world's cultures and languages with ideas that arose more than twenty-five centuries ago.

In some sense, this journey is a pilgrimage—a mission to seek some deeper truth about yourself and the world—and it may require of you the

This trip to Greece was the third gathering of the Berkana Exchange. Our first took place in Nova Scotia in 2005 and lasted only three days. The second, five days in length, followed a year later in Oaxaca, Mexico. Then, in May 2007, we arrived in Greece, forty-six people gathering for ten days on the land of one of our own community members. We wanted to learn together about the "art of learning centering," the practice of hosting places where people explore and invent ways for communities to become healthy and resilient—places like Unitierra, Elos, The GreenHouse Project, Kufunda, and Shikshantar, which you've just visited.

Ten days, by Western standards, is a long time to be away from the workplace. It's a long time to be apart from family and friends. It's a long time to spend doing something that has no predictable outcome.

And yet, our community was certain that we couldn't get done what we needed to get done in less time. Because what we needed to "get done" was to weave the fabric of our friendship deeper and tighter so that learning could flow more easily through our network. We knew we had enough common interests—food sustainability, ecobuilding and upcycling, health and healing, intergenerational leadership, and more—to trust that we each would initiate the conversations and experiments we most needed to have. There were no experts, no panels, no workshops, no teachers. Just us, turning to one another to explore our differences and our similarities, our triumphs and our challenges. Like a family reunion, we gathered to discover the joys and frustrations of being together, all the while remembering that we're family.

Deborah

pilgrim's patience and perseverance along the way. For however many flights it took you to arrive in Greece, much of the road still lies ahead. After you land in Thessaloniki, you'll need to find the KTEL Intercity Bus for the two-and-a-half-hour ride to Volos, the last big city you'll see for the next ten days, which sits in the northwest corner of the Pelion peninsula. The next forty miles of your journey will take another two hours on the local bus, rising, plunging, and twisting its way along the precipitous route to Platania, the local fishing port at the bottom of the peninsula. Pelion is a cloak of green that divides the Aegean Sea from the Pagasitikos Gulf. The landscape is dense with beech, oak, birch, and fir trees; with orchards of fig, plum, walnut, quince, and currant. And everywhere, groves of olives waiting to be picked, pickled, brined, stuffed, and pressed.

Night has already fallen by the time you step off the bus in Platania, weakened by the dizzying ride. Sarah Whiteley waits patiently by her truck to shuttle you the final leg to Axladitsa-Avatakia. A lanky and tranquil Brit, Sarah moved to Greece to co-steward this twenty-four-acre parcel of land that slopes down toward the Aegean Sea. Sarah has the air of Persephone about her—that is, at once in union with the abundance of nature and with some darker mystery, a link between the underworld and the earth. En route, she tells you her story of a ten-year search that led to this magical land, a land that is her teacher and she its guardian. These last ten minutes of the journey become increasingly wild, bumping and rolling over unkempt roads until you swing a left onto the dirt driveway that spills down toward the red-shingled roof of the main house.

At the sound of the truck, Maria Skordialou rushes out to greet you, a petite, black-haired Hestia, one who is ever ready to feed and shelter weary travelers. A Greek nomad who has returned to her homeland to co-steward Axladitsa, Maria clasps you in a tight hug and hands you a glass of *tsipouro,* the fiery distilled liquor that revives you just enough to make the final trek down to your campsite. You will have time in the morning to properly greet this land and her guests. But now it is late and you must rest, for we'll be working hard in the days ahead.

Leave the flashlight behind; the moon is full and will escort you gently down the *rema,* the dry riverbed that leads to your tent. The moonbeams glint off smooth-shouldered rocks and shimmer in the leaves of the crooked olive trees. Every so often, call out your greetings to the wild boar so you don't surprise him and excite an unwanted response. You are trespassing in his land and must pay your respects. As you nestle into your

The Pelion peninsula is a cloak of green that divides the Aegean Sea from the Pagasitikos Gulf.

FROM INTERVENTION TO FRIENDSHIP

tent, listen to the night calls of the screech owl, the honey buzzard, and the nightingale. These were the same lullabies that rocked the giants to sleep—Ajax and Agamemnon, Atlas and Achilles, Aristotle and Aeschylus. Welcome to the land of gods and goddesses, great warriors and philosophers, Muses, bards and comedians. You are sleeping at the crossroads, a world that is neither North nor South, neither East nor West, but stretches out in every direction—where everything is possible.

Kaliníhta. Oneira gluka. Good night. Sweet dreams. May your sleep be filled with ambrosia and nectar.

•• • ••

Yassas! Kaliméra! Cries of morning greetings echo out across the ravine and bounce back at you from the neighboring hills. You poke your head out of the tent to see the brilliant Aegean sunshine illuminating a garden of herbs, wildflowers and grasses. Nearby stands a ten-gallon jug filled with spring water that you can gulp down and splash on your face before dashing up to the main house to discover who is here.

There are many faces that might look familiar, folks you've already met on this journey: Mabule from South Africa is here with his colleague, Tshideso; Ticha, Sikhethiwe, and Jackie are here from Kufunda. The inseparable Brazilian trio of Rodrigo, Edgard, and Mariana are here. Sergio from Unitierra has brought along Aline and Melisa. Manish has a whole contingent of Indians with him: Nitin and Anita with their fifteen-year-old daughter Sakhi, Sujata, Shammi, Sanjoy, and Ravi. There are new faces as

Friends from Unitierra, Elos, Joubert Park, Kufunda, Shikshantar, and beyond gather for breakfast. Maria, Panayiotis, and Sarah relax on the hillside that will become the terraced garden.

WALK OUT WALK ON

well: Nora from Slovakia; Filiz from Turkey; Jane, Todd, Vanessa, Emma and Tim from Canada; Juan, Yvette, Aerin, Lauren, Deborah, Teresa, the Stilger-Virnig family, and the Mates family from the United States. And of course, Maria and Sarah along with their neighbors and friends, Panayiotis, Stathis, Mr. Michalis, and another Maria. Only our Pakistani friends (Afshan and Asif) and two more Indians (Sumitra and Sandip) are absent, held up by bureaucratic wrangling with the Greek visa offices.

Greetings, hugs, and hearty laughter sail across the checkered breakfast table beneath the thatched shade of the patio with its grand vista of the woodland sloping down to the sea. At least half of these folks have been together before. This is the third annual Art of Learning Centering, a gathering for the members of the Berkana Exchange, all of whom, in their own unique way, are working to build healthy and resilient communities at home. We think of one another as family—as "family of choice" rather than of origin—and for ten days, we will live, cook, work, eat, play, and dream together, learning from one another how to build the world we wish for.

There is much building to do.

CREATING AND PREPARING THE SPACE

Maria and Sarah came to Axladitsa-Avatakia in August 2006 with a vision of hosting a place where local people and those from afar could learn how to listen to and tend the land, ourselves, and one another so that we can live sustainably and harmoniously. That would mean growing and producing organic food, sourcing energy from renewable resources, building infrastructure that would produce zero waste, and practicing leadership that engages everyone's gifts and creativity.

Little pear tree and place that is difficult to traverse. That is what Axladitsa-Avatakia means. It is an ancient name for this land that bridges two valleys. Axladitsa is an untamed landscape of ravines with steep edges, ten acres of protected woodland and fourteen acres of agricultural land, laced by four streams and a narrow winding footpath that meanders down to the beach at Kastri. It is home to the lethargic but deadly horned viper that sunbathes on hot black rocks and to poisonous scorpions that sneak into tents and open-toed shoes. Its ochre soil hosts 350 olive trees that produce hundreds of kilos of cold-pressed olive oil in a good year. It is land that is at once alive and pulsing, enchanted and wise.

Maria and Sarah purchased this land from a family friend of Maria's who preferred selling it to someone he knew rather than turning it over to a stranger. Now, they have an opportunity to develop it. Conventional wisdom would have them take advantage of any number of economic incentives for development. They could plan an integrated resort or conference center that would attract upmarket tourists by providing seaside lodging, local gastronomic adventures and the region's unique Thassalotherapy seawater spa treatments. (Club Med, in fact, had been rumored to be preparing a bid for the twenty-four-acre parcel at the time Maria and Sarah closed their deal.) They could leverage agricultural incentives, building out their farmable land; the region's mountainous topography has prohibited large-scale farming, making it wise to shift to more labor-intensive—and potentially lucrative—organic farming. They could chase incentives for wind, solar, geothermal, and biofuel development, for youth programs, for agrotourism, and for microenterprise. They have endless choice, many of which are advocated by the banks, by municipal government, and by development agencies, ensuring access to loans and other forms of development assistance—and a rapid return on investment.

Instead of following the advice of experts, however, Maria and Sarah decide to invite their friends to join them at Axladitsa to collectively discover what this place might become. And so here we are, nine months later, forty-six of us gathered on the land to begin this odyssey.

BRINGING FORTH OUR GIFTS

There is a rhythm to our days, and it goes like this: *Morning practice . . . Breakfast . . . Check in . . . Opening the space . . . Lunch . . . Digestion . . . Community conversation . . . Check out . . . Reflection . . . Dinner . . . Evening offerings.*

Morning practice is the base beat, the foundation for the day that wakes you up and gets your body present on the land. You can join Shammi for yoga on the patio by the main house, or sit in meditation in the *platia,* the new red-shingled rotunda that crowns the property. Juan and Yvette are leading a walk down to the beach for a morning swim—this will be Ticha and Sikhethiwe's first time ever seeing the sea. Those who signed up on "the matrix" for morning chores will be preparing breakfast in the open-air kitchen, fetching water from the spring or sweeping out the community spaces. The matrix is the tool that allows us to organize ourselves for living together on the land—preparing meals, collecting water, managing waste, maintaining sanitation—without having anyone in charge. Now would be a good time for you to sign up for your contribution. Choose whatever you want, but consider that the matrix is built on the assumption that each member of the community will shoulder a fair share of the difficult tasks.

After breakfast, we gather in the platia for check-in. Check-in and checkout are the tonic notes—that is, the chord to which everything else resolves. This morning, Filiz is hosting the check-in, inviting us into a Turkish circle dance. We hold hands and stomp our feet as we travel around the edge of the platia, nearly tumbling out as the dance speeds up. We follow this with a question, a chance for people to voice their reflections, share a story, or simply sit in silence. Ticha offers a poem. Sarah lights a candle. Maria rings a bell. We are here.

The rest of the morning is Open Space, the agenda-free process that invites people to self-organize around the projects and conversations that grab their attention. This is the moment when the full ensemble explodes into sound, each group playing its part according to our agreements: that we are here to give Axladitsa shape and form, and in so doing, to exchange with one another what we know. Manish and Mabule call together those who wish to transform the grassy knoll by the main house into a garden. Rodrigo and Melisa plan to carve a stone staircase into the steep slope that runs up to the rotunda. Aerin and Sergio want to finish digging holes for the outdoor toilets and encasing them for privacy in chicken wire woven with straw. Nora will be constructing wooden toilet seats from discarded plywood in the shed. Where do you feel called? Join that group, create your own project, or sit quietly and settle into the land.

The afternoon community conversations are about how to support one another in advancing our work back home. How might the Warriors

Mornings, we work on the land. Afternoons, we gather in the platia to explore questions that challenge us, teach us, and deepen our friendship.

FROM INTERVENTION TO FRIENDSHIP

Without Weapons program in Brazil spread trans-locally through other communities? What is the next stage of supporting young people in India in developing right livelihood? How do we practice zero-waste living? How do we feed ourselves sustainably? How do we deal with leadership succession planning in our organizations? What would happen if we worked together regionally? Why does gift culture matter? What strengthens or diminishes our political power?

These conversations are intense, sometimes tearful, sometimes jubilant. We don't agree on everything, and sometimes the differences are hard to bear. But the quality of our friendship allows us to go as deep as we need to go, exploring some of our most closely held beliefs. We shift in and out of different shapes—pairs, triads, small groups, large groups, the whole. The afternoons are long and often wearying as we push the edges of this composition, exploring dissonance and cacophony before resolving back to the primary tones of our checkout together. It is a perfectly Greek moment: Legend has it that Pythagoras himself is credited with discovering the nature of harmony when he passed by the blacksmiths at work and noticed the beautiful tones they created as they struck their anvils with their hammers.[76] Consonance is proportionate, predictable; dissonance is surprising and follows no order. It makes things interesting. It keeps us learning.

Mealtimes are the chorus. Everyone comes back together, gathers around the checkered tables and raises their voices in a refrain of storytelling, inquiry and debate. Lunch and dinner are a bizarre fusion of culture depending on who signed up for meal prep. Fresh bread, olives, and feta cheese make up the Greek staples—the rest is up for grabs. Melisa and Aline bring *mole* and solar-roasted chocolate from Mexico. The Indians contribute bagfuls of mangoes and handfuls of coriander, turmeric, cardamom, cumin, and red pepper to prepare curries. The Greek neighbors will teach us how to deep-fry oregano, wild greens, and fennel collected from the land to prepare *riyanokeftedes*; how to whip yogurt, cucumber, and garlic into *tzatziki*; and how to grill skewered lamb in the wood-fired stove to make *souvlaki*. You'll sip homemade *retsina*, Turkish coffee, and Indian-spiced chai. And when dinner is finished, you'll dance fandango to the music played by Sergio and Aline on their eight-stringed, guitar-shaped *jaranas*, you'll sing melancholy tunes by candlelight with Rodgrigo and Edgard, you'll huddle around laptops to watch movies brought by Nitin and Manish, you'll pull tarot cards with Maria and Sarah, or you'll sit out on the hillside gazing up at the stars and wonder why the world isn't always just like this.

DIGESTING THE MEAL

While Pythagoras revered consonance, the Athenians must have delighted enough in dissonance to have embraced democracy. More than 2,500 years ago, the Athenians decided it would be a good idea if every adult citizen (excluding women and slaves, of course) had the right to have his say and vote on legislation. All that was required to speak or propose a law was *Ho boulomenos*, "he who wishes"—someone willing to take the initiative and stand in front of his fellow citizenry to speak on behalf of what matters. With a quorum of six thousand people in the assembly, one can imagine that there was probably a mighty amount of discord, not to mention inefficiency, inconsistency, and unpredictability. After all, this was a state run by amateurs.

As we sat under the night sky—friends from India, Europe, Africa, and the Americas—we reflected on how right it felt to be here in Greece, the crossroads between us. Ironically, this was the culture that sculpted the heroic leader archetype, one who demonstrates courage and self-sacrifice to lead others to safety—and none of us wanted to be heroes.

We'd come together to explore a very different model for how to get work done—as friends, as community. We talked about how we didn't want to save anyone, that we didn't want to stand out in front and pronounce, "I have the answer." We yearned to work side-by-side with our friends and neighbors, finding solutions to problems together, all of us satisfied when we accomplished good work together

That desire was as clear as the stars that night. Yet I know my heroic side is always there, too, the leader who wants to leap up and say, "I *know* how to solve that problem! Follow me!" Then I forge ahead, bent on solving the problem myself, losing friends and colleagues along the way. And of course, my single-minded approach doesn't solve the problem, it just creates more of them.

I'm learning how to control my heroic urges. When I'm in meetings or with a group, sometimes I literally sit on my hands, reminding myself to refrain from offering a solution. I've learned that when I listen rather than tell, when I wait for the community's wisdom to surface rather than impulsively offer my own, then so much more is possible. We are smarter together than we are apart—an assumption that lies at the root of democracy. Perhaps Greece, the birthplace of democracy, was the perfect place for us to be together after all.

Deborah

FROM INTERVENTION TO FRIENDSHIP

And yet, the city-state of Athens was among the first to invite in the full bounty of its citizenry's gifts and, as a result, to thrive (that is, until its trouncing in the Peloponnesian War). Ever since, democracy has steadily ebbed from the rough hands of its citizens into the polished gloves of its professional representatives. Today, we find ourselves in the unenviable position of depending on experts to intervene on our behalf in nearly every aspect of our lives—governance, justice, health, education, security. Inevitably, it seems, few of those experts agree on how best to solve our problems. In fact, argues Nassim Nicholas Taleb in his book *The Black Swan*, "certain professionals, while believing they are experts, are in fact not. Based on their empirical record, they do not know more about their subject matter than the general population, but they are much better at narrating—or, worse, at smoking you with complicated mathematical models. They are also more likely to wear a tie."[77]

Intervention (from the Latin for "to come between, interrupt") has emerged as the modus operandi for our culture's appetite for problem solving. It wasn't always so. Until the beginning of the twentieth century, the United States had an isolationist mindset, uninterested in meddling in the affairs of other nations. But after two world wars and America's rise to supremacy, interventionism as foreign policy took center stage—and with the emergence of the Cold War, shifted from overt (military) to covert (nonmilitary).[78] It became the dominant theme of development and assistance, both within our borders and beyond. In education, there are interventions in early childhood development, for minority students, for poor test takers, for children with psychological problems. In addiction therapy, there are prescriptions for family interventions, workplace interventions, adolescent Interventions, and professional Interventions. There are cognitive interventions, behavioral interventions, economic interventions, environmental interventions, and art interventions. In his March 2000 report to the United Nations, Kofi Annan challenged the international community to step up to its responsibility to engage in humanitarian intervention.

However well intentioned the intervention might be, it is always rooted in the belief that people need help, they can't help themselves, and it is our duty to "interrupt" their experience on their behalf. Perhaps nowhere more so than in international development has the notion of benevolent intervention been so broadly embraced, under the moniker of "aid." According to Zambian author Dambisa Moyo in her book *Dead Aid*, "Deep in every liberal sensibility is a profound sense that in a world of moral uncertainty, one idea is sacred, one belief cannot be compromised: the rich should help the poor, and the form of this help should be aid."[79] Since the 1940s, the rich countries have put more than $1 trillion in development assistance into Africa alone.[80] Certainly, this is evidence of our generosity and open-heartedness. And yet, what is so heartbreaking is that the poor are poorer and dependence is more systemically entrenched.

Stories of intervention gone awry abound with laughable absurdity—were it not for the deadly serious suffering they inflict on people's lives and livelihoods. Yemen is on the brink of a water crisis after replacing its centuries-old practice of harvesting rainwater for crops with a World Bank–driven approach to irrigated agriculture that has tapped out underground aquifers.[81] In the Pacific Island nation of Kiribati, aid organizations extended economic incentives to the islanders to produce coconut oil in an effort to stem overfishing of tropical reefs; with all that extra money, islanders spent their new leisure time back at sea . . . and fish populations plummeted.[82] International Monetary Fund policy in Jamaica wiped out the local dairy industry when it flooded the market with cheap European and American milk powder.[83] And we've already heard (during our visit to Zimbabwe) about Bill Clinton's apology for U.S. policy in Haiti that destroyed local rice production.

We are so attached to our interventionist mindset that we cling to it perversely in the face of disconfirming proof. As Moyo writes:

> One of the most depressing aspects of the whole aid fiasco is that donors, policymakers, governments, academicians, economists and development specialists know, in their heart of hearts, that aid doesn't work, hasn't worked and won't work. . . .
>
> Study, after study, after study (many of them the donors' own) have shown that, after many decades and many millions of dollars, aid has had no appreciable impact on development. . . .
>
> Even the *most* cursory look at data suggests that as aid has increased over time, Africa's growth has decreased with an accompanying higher incidence of poverty. Over the past thirty years, the most aid-dependent countries have exhibited growth rates averaging *minus* 0.2 percent per annum.[84]

Intervention is not fundamentally flawed. In fact, it is essential for protecting people who are being victimized by brutality greater than they can withstand—from domestic violence to genocide. But it's a short-term strategy for the immediate situation; any longer-term change requires the engagement of the person or people. So as a community- or nation-building strategy, it can't ever work. Why, then, do we persist in our belief that we must intervene? Why do we come between people and their problems?

There is, perhaps, an assumption we hold about the nature of knowledge and expertise that Plato illuminates in his text *The Symposium*. At a drinking party, Agathon invites Socrates to sit beside him and impart his wisdom. In response to the request, Plato writes, "My dear Agathon, Socrates replied as he took his seat beside him, I only wish that wisdom *were* the kind of thing one could share by sitting next to someone—if it flowed, for instance, from the one that was full to the one that was empty, like the water in the two cups finding its level through a piece of worsted. If that were how it worked, I'm sure I'd congratulate myself on sitting next to you, for you'd soon have me brimming over with the most exquisite kind of wisdom. My own understanding is a shadowy thing at best, as equivocal as a dream."[85]

This empty-vessel paradigm of learning is one of the foundations of our interventionist mindset. It posits that the trainer is full, the trainee is empty, and it is only a matter, as Socrates says, of pouring knowledge from one into the other. It assumes there is a right way, the expert has mastered it, and it only needs to be transmitted through training and intervention to an "undeveloped" or "underdeveloped" individual, community or nation. It relies on our belief in our own superiority—we are good and generous people with skills, knowledge, and gifts to bestow upon others who are less fortunate. And so, despite mountains of evidence to the contrary, we persist in pouring our wisdom—which may be far more shadowy and equivocal than we believe—down the throats of people who are living differently, of people whose own wisdom points them in a direction we don't value or understand.

It is time to walk out of the interventionist mindset of outside experts. Now more than ever as humanity's challenges converge, we need to learn from one another. At the Art of Learning Centering in Greece, our friends are walking on to a different learning paradigm: one that replaces intervention with friendship and the empty vessel with the plentiful potluck, the unplanned meal where each and every person makes a contribution. It isn't that the potluck always works out as a perfect meal; sometimes there's a mishmash of things that don't taste good together. But they are offered in a spirit of love and friendship, and somehow we always end up with a rich and full meal. No story demonstrates this better than the Great Toilet Paper Debate.

THE GREAT TOILET PAPER DEBATE

The ancient Greeks preferred clay and stone, while the Romans opted for a sponge on a stick. The Nara-period Japanese pulled off the sponge and used the stick as a scraper. Henry VIII had his very own Groom of the Stool (a highly respected position) who provided hands-on ministration to the King. And until the Scott brothers introduced toilet paper on a roll in 1890, Americans preferred the old *Farmer's Almanac* and Sears Roebuck catalog as their outhouse attendants.

Today, toilet paper is a multibillion-dollar industry in the United States alone.[86] Someone even took the time to figure out that Americans, on average, use 57 sheets a day[87] and 23.6 rolls per year.[88] That's more than seven *billion* rolls of toilet paper consumed by the U.S. population each year, less than 2 percent of which is 100 percent recycled. And thus it is that we cut down about seven million trees for that "one kind thing you can do for your behind"[89] fluffy, luxurious wipe.

But dead trees are not what have Mabule and Sergio's knickers all in a knot. It's the dioxin—the carcinogenic chlorine bleach that impregnates most toilet paper, and certainly the toilet paper that we have available to us at Axladitsa-Avatakia. From a distance, you can see Sergio standing by one of the eco-loos, waving his arms about and from time to time stamping one foot. Mabule has his arms crossed, quietly listening and shaking his head no. Sergio is advocating that we burn our used toilet paper so that the bleach doesn't leach into the soil, compromising the food chain. Mabule is equally resolute about not releasing the dioxins into the air; we should, instead, bury our toilet paper.

Aerin Dunford digs a hole for an outdoor toilet. Panayiotis is the local keeper of wisdom; it is his knowledge of the traditions and practices of this place that guide our efforts.

The two are at an impasse, so for the next few days, our toilet paper accumulates in garbage bags, awaiting a breakthrough strategy for disposal.

The Indians have one: Why not bypass toilet paper altogether and tidy up Indian style, with water and the left hand? The Indians are beaming, smug with their incontestable solution—until chaos breaks loose as a few North Americans stand in shock, stunned at the notion that some people actually *use their hand* to wipe their behind.

But it will take more than the delicate sensibilities of a handful of North Americans to squash this proposal. The Greeks are aghast as well, since we are in the middle of a *drought* and are *already* spending several hours every day fetching water from the spring to hydrate, feed, and wash this community. Water, they declare, is not the solution.

Back to the impasse. As several more days go by, a small mountain of garbage bags accumulates at the shed near the driveway. Tensions and tempers escalate as people who have devoted their souls to the health and well-being of the earth, air, and its inhabitants stand witness to their collusion in creating a new mountain of toxic waste.

On Day Six of the gathering, Manish has a new proposal for the community: "Let tomorrow be the Toilet Paper Challenge Day. I invite each and every one of you to experiment with what it might be like to have a toilet-paper-free day!" Turning our trouble into a game is just the right spirit for reengaging our creativity. While several people opt to keep their investigations to themselves (toilet etiquette being a rather personal preference), others eagerly dispense their newfound wisdom. There are those who try water for the first time, and those who praise the virtues of the smooth, long rock. One gentleman (who prefers to remain nameless) decides to time his shower for just after his morning movement.

But the greatest excitement occurs when Susan, a hiker from Washington State, returns to the group at lunchtime with wads of green bunched up in her hands. "Hiker's Toilet Paper!" she crows, showing off the thick, velvety leaves of the mullein plant favored by campers for its fluffy, flannel-like texture. A sun-loving weed, mullein thrives on dry, hillside soil with high clay and stone content—and so has blanketed itself all over the upland slopes of Axladitsa.

Who would have guessed that it would take the combined wisdom of a Mexican, South African, Indian, Greek, and American to invent a solution that would engage the whole community? One could argue that we might have gone straight to the solution from Day One—skipping over the unnecessary accumulation of toilet paper that would now be sent to landfill—had the right person bestowed the right knowledge upon us. Our participation in that solution would likely have been halfhearted, if we complied at all. (Imagine, if you will, arriving in someone's home, only to be told that despite an abundance of toilet tissue, you will be instructed to wipe your bum with an unfamiliar fuzzy green leaf.) Instead, we discovered the resources available among us by acting together, in friendship, experimenting with what we could co-create, rather than being passive recipients of others' knowledge.

This collective discovery process plays itself out again and again during our ten days together. We debate how to design the garden using permaculture practiced in Zimbabwe, natural farming practiced in India, and terracing practiced in Greece; whether to cook without oil and eat vegetarian or embrace the local culture's abundant olive oil and lamb; how to upcycle our trash into jewelry, toys, and practical devices rather than send it to the local dump; how to build the stone stairway by making mortar out of the red soil. Our experiments have a light touch; we are not concerned with getting it right, but rather with learning from one another. Panayiotis is here at every turn to keep us grounded in the local reality, reminding us about the Greek way that has arisen from the unique knowledge of time, place, practice, and tradition. As architect Christopher Alexander writes:

> If I build a fireplace for myself, it is natural for me to make a place to put the wood, a corner to sit in, a mantel wide enough to put things on, an opening which lets the fire draw.

 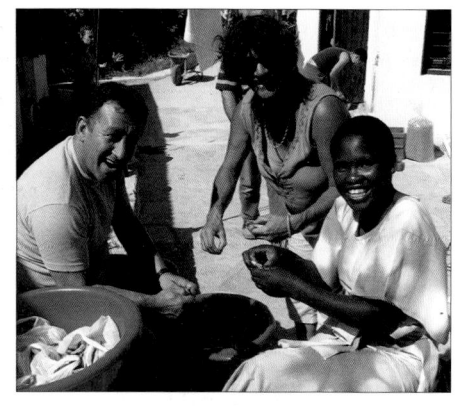

We terrace the garden by laying rocks and making mortar out of the red soil. Under Stathis's guidance, Jackie and Sikhethiwe of Kufunda prepare a traditional Greek fish recipe.

FROM INTERVENTION TO FRIENDSHIP

But, if I design fireplaces for other people—not for myself—then I never have to build a fire in the fireplaces I design. Gradually my ideas become more and more influenced by style, and shape, and crazy notions—my feeling for the simple business of making fire leaves the fireplace altogether.

So, it is inevitable that as the work of building passes into the hands of specialists, the patterns which they use become more and more banal, more willful, and less anchored in reality.[90]

It will be Maria and Sarah, Panayiotis, Stathis, and Mr. Michalis who will inherit whatever we create; they are the ones who will continue to tend the garden, maintain the steps, and manage the water supply long after we've all left. Our individual expertise matters far less than how we listen to one another, how we each offer our gifts to produce a banquet that nourishes us all. And our individual expertise becomes far more useful when it is enriched by the reciprocity of friendship.

MUTUALITY, TRUST, AND FRIENDSHIP

Aristotle distinguished three kinds of friendship: friendship based on utility, on pleasure, and on goodness. Only this latter kind, which he called "perfect friendship," merited his full respect. Perfect friendship requires equality; each person sees the other as a peer and extends toward the other good will (*eunoia*). The friendship becomes imperfect if they see each other as unequal or if they seek to gain some advantage through the other.

Our industrial age has been one of imperfect and unequal relationships that privilege production and profit over learning and friendship. When we seek to intervene on behalf of others, more often than not, we do so because we see them as lacking and are blind to their potential. That is not a friendship of equals. Austrian philosopher and social critic Ivan Illich held a vision of a society based on Aristotle's perfect friendship that he called "convivial." The convivial society, he said, invites all its members to offer their gifts autonomously and interdependently.[91] What satisfies the needs of society's members is the opportunity to experience the joy of engaging in creative activities alongside one's neighbors, friends, and family. There is joy in the act of gathering together with friends to create, invent, and experiment; there is compliance in the act of receiving knowledge that will increase our productivity and potential. Illich believed that friendships require mutuality, and that only out of a society that cultivates "disciplined, self-denying, careful, tasteful friendships" can healthy community life arise.[92]

Reflecting back on the gathering a few weeks later, I found our toilet paper angst hilarious. There we were, a group of highly intelligent and motivated social activists completely unable to agree on how to wipe our butts. But at the time, this was one among many conflicts that arose as we confronted our differences. As an intercultural group, we were often operating from different assumptions.

One of my most important lessons about difference came late one afternoon when we were engaged in a dialogue that was stretching far into the dinner hour. We had asked one another to speak for only three minutes, and speaker after speaker were, in my mind, rambling on and on, far longer than their allotted time. I became increasingly frustrated. People were being self-centered, more concerned with expressing their thoughts than attending to the needs of the whole. And so I interrupted, naming the behavior and asking people to stick to three minutes.

What was swiftly pointed out—and I hadn't noticed—is that for each of the speakers I had criticized, English was not their first language. I had the advantage of speaking in my native tongue, finding exactly the right words to express myself. They did not. Once again, I was in a position of privilege, with friends from the South—from Africa, India, and South America—adapting themselves to meet my needs. The conflict that arose from my confrontation was painful—for me, for those who had spoken, and for everyone who witnessed our reenactment of a classic intercultural dynamic. Had it not been for the strength of our friendship—for the good work we'd been doing for days together—things might have fallen apart, dissolving into accusations and finger pointing. Instead, we gently rewove the torn fabric, both one-on-one and collectively, turning this conflict into an opportunity to deepen our understanding of one another, of the many hurts we carry from the past, and of the fears and desires we hold for the future.

Deborah

The convivial society built on friendship is messy but enduring. It listens to each and every voice, it receives all contributions. It values as equal the wisdom of people who live differently. The empty-vessel paradigm of learning is fundamentally founded on the inequality between the professional and the amateur, the expert and the ignoramus, the so-called developed and underdeveloped. It's like the nutritionist who prescribes a perfectly balanced diet. But nourishment that satisfies the body and soul requires far more than the right blend of vitamins and minerals. True nourishment arises from the intimate connection between human beings, the

FROM INTERVENTION TO FRIENDSHIP

precious moments of mutuality and trust that emerge when we turn to one another. True nourishment is about the joy of sharing a meal, including the messiness of preparation and the hard labor of cleaning up, the botched brownies and the victorious soufflé, the stories, laughter, and tears that show up whenever people open their hearts to one another, whenever we offer our friendship.

Walking out of intervention does not mean we surrender our concern for the world's ills and injustices. New models of profound social change that rely on mutuality, trust, and friendship have burst onto the community development scene over the past decade. Microcredit, pioneered in Bangladesh by Nobel Peace Prize laureate Muhammad Yunus and Grameen Bank, provides small loans to poor people who have no access to credit. (Yunus made his first loans in 1976 to forty-two people; the total amount was $27.) At first glance, it sounds like another example of economic intervention—until you dive a little deeper into the relationships that anchor the practice. Small circles, mostly of women, are bound together to shoulder responsibility for repaying each member's loan—resulting in an impressive 96.7 percent loan recovery rate. "Solidarity lending" is the fancy term professionals have given to this most natural of human impulses: groups of peers sitting in circle together, turning to one another for support. The results of these friendship circles have been astonishing: As of March 2010, 68 percent of Grameen Bank's eight million borrowers have crossed out of poverty.[93] What's even more surprising is that from the beginning, Grameen Bank has passed along ownership of its equity—95 percent—to the borrowers themselves. Following on the success of Grameen Bank, thousands of organizations have launched microcredit programs. Very few of them, however, have maintained (or even noticed) Grameen's emphasis on the role of friendship among borrowers to encourage high returns.

Grameen Bank trusted this unconventional approach to poverty because it knew that poor people have all the skills, creativity, and ingenuity they need; it is the economic and societal barriers embedded in our cultures that are inhibiting their success. "Government decision-makers, international consultants, and many NGOs usually start from the opposite assumption—that people are poor because they lack skills," Yunus writes in his book, *Creating a World Without Poverty*. "Based on this assumption, they start anti-poverty efforts built around elaborate training programs. This seems logical, based on the underlying assumption—and it also perpetuates the interests of the anti-poverty experts. . . . To be fair, most anti-poverty experts are well-intentioned. They opt for training because that is what their flawed assumptions dictate."[94] Grameen Bank has walked out of training and walked on to create multiple ways of supporting poor people in exercising their innate skills to survive, to invent, and to make life better for their friends and neighbors.

There are other compelling examples of the power of friendship to evoke creativity, learning, and support. One is "Communities of Practice," groups of people doing similar work who informally find one another at conferences, professional events and through the Internet. In these self-organized relationships, participants exchange information and experiences and develop trusting relationships. Their mutual exchanges lead to new competencies and solutions, and people feel supported and less alone in their work. Communities of practice have self-organized among teachers seeking to transform the high-stakes testing culture in schools, among commanders in the U.S. Army who need to generate real-time information and learning faster than the traditional chain of command, among urban youth pioneering innovative approaches to food security. They're embodying Aristotle's third model of friendship: reciprocal good will among peers who share their gifts.

Among the Internet's many effects, one valuable one has been the ease with which people can find like-minded peers and the information they need on virtually any subject. Today, we turn to one another to tell stories, create software platforms, build political campaigns, solve health problems, choose schools, design neighborhoods, even make loans. Ordinary people—the amateurs—no longer need the professionals to intervene on our behalf; we can find new friends who share our interests, values, and desires to create together. Imagine what would be possible if we brought that same curiosity and commitment to finding like-minded friends in our local communities, where together we could create solutions to the issues affecting us at home.

Friendship creates a container in which we can co-create, support one another, and bounce back from the conflicts that arise. Conflict is an inevitable consequence of interdependence; the more interdependent we are, the more conflict there's likely to be. But when friendship is present, so, too, is our commitment to stay together and work things out. We open our hearts to each other, knowing that we need kindred spirits—*especially* when the going gets tough. We can walk out alone, but we can only walk on in friendship.

FROM INTERVENTION TO FRIENDSHIP

PREPARING TO GO BACK HOME

It is our final night together on this wild land of Axladitsa-Avatakia, herself seeming like an ancient goddess, one who has helped us see each other more clearly. She is inviting us now to listen to the future: a garden will come, filled with peas and broad beans, cauliflower and cabbage, wild greens and garlic and onions; olive trees and grape vines will yield oil and wine; small tents and yurts will shelter the many guests who will recognize this place as a true home. Axladitsa-Avatakia will host large group gatherings and individual retreats. She will speak Greek and English, Portuguese and Zulu, Hindi, Turkish and French. She will not yield to development, to profit, or to economic intervention. She will invite all those who pass through to ask questions that matter. She will inspire us to learn together in a spirit of friendship that arises out of a sheer sense of joy, *gratis*, with no ulterior motive. And she will inspire us to poetry. So on this, our final night together, she will tell us through Nova Scotia–based poet Tim Merry what it feels like to walk on to friendship.

Love, truth,
No roof
No limit to potential
Where learning is truly exponential
Belief in human goodness essential
The feeling of community
More important to me
Than any mental model or theory.
It is the feeling that allows me
To act clearly
From internal intention
From collective question
The experience that tells me when to sit back rather
than make an intervention.

What is the feeling to be gifted?
What internal world shifted?
What new reality uplifted?
That will support my work at home
Support us feeling in Yarmouth less alone
Strengthen the skeleton bones
We are building for new community,
A body that nobody owns
But we all dare to share.
I'm here because I care.
Friends are where I go
To tune in to deeper flow
To understand what I already know.

Every breath is precious,
A precious wake-up call.
I'm grateful to be here
And with you all.

INTERVENTION

Greece is the source of myths and ideals that have swept round the world and continue to influence us visibly and invisibly. So it's good to return here to be reminded of what some of these ideals originally meant, especially friendship. This is a time when many of us feel isolated and alone, disconnected from ourselves, from each other, from what's possible. Still, we have a deep yearning to connect, but it's become more and more difficult to find time to be friends.

There are other factors here besides our being so busy. Some of this fragmentation has been created by our culture of expertise. When was it that we stopped caring for each other as good neighbors? When did we start offering help not from friendship, but as experts with superior knowledge?

When friendship fades and we no longer feel responsible for taking care of each other, what also disappears is our own sense of personal competence. Where do we turn when we need advice? Do we consult our own experience or immediately ask an expert? When there's a problem at work, do we come together as colleagues to try and figure things out, or do we import a solution from elsewhere? If a friend comes to us in crisis, do we offer our companionship, or do we refer him or her to a book or DVD? Experts are important, absolutely. But it's our dependence on them as the first or only choice that bears watching.

The word *intervention* means "interruption," an action that breaks a pattern and opens up new possibilities. But current interventions break us into categories. People are either victims or helpers, those with problems or those with solutions. The people we came to help end up objectified as a collection of problems. Even though we want to make a difference, our good intentions get derailed by this break in human connections, by the absence of friendship.

Aristotle said that perfect friendship is a relationship between equals who offer good will to one another. By his definition, most of the time we're not acting in friendship. We're not friends if we're feeling pity or guilt for the other. We're not friends if we feel even slightly superior, or if we think we know what's wrong with the other person and how to fix them.

What if we stopped pursuing the perfect problem-ending technique and decided to become experts on being there for each other? We could begin by remembering that we're all humans, so we must be equals.

When have you experienced someone trying to "help" you? What happened to your relationship?

FRIENDSHIP

Maria and Sarah took a big risk when they chose to develop Axladitsa-Avatika by relying on their friends rather than the advice of experts. But that wasn't the biggest risk. What was most risky was opening their land and their dreams to their friends and being willing to trust they'd work things out through friendship.

Friendship becomes strong and trustworthy if we're willing to commit to each other. We agree we'll stay together no matter what, that we won't flee when things get difficult. Walk Ons rely on friends to provide energy and inspiration. When we work together, great ideas take shape. When we feel angry, sad and frustrated, together we can admit our exhaustion and open our hearts to break. We cry, fight, yell, laugh, sing, complain, dream, celebrate, weep. It's here, inside our friendship, that we explore what it means to be present, vulnerable, open—in other words, fully human.

Friendship isn't easy. When we care about something deeply (for example, toilet paper), we don't want to discuss it. Our solution is obviously the best one; of course we're right. Let's not go through the endless conversations and dramas of people arguing, getting upset, accusing each other of not listening, threatening to leave. However frustrating this is, it's absolutely necessary if we're to find a solution that everyone supports. Without friendship to hold all of this, we'd never stay together long enough to discover that solution.

Friendship takes time. The easiest way to discover its strong threads is to work together. This company of friends, who traveled from afar to labor on a Greek hillside, knew this from their own experience. They'd learned, as we've seen in every visit, that the most reliable way to develop good relationships is to engage together in hard work that has a tangible outcome. Working side-by-side, we learn things about each other, we notice skills and talents, we focus less on interpersonal dramas than on figuring out how to get work done. We often become friends even with people we at first had no interest in.

So much more becomes possible when we put work at the center. Yet as we do our work, we can be assured that we'll have challenges and conflicts. Conflict is unavoidable; it's a consequence of interdependence. We argue because we're connected, we fight because we all care. This is good to remember when we're struggling so much, when we'd rather just leave.

But we can't leave. We're friends. We're in this together.

What have you learned about the difficulties and strengths of friendship in your own life experience?

FLAWLESS

For far too many years
I have wanted to be flawless,
      perfecting my pursuits,
      I bargained all for love.

For all these many years
I've made masks of my own doing,
      pursuing my perfection,
      I found I was pursued.

And then
one day
I fell
      sprawled
      flattened

      on the fertile ground of self.

Naked in dirt
no mask
no bargains
I raised my soiled face

      and there you were.

      I struggled to stand.

      Dirt from my body fell in your eyes.

      Your hand reached for me.

Blinded, your hand reached me.

There is, in all of us, a place of pure perfection.
We discover its geography together.

—Meg Wheatley

UNITED STATES
COLUMBUS, OHIO
FROM HERO TO HOST

You Are Brilliant, and the Earth Is Hiring

You are going to have to figure out what it means to be a human being on Earth at a time when every living system is declining, and the rate of decline is accelerating. . . . Basically, the Earth needs a new operating system, you are the programmers, and we need it within a few decades.

Forget that this task of planet saving is not possible in the time required. Don't be put off by people who know what is not possible. Do what needs to be done, and check to see if it was impossible only after you are done.

—Paul Hawken, 2009 Commencement Address

Columbus, Ohio? They're taking us to Columbus, Ohio? you might wonder as your plane angles down toward the neat, gray grid of America's sixteenth largest city. A city that gave birth to Wendy's and Value City. A city whose residents oddly boast that it's one of the United States' cloudiest (ranking fourth—just behind Seattle).[95] A city that is known for its year-round culture of Buckeye Fever where one-tenth of its population fills the stadium on fall Saturdays for Ohio State football. (This fever went off the charts when the Buckeyes won the Rose Bowl, January 1, 2010.)

On a journey that's danced through the *cortiços* of Brazil, locked eyes with the Zapatista rebel army, cycled through India money-free, popped corn on South Africa's solar panels, dug toilets in Greece and filled them with trees in Zimbabwe, you just might be wondering what Columbus has to offer.

But Columbus is the perfect place to end our journey. It's the perfect place because it's a mirror of the United States, reflecting its mix of race, income, immigrants, neighborhoods, and problems.[96] It's the perfect place because it's in the middle of the country. It's the perfect place because it is utterly, exceptionally *ordinary.* So if something extraordinary can happen here, it can happen anywhere.

And something extraordinary is definitely happening in Columbus. Leaders in some of America's largest institutions—health care, academe, government—are changing how they lead. They've given up take-charge, heroic leadership, choosing instead to engage members of their community in difficult social issues that other communities still find intractable. As formal leaders, they're using their influence to host conversational processes that bring in all voices, especially those that have been silent or silenced. More and more citizens are learning how to use these processes to think and work together. They're rethinking how to solve hunger long term, how to deal with homelessness, how to transform health care from sickness to wellness, how to shift relationships in academia from competition to collaboration, and much, much more.

Leaders as hosts, not heroes, are sprouting up everywhere now in the fertile soil that's been cultivated by several formal leaders since 2002.

•• • ••

Tuesday Ryan-Hart is weary. Eily, her seventeen-month-old, has come down with a cold, and Zane is being sent home from kindergarten because he just vomited in class. Nonetheless, here she is curbside, lounging against

I meet many people who are tired of command-and-control tactics. They want to find new ways of leading, but they don't know how. They often say, "I just need to get out of the way." This statement scares me. Leaders have critical work to do to engage people and redistribute power. The leaders we'll meet in Columbus didn't get out of the way; instead, they've used their power to create the means to engage people and communities in solving their own problems.

As you'll soon learn, the leadership revolution in Columbus was initiated by Phil Cass, a CEO. I've had many thoughtful conversations with Phil in which he's spoken candidly about his struggles to give up power, when he had to stop himself from reasserting control. Yet he also had to use his power effectively with his own bosses and boards, convincing them that this was the right direction. I've been in many similar conversations with senior leaders, and it's never easy. They can be quick to notice the power they're losing, rather than the capacities they're gaining by bringing in other voices. And sadly, too many leaders don't believe that people are worth the effort. They don't trust us. The most horrifying comment I've heard in thirty-five years of consulting was when a Senior VP criticized a leader's success in engaging his workforce: "Your people think too highly of themselves."

I treasure the leaders in Columbus for their willingness to transfer power and for the consistent faith they've demonstrated in people.

Meg

her worn-in RAV-4, eagerly prepared to drive you around Columbus to meet people and see places where this new leadership is in full bloom.

A few years ago, Tuesday quit her job as an assistant director for women's issues at The Ohio State University to devote herself fully to this wave that is sweeping through Columbus called the Art of Hosting. She's going to explain it to you, but be patient. It's more than one thing; it may not fit any familiar categories. People come to Art of Hosting events to learn how to host a variety of conversational processes. These conversational processes are used with diverse groups to resolve conflicts, develop strategy, analyze issues and develop action plans. But it's more than a collection of problem-solving tools. At its core, and what allows it to flower in so many different forms and places, the Art of Hosting is a philosophy, a set of beliefs and values that are embodied in every process and in every person who learns how to host.

WALK OUT WALK ON

Art of Hosting practitioners describe themselves as a self-organized global fellowship. On their website, they describe their core assumptions: "It is common sense to bring stakeholders together in conversation when you seek new solutions for the common good. We believe that when human beings are invited to work together on what truly matters to them, they will take ownership and responsibility for moving their issues and ideas into wiser actions that last." As a web of practitioners, they "invite leaders, CEOs, managers, teachers—pioneers from all walks of life—who want to see and act wisely from a different perspective and practice of leadership where other people's courage, creativity, intelligence, and wisdom are set free."[97]

Tuesday's personal description is that Art of Hosting "is a *practice*, like yoga or meditation. There are tools in it, for sure—social technologies like circle, Open Space, and World Café that surface a group's collective intelligence through conversation. But there are deeper patterns present in the Art of Hosting that invite us to be authentic, to stay in inquiry, to build community."

If it sounds abstract, don't worry, Tuesday promises. Because we're en route to the Mid-Ohio Foodbank, and it's hard to get more real than forty-seven thousand meals per day. Here's where we'll see and feel what a shift in leadership can inspire others to create.

FROM FINDING FOOD TO ENDING POVERTY

In October 2009, the Mid-Ohio Foodbank relocated to its new head-quarters: a gigantic former mattress outlet that moves thirty-three million pounds of food per year onto the tables of Central Ohio's hungry citizens. The Food Bank's president and CEO, Matt Habash, greets you in the cavernous lobby to walk you through the building. He's straight out of Central Casting for the midwestern executive: earnest and humble, a quiet voice and wide grin, and eyes that light up when he talks about food logistics. But he moves at New Yorker speed as he tours you around the building, streaming a narrative that highlights the building's LEED-gold status (an internationally recognized green-building certification system)—the repurposed fixtures and recycled carpets, the cold storage layout that makes efficient use of cooler and freezer space, the organic recovery program that sorts leftover produce from grocery stores, the waterless urinals that save forty thousand gallons of water a year *each*. He points out the proposed site of community gardens and greenhouses on the 14.5-acre property, where starter plants will one day be distributed through food pantries so that people may have their own gardens.

But his pride and joy appears to be the Community Room, a high-ceilinged, modular meeting space filled with round tables and brightly colored chairs that is perfectly suited, he says, to hosting World Cafés.

Matt was introduced to the World Café in an Art of Hosting workshop in March 2005, invited by his friend Phil Cass, the CEO of the Columbus Medical Association and Foundation. World Café was one of many conversational processes taught at that event. Co-founded in 1995 by Juanita Brown and David Isaacs, the World Café is a process designed to create intimate conversations, even in large groups. Participants meet at small tables in groups of four or five to explore a powerful question. They rotate to different tables, always meeting more people, and, by the end, when the conversations are harvested, there's a clear sense of what the whole room's been talking about. Most often, as different ideas link and connect from table to table, a collective intelligence becomes evident; people feel a sense of unity, direction, and appreciation for everyone in the room. What got Matt's attention, he says, was the power of intentional conversation. "I spend so much of my time in conversations that do not matter," he explains. "I just didn't want to have another useless conversation."

So in the fall of 2005, he decided to take a leap. "The staff didn't know what I was doing," he recalls. "I ordered round tables, four chairs at every table, even checkerboard tablecloths. I put out an invitation to one hundred people; sixty showed up. And then I asked them a question: What does ending hunger mean to you?" Apparently, that was a radical question. "To some food bankers," Matt continues, "that might mean there's enough food that the

The Mid-Ohio Foodbank moves thirty-three million pounds of food per year onto the tables of Central Ohio's hungry citizens. Matt Habash is the Foodbank's director.

WALK OUT WALK ON

food pantry doesn't run out. But that doesn't solve the problem. I wanted to move down the continuum from finding food to ending poverty."

That first Café spawned questions that would transform the Mid-Ohio Foodbank's approach to its mission. They participated in a regional food movement across seven counties exploring how to shift the proportion of food produced locally from 1 to 10 percent. They turned over the design of the on-site food pantry to its stakeholders—nutritionists and clients—who opted for a revolutionary grocery store–like "Choice Pantry" that gives power back to its clients. They developed new kinds of partnerships with local organizations that reconnect schoolchildren to local food and support urban agriculture and local farmers.

For Matt, these changes point to a profound shift in the Foodbank's purpose from handing out food to transforming the system that links food, hunger, and poverty. To maintain this focus, he's integrated Art of Hosting practices throughout his organization—in fundraising campaigns, at senior staff meetings, with the board. "I don't hardly talk at board meetings anymore," he says. "I used to run them—you know, 'the world according to Matt.' Instead, we move to a strategic level of conversation by using Café or sitting in a circle." He points to three stones on his desk with words carved out: *Create. Imagine. Hope.* "I still struggle with how to introduce talking pieces [like the globe that was passed in circle at Kufunda]. That stuff can look hokey. But when people get engaged in the conversation, the process sells itself. It's easy to do. What I like about the talking piece is it slows the conversation down. You put the rules on the wall—speak with intention, listen with attention—it changes the dynamic. All of a sudden, you put the BlackBerry down and pay attention. You don't talk over people. You learn to deeply respect other points of view."

The results, he says, are giving the Mid-Ohio Foodbank a leading role in the transformation of Central Ohio's food system. But what's most important, Tuesday points out, is that Matt is just one of many leaders throughout Columbus who are laying out checkered tablecloths and welcoming the whole community to create solutions to their most intractable problems.

HOW DO WE BE TOGETHER BETTER?

Back in the RAV-4, Tuesday's story trickles out. "We did a workshop once where we asked, 'If you were born a question, what would it be?'" she recalls. "I started to think, What was the question I was born? What was the question I was brought forth in this world to be? I realized that at least one of the questions I was born was, How do I help people be together better? At a fundamental level, you people are just not being together well! How can I help this?"

In 1974, Tuesday was born in Ohio's Rust Belt to a young white mother and a black father in a time and place that didn't take well to interracial families. When Tuesday was five, her mother got out of the abusive relationship, and she and Tuesday were on their own to navigate a chaotic world of race and gender dynamics. Eventually, her mother healed and moved forward with her life, and Tuesday vowed to dedicate her own life to work with, by, and for other women. She became a therapist, working first at a rape crisis hotline and then in a domestic violence center. "That's where I really learned," she says, "that people aren't stupid. They do what they need to do to adapt and be resilient. They have these wonderful spirits that are experiencing these really hard things, but they keep going."

And then one of her clients was murdered by her husband, and Tuesday was suddenly confronted with the futility of her work. "I felt like I could put myself on a recorder and say the same thing to every woman who walks through the door, and it's not changing anything. It's our system that says it's okay to hurt women and children. That's the problem here." Tuesday began to question whether there was another way to act on behalf of women in the world. So she took a job training domestic violence workers to be more effective, hoping that something entirely different might be possible.

Then Zane was born with a bad case of allergies and asthma, and Tuesday needed a job that would give her the flexibility to take care of her sick son. Which is how she found herself employed at The Ohio State University, where we're heading now.

Tuesday Ryan-Hart and Phil Cass are inviting people in Columbus's big systems—food, education, health care, homelessness—into hosting as a leadership practice.

WALK OUT WALK ON

STEALTH HOSTING AT OHIO STATE

More than 55,000 students spread across 1,762 acres. Twelve thousand courses offered in 457 buildings. Income of $4.45 billion.[98] Ohio State is an empire of learning, the largest university in the country (until fall 2009, when Arizona State scraped ahead by enrolling thirty-eight more students). It is a place where rankings matter: OSU boasts top twenty-five in *U.S. News & World Report's* 2010 ratings of the nation's best public universities; faculty are lauded for the number of Nobel Prizes, Guggenheims, and Fulbrights they're awarded.

Academia. On the one hand, revered as a source of ingenuity, critical thinking, and the transmission of wisdom across the generations. On the other, criticized as the land of the lone wolf where collaboration might compromise academic freedom, where there's a rigid hierarchy of presidents and provosts, deans and chairs, associate professors and assistants, those who have tenure and those who don't.

This is the world Tuesday walks into when she takes a job in 2006 at the Women's Place, whose purpose is to make institutional change on campus for women faculty and staff. Her reaction is immediate distrust. "I knew it was absolutely not where I belonged from maybe the second or third day," she explains. "I'm all about leveling hierarchies, getting people to be together better. I've been a relatively successful person, so it's not like the hierarchy keeps me down—except where as a woman of color, I've experienced sexism and racism. But I inherently believe in equality and egalitarianism. Sometimes, preservation of hierarchy can be cloaked in talk of academic freedom. It works for those who have made it to the top of the hierarchy—they have a lot of investment in keeping the system going. But it doesn't work for those at the bottom."

She likely would not have stayed had it not been for her boss, Deb Ballam, a self-proclaimed rabble-rouser who was up for the task of disrupting the status quo. When Phil Cass (the Medical Association CEO who put Matt Habash on his hosting path) invited Deb to attend an Art of Hosting workshop in November 2006, she sent Tuesday in her place. Neither woman had any idea what this one act of saying yes would unleash on campus.

•• • ••

Just northeast of the football stadium, The Knowlton School of Architecture is a straight-backed, sharp-shouldered sentinel of concrete, marble and stone. The 165,000-square-foot facility is a paean to planning, a place where students study precision and technology, a structure that breathes order and discipline.

Which is why you might find it a little disconcerting when you stumble across twenty-six folks sitting in a circle of chairs around a centerpiece made of a green cloth, a black stone, tingshas (Tibetan cymbals), and a toy walking man made out of green foam. Taped to the walls are simple drawings of a butterfly and a bumblebee, a page that reads "Law of Two Feet" and another with a yin-yang drawing labeled "Passion/Responsibility." Another page explains the principles of Open Space Technology, a process that invites participants to self-organize to create their own agenda rather than work from a predetermined one.[99] So much for planning.

The chime of the tingshas reverberates through the room. A tall, silver-haired woman in a white turtleneck sweater introduces herself. "Good morning and welcome," she says. "I'm Hazel Morrow-Jones, Professor and Associate Dean in City and Regional Planning. Our purpose for today is to connect people's practice experiences, to connect with mates [an Art of Hosting term for fellow practitioners], to share our learnings, and to strengthen our understanding of the deeper patterns of the Art of Hosting." She points to another flip chart page that outlines the flow of the day and then reminds people of their shared practices for how to host a circle: "Listen with attention, speak with intention, and take care of the well-being of the group," she says. "Offer what you can; ask for what you need. Listen for what's happening in the middle that nobody brought into the room but maybe we can all take out." These agreements were developed by Christina Baldwin and Ann Linnea of PeerSpirit, who've spent many years teaching and writing about how to host circles to create space for deep conversations.[100] Their circle practice is a core element in the Art of Hosting.

These twenty-six people sitting in circle are all experimenters; they're learning what it means to lead as a host. They come together every three months as a community of practice to encourage, support, and learn from one another. They come from all over Franklin County—from health care and food systems, municipal government and the Board of Regents, youth work and homeless shelters. And a large number of them come from OSU.

Tuesday and Deb Ballam called the first Art of Hosting at OSU in April 2007. Since then, the Art of Hosting has sprung up in Arts and Sciences, Comparative Studies, Political Science, City and Regional Planning, Veterinary Medicine, Dentistry and Social Work; in the University's Human

Resources department, Service Learning and Student Life, the President's Council on Women and the Institute on Women, Gender and Public Policy. Those are just the places Tuesday and Deb *know* about. They have initiated more than 150 people into the practice, people who then introduce it in their own departments and beyond. In fact, Oregon State, Indiana State–Bloomington, and Iowa State have all visited OSU to check out what's happening.

Tom Gregoire is the Dean of the College of Social Work. This is his third time meeting with this community of practice. He keeps returning, he says, because here he can exchange stories, share successes, and tackle tough questions with fellow hosts. He's using his hosting skills in a remarkable way within the College, transforming how they develop curriculum, a notoriously combative process. "We didn't have much of a history of successful conversations about curriculum—or anything else," he explains. "I sought a process that could help us think very creatively and collaboratively about curriculum. I also desired greater collegiality within our faculty and between our faculty and the community." This time around, Tom wanted to engage all stakeholders in the process: faculty, staff, students, and local social workers. But he feared that might trigger some egos. "There was a tradition in our faculty, with just a few exceptions, of being relatively isolated from the practice community," Tom adds. "Generally, our faculty saw the community as out of step with best practice, the community thought our faculty relatively clueless when it came to practice in 'the real world,' and nobody in particular valued the student's voice."

Tom invited Hazel Morrow-Jones and Phil Cass to help him design and host a Curriculum Café for ninety-two participants to co-create principles

The Knowlton School of Architecture seems an unlikely place for folks to sit in a circle around a centerpiece made of green cloth, a black stone, tingshas, and a foam walking man.

for the College of Social Work's curriculum development. Following the Café, a group of eighteen volunteers—students, staff, practitioners, and faculty—distilled the agreements into ten principles that shape every curriculum conversation. "Those principles are beginning to pervade our faculty as a number of us try now to host rather than facilitate our meetings," Tom says. Today, that Café is fondly recalled as a turning point that's led to greater community involvement and good will throughout the College of Social Work.

Similar stories surface from others at OSU, although outside the community of practice, they're often kept below the radar. "We call it stealth hosting," Deb explains. "The department chairs want to bring it in, but they know they can't call it 'World Café' with their faculty. Faculty can be pretty mean to each other. And they don't want to be laughed at. You put your reputation on the line when you try something new." So Tuesday and Deb find other ways to bring it in, knowing that good things will emerge. "Particularly in faculty culture, people are desperate for connection," Deb adds. "At the end of a program, people will come up to us and say, 'This is the first time I've felt part of something—part of human connection and part of community.' That is what we're all thirsty for."

Is the Art of Hosting becoming clearer to you now, Tuesday wants to know? The reason it can be difficult to see is because the Art of Hosting is an operating system, like Windows, Mac OS, or Linux. So far, all you've seen are two different applications, the Foodbank and OSU. Operating systems aren't invisible; it's just that most of us don't have to know how they work. They're great examples of the power of self-organization to achieve order without control. So let's try to take a glimpse, then, under the proverbial hood.

ART OF HOSTING AS AN OPERATING SYSTEM

Computers can't function without an operating system. The operating system manages all interactions and communications between the computer hardware and its software. Whenever we download new programs or plug in a new toy, the operating system does the work of integrating the new applications—ideally, without crashing. Within this complex computing environment, order is achieved by specifying that every application be built using the same source code (instructions written in a programming language). Programmers work from this code to create new apps, games, and gizmos. No matter what they create, the source code they use is the same.

Microsoft keeps a strong proprietary grip on its source code; only those who sign a formal agreement can work with it. The corporation charges expensive licensing fees and maintains control over the system's boundaries, expressions, and uses. By contrast, the Linux operating system (which entered the market in 1991) is a free and open source, meaning anyone can use its source code. Without fees and entrance barriers, this open system promotes creativity and experimentation. Developers agree to freely share their work. Whatever's created can be used, modified, and redistributed among an unbounded community of software developers. As a by-product of these exchanges, the Linux culture has become one in which people feel "we're all in this together."

In Western culture, most leaders behave more like Microsoft. They hold power close and tell people what they can and can't do. Rather than engaging everyone's creativity using the same source code—the organization's values and principles—they design rigid hierarchies and assign tasks. But hierarchy isn't interested in new apps.

The Art of Hosting is like Linux, freely offering its source code for leaders to achieve order without control. Its code is a set of principles and practices for how to host conversations that matter: setting intention, creating hospitable space, asking powerful questions, surfacing collective intelligence, trusting emergence, finding mates, harvesting learning, and moving into wise action. Like Linux, the Art of Hosting operating system encourages experimentation and sharing worldwide. What's emerged is a vibrant global community of people discovering that the wisdom we need exists not in any one of us, but in all of us.

So let's see how powerful this operating system can be when it takes on one of the United States' most intractable, complex problems: health care.

AFFORDABLE, SUSTAINABLE HEALTH CARE FOR ALL

You're back in the RAV-4, this time listening to Tuesday tell you how she met Phil Cass, who's been the catalyst for this revolution in Columbus. It was November 2006 at the Art of Hosting workshop she was sent to by Deb Ballam. Zane was sick again, and Tuesday was feeling distracted and guilty about being away. Toward the end of the three-day program, Tuesday was intrigued by the process but a little confused. "I told the facilitators, 'You guys are painting a nice picture here of what Art of Hosting could do in the world, but how do I fit in?'" she recalls. They invited her to call an Open Space on her question, which she did. Phil showed up, a giant, gentle man with silver hair and piercing blue eagle eyes, and before the day was over, something had shifted. "Before I left, Phil said to me, 'We've got work to do.'" Tuesday's eyes fill with tears. "It really changed my life. It was just like, oh. *Oh!* I believed him, but I don't know that I had any sense that it would be so big. You can feel the generosity of his soul. He just said, *We have work to do.*"

That work would begin the following week at the sixth assembly of Our Optimal Health, a project committed to creating affordable and sustainable health care for all people in Franklin County. Tuesday is driving you now to the Columbus Medical Association and Foundation office, where the hosts of Our Optimal Health project are having their monthly meeting. Here, you'll finally meet Phil, as well as Marc Parnes, Deb Helber, and the rest of the core team who are engaging Franklin County in a conversation about health care that's creating some innovative initiatives.

Stories don't always have a clear beginning, especially when they involve friends supporting and inspiring one another. Tuesday stumbles about a bit before settling on June 2001, when Phil Cass decides to attend Meg Wheatley's module at The Shambhala Institute—Authentic Leadership in Action (ALIA). There, he meets skilled practitioners of circle and community building and gets inspired by the concept of self-organization; his whole approach to leadership as a CEO begins to change. He returns to Columbus, eager to experiment in his own organization, which includes a professional association for physicians, a medical association foundation, a trauma center, and a physicians' free clinic. He returns to ALIA in 2002 and enrolls in a course called "The Art of Convening Strategic Conversations" taught by Marianne Knuth (whom you met in Zimbabwe) and Toke

Phil and Tuesday host a community in discovering what they can create together. Participants meet in World Café to generate a collective vision for "optimal health."

WALK OUT WALK ON

Møller of Denmark. At this time, the Art of Hosting as a movement is just being born. And yet for Phil, something powerful and irreversible lands on him. Hosting becomes his leadership practice, and he will use it to invite into conversation all those who care about health care in Franklin County.

The first Columbus Art of Hosting takes place in March 2005 for thirty-six leaders. During the workshop, Dr. Marc Parnes, an OB-GYN and president-elect of the Columbus Medical Association, uses the Open Space time to host a conversation about the role of the community in changing the health care system. Together, Phil, Marc and a few other community leaders dream up a plan to launch an exploration into affordable and sustainable health care. They experiment with a number of processes for how they might engage the whole community—physicians, hospital administrators, insurance company CEOs, community organizers, politicians, and patients—ultimately creating a series of assemblies where more than one

Now that I'm older, I enjoy conversations with those I work with about our past. Where'd we first meet, what ideas showed up when, how did we use each other's work, where did we carry the work, how far did it travel? We're trying to recall the web of connections that got us here, and of course we never can. But it's great fun to explore this—we always end up feeling grateful and more connected.

Columbus is a great place for this kind of conversation. Over the ten years I've known Phil, Tuesday, Deb Ballam, and other Columbus leaders, we've woven in and out of one another's work. I haven't always known about their most recent project or newest idea, though I thought I had a pretty good idea of what was going on. But I have to admit I'm surprised—and delighted—to see what's emerged here, ten years later, a new form of leadership in use throughout the city.

Emergence has always been my favorite subject to teach and write about. It's life's process for change—small acts with limited power converge to create something powerful and influential. I've often said that when we understand emergence, we'll have truly shifted paradigms.

Emergence is always a surprise, we can't see it coming. We work hard for years, but it doesn't look like anything's changing. And then one day it all shifts, and an entire city is using a new form of leadership.

Columbus is a wonderful surprise to me, and that's just as it should be.

hundred participants gather each time to identify strategies for advancing health care.

And then they discover they've been asking the wrong question.

It is at the third assembly when Toke from Denmark (whom Phil invited to host the gatherings) asks Phil if he's ever been involved in a conversation about the purpose of the health care system. Phil's response, as Toke recalls, is a great surprise:

> Phil said, "In all the forty years I've worked within the health care system, I've never been in that question, and I've never heard anyone ask that question." I said, "Are you telling me that you're spending $7 billion a year in health care—if you count all the activities—and you guys have never talked about the purpose of what you're doing?" And he said, "I'm ashamed to realize that we've never talked about it. It's about time." We got so excited! We knew this was the wicked question.
>
> This was one of the most profound large-scale assemblies I have ever been a part of. We had a four-hour World Café around the question, "What should be the purpose of the health care system you want and need for this city and its future?" We had 120 people rotating through 25 tables. At the end of the Café, we put a microphone into the center and invited people to share one sentence about what the health care system should be. I thought five to seven of them would speak. But one after another, they came to the microphone—we couldn't stop them! They were all saying the same thing: We want optimal health.[101]

Optimal health, as this group defines it, is about being as healthy as you can be, given what you've got—your individual physical, emotional, and mental abilities. That means that optimal health is different for everyone—and attainable for all. But optimal health is not the purpose of our current health care system. "The system that we've known has been built on the wrong platform," Phil explains. "It's been built on a sick platform. As long as it operates on a sick platform, it will be unsustainable. When it's built on a sick platform, you're engaged in a zero-sum game: a fixed amount of resources are divided across sickness."[102] In Franklin County, that zero-sum game is abandoning 12.3 percent of the population, more than 134,000 people who are without health care—despite spending more than $6.4 billion annually on health care services.[103] "Like life," says Phil, "there is no zero-sumness to health. There are millions of ways, infinite possibilities for how we can support each other's health."

Marc, the physician, joins in. "We'd been looking at how to change the sick system and not at how we promote wellness within our community so that the rescue system doesn't have to be as huge," he says. "Everybody is talking wellness. It's sort of one of those *duh!* type of things. But this time, the whole community came to it together. Producing wellness becomes a personal responsibility. It's not how am *I* going to make you well. It's how are *you* going to make you well."

Our Optimal Health is inviting citizens to explore ideas around a new and different system of health care in Franklin County. Here's just one example: In Clintonville, a neighborhood of Columbus, residents are seeking to organize their own parallel health care system. "They're saying, 'To hell with the health care system!'" Phil exclaims. "'If we can attract five family practice physicians and five nurse practitioners, we'll build our own primary care system and make it available to everyone in our geographic community.' They're not there yet, but I think that's where they're going to end up." The Clintonville Neighborhood Initiative is experimenting with Health Block Watches, a riff off Crime Block Watch, so that neighbors pay attention to one another's well-being, inviting each other into local walking clubs, spreading the word about yoga classes and nutrition events, and checking in on seniors and homebound residents. They are recruiting local dentists to provide free care to neighbors who can't afford it. And they are enrolling volunteers in transporting people in need to medical appointments.

Yes, it's a drop in the bucket. And there's no guarantee that it will ever take off. But for Dr. Marc Parnes, that's not the point. "Clintonville is a microcosm showing what's possible," he says. "A group of people are saying, 'We can do this. We don't have to wait for it to trickle down.' I am

Deb Helber shares the Art of Hosting with leaders wanting to transform their organizations and communities. Dr. Mark Parnes (in scrubs) invites fellow health care practitioners to shift their focus from sickness to optimal health.

so frustrated with our government and all the talk and effort being made to reform health care. In this short period of time, we've done much more exploring than I know them to have done. The only way I know to change the national conversation is to experiment with it locally and invite others into the conversation."

Which is exactly what has happened to the conversation around homelessness.

A NATIONAL CONVERSATION ON HOMELESSNESS

It is the summer of 2009 when Barbara Poppe, head of the Community Shelter Board in Columbus, gets a call from the Obama administration. Housing and Urban Development Secretary Shaun Donovan needs to present a new national plan to end homelessness to Congress by May 20, 2010, and is tapping her to head up the United States Interagency Council on Homelessness. Everything moves very quickly. She reports for duty in Washington in November with the mandate to get federal, state, local, and private agencies working well together to design strategies that will end homelessness. Once in office, she has only ten days to come up with a framework for Secretary Donovan and the White House for how those strategies will be developed. With that kind of time pressure, she turns to what she already knows: the Art of Hosting. She's been relying on its beliefs and practices since 2005 and trusts its power. Perhaps, she thinks, it can change the way policy is informed in DC.

If we go back a few years, again we'll see Phil Cass's hand in this. In 2005, he invited Barb to attend an Art of Hosting and, for her, it was love at first sight. "When I went to the Art of Hosting, it was deeply familiar," Barb says. "Folks sitting in circle, everyone having a voice, processes that engaged community. It aligned so closely with my life values. I was struck—oh, my gosh, I'm returning to something I know!" She had led two meetings for Rebuilding Lives, a community-based strategic planning process on homelessness convened by the Community Shelter Board, when she tossed out their conventional approach to facilitation and tapped Deb Helber to, as she says, "go whole hog with Art of Hosting."

The community meetings became entirely open processes, attended by shelter service providers and funders, advocacy groups and businesses, and former and current homeless citizens. Participants developed ninety-six strategies, which collectively they winnowed down to eleven priorities focused on pressing issues such as how to coordinate emergency assistance, accelerate rehousing, and find employment opportunities for Franklin County's more than eight thousand homeless people. Throughout the process, Barb herself had no vote. This is the community's plan. They vote on it, they stand behind it, they own it. And when she leaves for DC, they continue moving ahead, unperturbed by the loss of their leader. For as charismatic as Barb may be, she's not the hero of this system that's fighting homelessness in Franklin County. She's been a skilled host, and it no longer depends on her for its stability—it has become resilient.

Barb couldn't have known at the time that the Community Shelter Board would be her trial run for a process she'd repeat at the national level. But hosting in the hospitable environment of Columbus is one thing; running it through government bureaucracy is entirely another. Would this process—at times called "hokey" and "stealth" by its own practitioners—work among federal employees? "The current methods of collaboration weren't working," Barb reflects. "If it's broken, what do you have to lose in trying something new? I had learned to trust the process. Government is made up of people, and if we can tap the passion of people, we can do this."

Less than two months after she moves to DC, Barb is ready to take World Cafés national. On a cold Sunday night in January, Tuesday has just finished fixing dinner and getting the kids to bed when she finds herself in a rapid-fire email exchange with Barb. Barb needs Tuesday to dig up hosts for World Cafés—the first of which is just two and a half weeks away. (Oh, and the hosts all need to be volunteers.) Four weeks later, more than 750

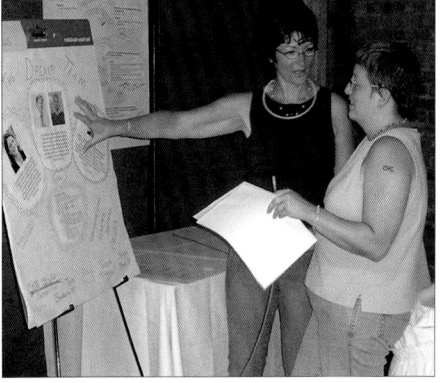
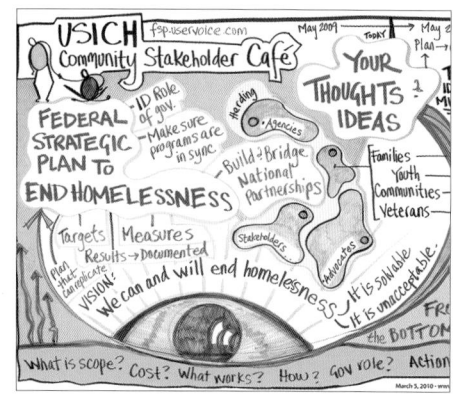

Barbara Poppe carries her Art of Hosting practice from Columbus to Washington, DC, to create a federal strategic plan on homelessness.

FROM HERO TO HOST

people in six cities have gathered in World Cafés to inform the national strategic plan on homelessness. As in Columbus, they represent the full range of stakeholders, including the homeless themselves, who seldom if ever are included in conversations about their future. The output of the Cafés is sent to a sixty-person decision council that Barb assembles from the nineteen federal agencies that need to approve the plan. She laughs as she describes the reaction to the Café process by a jaded advocacy worker: "What do you mean every person had a vote? There was democracy in the federal government?! Has that ever happened before?"

Barb doesn't stop there. Once the Cafés are done, she sends an email to Tuesday thinking about how the Art of Hosting might be used to implement the plan locally, in communities throughout the United States. (In June 2010, Tuesday and Phil go to DC and offer the Art of Hosting to Barb's staff to strengthen the hosting skills they'll need to implement the federal strategic plan.) "Under the Obama administration, we're supposed to be breaking down silos, creating open government initiatives. Our old practices don't work for that. I'm fascinated to see how the Art of Hosting fits. I've been wondering whether we should tell people what we're doing or just act like this is normal practice—this is just how we do things. We'll see whether it becomes viral, whether people start using it simply because it works. For now, what I know is people tell me they've gone to other interagency meetings, and they like ours better."

As for Columbus, the Art of Hosting has unequivocally gone viral. Phil and Tuesday constantly stumble across yet another place that's using hosting as an alternative form of leadership. It's worked its way into the Chamber of Commerce, government-convened task forces and the city of Upper Arlington. Arlington, says Phil, is the icing on the cake: The police force and fire department, America's archetypal heroes, are walking on to experiment with hosting as a leadership practice.

FROM HERO TO HOST

Being a hero is about the shortest-lived profession on earth.

—Will Rogers

America loves a hero. So does the rest of the world. There's something in all of us, perhaps, that keeps hoping that somebody somewhere knows what to do and will get us out of this mess. If a hero rushes in, then we're off the hook for solving our own problems. We're so hungry for heroes that we create them out of thin air, no act of bravery required. Celebrities become heroes simply because they're famous. Businessmen who make billions are believed to have superhuman insights into the future of global markets. Politicians paint themselves as flawless champions of the people—and then are brought crashing down by their imperfections.

Several beliefs feed our trust in heroic leadership: *Leaders have the answers. People do what they're told. High risk requires high control.* When we believe this, we willingly give away our power. We wait for leaders to direct us, assuming they know what they're doing. Many leaders enthusiastically accept the power we hand over. But we're all caught in a terrible illusion. When problems are complex, there are no simple answers; no one person, no matter how brilliant, can make things better. And even though some surrender personal freedoms in exchange for pledges of security, how can any leader these days guarantee that we'll be secure?

Submitting to heroic leadership may be effective in the moment; it may even feel good. But it assumes that someone's in control. In today's turbulent world, things that we have no control over—that *no one* has control over—can change our lives forever. No one is in charge of our food system. No one is in charge of our schools. No one is in charge of health care. No one is in charge of homelessness. These highly complex systems have emerged over time through thousands of small, local actions, and they cannot be solved even by the boldest visions of our most heroic leaders.

If we want to find solutions to our most challenging problems, we need to transform our ideas about effective leadership. We need to walk out of our reliance on the leader-as-hero and invite in the leader-as-host. Leaders who act as hosts are welcoming, caring, and respectful of the people they work with, just as if they were guests in their home. We've seen in Columbus how much becomes possible when leaders rely on other people's creativity and commitment. These leaders bear witness to people's capacity to engage in hard work, to work well together, and to stay engaged long enough to discover solutions. Leaders learn to trust that everyone has gifts to offer, and that most people want to work on behalf of something greater than themselves. In some cases, these leaders serve as mirrors, so that people can see their skills and potential, those that have been buried under years of disregard.

Over time, as conversational processes become the normal way of meeting, communities discover they have new skills. They can examine problems in depth, make use of each other's diverse insights, and create

FROM HERO TO HOST

robust solutions. Leaders, and those they happily host, take on large-scale, intractable problems and discover they're capable of solving them.

Maybe this is why the Art of Hosting as an operating system for change is spreading like freeware through organizations and communities all over the world.

ART OF HOSTING GOES GLOBAL

As an open-source operating system, the Art of Hosting has grown and developed through networks of relationships. It's been a multicultural, multigenerational, self-organized voyage of discovery, fueled by people's inventiveness, curiosity, and generosity. Art of Hostings get held wherever people call them, whenever people are willing to do the work of inviting a group together to have conversations that make a difference.

The result today is a vibrant global community whose breadth and impact is impossible to measure. In 2010 alone, Art of Hosting trainings have been held in the United States, Canada and Mexico; in Belgium, Croatia, Denmark, France, The Netherlands, Sweden, and the United Kingdom; in Australia, New Zealand, and Japan. The movement also has spread to Brazil, South Africa, Zimbabwe, Israel, Greece, Slovenia, and Greenland. It is serving as the operating system for children and family service advocates, financial planners, public educators, and health service workers; for indigenous communities, rural villagers, union activists, and faith-based groups.

No one knows exactly how many people have experienced the Art of Hosting, or how many people are skilled to train others in the practice. That's because no one owns, runs, or measures this movement. Despite the increasing demand for their hosting skills, the Art of Hosting community has remained self-organizing and passionate. They function as a community of practitioners, maintaining their identity and coherence through clear values, a shared worldview, agreed-on practices, and a commitment to supporting one another. That integrity magnetizes people to them, resulting in rapid growth—without ever having a growth strategy. People practice the Art of Hosting because it works. They practice the Art of Hosting because it invites us to do what humans do best: connect and create together.

The citizens of Columbus, Ohio, are slowly but steadily walking out of a model of heroic leadership that most Americans assume is the only way to lead. "This country's culture, its basis for understanding itself, is based on rugged individualism," Phil says. "It's been what we've been proud of, counted on, and pointed to as our success over the years. And it's fundamentally not working anymore. It's a huge countercultural act to do something as simple as dropping a talking piece into the conversation. People *like* the solutions that come out of a more collective way of operating. I believe hosting taps into a basic human need to be connected and to be connected in as unconditional a way as possible."

For Tuesday, hosting can hold the paradox of our differences and our commonality. "Hosting lets us voice our differences while connecting us with each other," she says. "It's a space where you can show up, be safe, be who you are, and have deeply meaningful and authentic conversations and relationships. There's a willingness to let folks be, whatever that looks like."

Throughout this learning journey, we've met a wonderful variety of leaders-as-hosts: Sergio and Raymundo in Mexico hosting learners through self-directed learning processes; Edgard and the Elos team hosting the people of Paquetá in discovering the resources already available in their community; Dorah and Mabule hosting the Joubert Park community in trusting what will emerge if they *start anywhere*; the Kufundees hosting villagers in reconnecting to their innate wisdom and resilience; Manish and the Shikshantar community hosting gift culture; Maria and Sarah and the blessed land of Axladitsa-Avatakia hosting enduring friendships; Phil Cass, Matt Habash, Barb Poppe, and Tuesday Ryan-Hart hosting a community's capacity to take on its largest, most complex problems.

Leaders-as-hosts invite us to experiment and take risks—rather than to avoid failure. They invite us to discover new and surprising connections—rather than to stay inside our box on the org chart. They create the conditions for information to flow freely and abundantly—rather than to manage the message. And they call forth the visionary leadership of the many, rather than the few.

For Tuesday Ryan-Hart, when we practice hosting, we are learning how to be together better.

HERO

This journey, at its deepest level, has been a quest to understand the human spirit, to see more clearly what motivates us, what keeps us engaged and persevering through trials and setbacks, what calls us to discover new talents and capacities and to offer those to the people and causes we care about. Leadership makes the difference here, so it's good that the final stop on our journey explores a kind of leadership based on a profound appreciation of who we are as human beings.

We have relied on heroes for far too long, perhaps because it's such an enticing promise. Somewhere, there's someone who will fix everything. Somewhere, there's the perfect leader who will lead us out of this mess. Somewhere, there's someone who's visionary, charismatic, brilliant, and we'll happily follow him or her. Somewhere . . . .

Well, "it is time for all the heroes to go home," as the poet William Stafford wrote. It is time for us to give up these hopes and expectations that only serve to make people dependent and passive. It is time to stop waiting for someone else to save us. It is time to face the truth of our situation—we're all in this together—and figure out how to engage the hearts and minds of everyone and get on with the work that needs us to do it.

And it is time for us to give up our own personal attempts at heroism. Are you acting as a hero? Here's how to know. You're acting as a hero when you believe that if you just work harder and put in more hours, you'll fix things; that if you just become smarter or learn a new technique, you'll be able to solve problems for others. You're acting as a hero if you take on more and more projects and causes, no matter how worthy, and have less time for the people you love and the activities that nourish you. You're playing the hero if you still hold the belief that it's up to you to save the situation, the person, the world.

Our heroic impulses most often are born from the best of intentions. We want to help, we want to solve, we want to fix. Yet this is the illusion of specialness, that we're the only ones who can offer help, service, skills. If we don't do it, nobody will. This hero's path has only one guaranteed destination—we end up feeling lonely, exhausted, and unappreciated.

WALK OUT WALK ON

It is time for all us heroes to go home because, if we do, we'll notice that we're not alone. We're surrounded by people just like us. They, too, want to contribute; they, too, have ideas; they want to be useful to others and solve their own problems.

Truth be told, they never wanted us to fix them anyway.

How often do you find yourself playing the hero?
What are the results of your attempts?

HOST

Leaders who journey from hero to host have seen past the negative dynamics of politics and opposition that hierarchy breeds, they've ignored the organizational charts and role descriptions that confine people's potential. Instead, they've become curious. Who's in this organization or community? What do people care about? What skills and capacities might they offer if they were invited into the work as full contributors?

Columbus, like any major city, is a collection of institutions locked in hierarchy and politics trying to do useful work. Recall the institutions and problems that leaders in Columbus took on: hunger, university politics, health care, homelessness, law enforcement, and more. Huge, seemingly intractable problems encased in giant unmovable bureaucracies.

Yet leaders here didn't begin by trying to dismantle hierarchy. They chose a simpler way based on their belief in people. They invited people to come together to explore a good question. What does ending hunger mean to you? How do I help people be together better? What is the purpose of the health care system?

They used their positional power to convene people, not to tell them what to do. They learned that their city—any city—is rich in resources, and that the easiest way to discover these is to bring diverse people together in good conversations. People who didn't like each other, people who discounted and ignored each other, people who felt invisible, neglected, left out—these are the folks who emerged from their boxes and labels to become interesting, engaged colleagues and citizens.

Hosting meaningful conversations isn't about getting people to like each other or feel good. It's about creating the means for problems to get solved, for teams to function well, for people to become energetic activists. The leaders of Columbus have created substantive change by relying on everyone's creativity, commitment, and generosity. They've learned that these qualities are present in everyone and in every organization. They've extended sincere invitations, asked good questions, used a robust operating system, and had the courage to experiment. Their courageous efforts moved laterally across the city, state, and nation, gaining ground where heroes had once prevailed. And now, people are discovering what's been there all along—fully human beings wanting to make a difference for themselves, their city, their children, the future.

Leader-as-host is much more gratifying than false heroics. People thank you for your leadership. They feel welcomed, appreciated, and valued. Conviviality and camaraderie inspire people, as we've seen many times on this journey. Heroes don't have this much fun, or see such good results from their work.

When have you trusted others to do the work
themselves? What were the results?

CAN YOU HEAR THEM NOW?

We began this journey as a quest to understand the human spirit. We willingly left the safety of home so that our beliefs and assumptions might be exposed and our imaginations stirred. We journeyed through urban parks and rural fields, dark warehouses and sunlit olive groves, misty mountain trails and dusty city streets. We traveled through human histories burdened by grief and discovered vibrant human beings creating the future.

And now we bring our journey to an end in the middle of a U.S. city. We chose to end here intentionally, in a place that feels familiar to many of us, a place that confronts the issues too many of us face—power, leadership, societal crises, dispirited people, fractured relationships.

Remember our warning about the demons of doubt that might assert themselves, saying no change is possible? In Columbus, leaders didn't listen to them; instead, they heard the voices of people discovering their own power, the joyful melodies of communities working well together. The same harmonious music we've heard throughout this journey.

Can you hear them now, the voices of friends working side-by-side, creating possibilities?

Can you hear them now, the magnetizing questions that summon people out of offices and fields, out of boardrooms and cortiços?

Can you hear them now, the murmurings of people gone unheard who have something to say?

Can you hear them now, the sounds of gifts freely exchanged, welcomed with delight?

Can you hear them now, the sounds of play and invention carried from place to place on the winds of friendship?

Can you hear them now, the voices of our ancestors, our histories, calling us forward?

Can you hear them now, the harmonies of community writing songs they'll sing into the future?

WALK OUT WALK ON

PART III
RETURNING HOME

My heart is moved
by all I cannot save
so much has been destroyed.

I have to cast my lot
with those who age after age,
perversely,
and with no extraordinary power,
reconstitute the world.

—Adrienne Rich

We invited you on this Learning Journey as an active learner, one who was willing to be surprised, even disturbed, by encountering worlds different from your own. We asked you to leave home—even while comfortably seated at home—and undertake a quest, a journey whose greatest risk was that you might change your mind about some cherished beliefs.

So how did it go? What's going through your mind now, at the close of this journey? What ideas and people do you still think about? Which ones are you challenged by? Are you seeing your own work or life differently?

We've journeyed far together. Our minds and hearts have visited what at times may have felt like a parallel universe—a world of Zapatista rebel armies, trash-picking warriors, park-patrolling photographers, dancing knitters, gobar collectors, and toilet-paper-free pioneers. It would be easy to let this Learning Journey recede into memory, into the world of dreams, or get lost in the barrage of daily demands. In our experience, we've found these people sometimes reappear as we go about our day. We wonder if that happens to you, too.

When you see a pile of trash, do you think of Edgard and a children's garden? When you pass a fruit tree, are you reminded of Ticha and his arborloos? When you walk through a dirty city park, do you imagine how the local community might get engaged? When you see your child struggling or being bored in school, do you think of the learners at Unitierra who create their own education? When you sit in a meeting, do you wonder how it might be different if Tuesday or Phil were hosting?

We hope these stories, these questions, these challenges, will live in you for a long time. The seven communities we visited—seven wildly different places, cultures, and practices—are part of a single story, a pattern that connects. It is the story of what becomes possible as we work together on what we care most about, freed from overbearing control, curious about one another's talents and knowledge, discovering the wisdom and wealth revealed when we turn to one another. This is a new story for our time, and it is also an ancient story we need to reclaim. It's filled with compelling and practical insights for how we can work together now to create a future that offers hope and promise. It's a future already in form, already being practiced not only in seven communities, but in thousands of places around the world.

RETURNING HOME

THE PATTERNS THAT CONNECT

If by now you've claimed the identity of Walk Out, or if you're eager to join this tribe, we'd like to illuminate the deep patterns that unite and connect the Walk Outs we just met. We find them helpful as we work to give birth to the new in the midst of the breakdown of the old.

Over many years of participating in the Berkana Exchange, people from these seven communities have come to know each other well. Theirs is a story of experimentation and connection, people visiting each other, teaching and encouraging each other, sharing successes and disappointments, and developing deep, enduring friendships. Along the way, they became aware that they shared congruent values, beliefs, and principles. While members of the Berkana Exchange express these in unique ways, they hold this root belief in common:

> We create healthy and resilient communities by relying on the wisdom and wealth available in our people, traditions and environment. This belief has led us to know that we must include the elders and the youth, we must invite in the wisdom of women, we must reinvigorate our history and traditions and discover their gifts for today's world.

In their actions, they aspire to follow eight principles. Woven together as a whole, these are a powerful and coherent theory for how to foster systemic change and create healthy and resilient communities. Here are their principles, with our commentary on where they were most visible in our visits:

Start anywhere, follow it everywhere. A few photographers agree to begin patrolling Joubert Park. The women of Rusape start sewing together. Mukesh Jat's family harvests gobar from Kali, his only cow. In each case, these small acts lead to other small actions and, eventually, what emerges is larger, systemic change. Systems change begins when a few people step forward to act on behalf of what matters to them, when they start with a problem that's right in front of them. They don't start with the ambition to solve their community's toughest problems, nor do they wait to develop a five-year plan. Instead, they start with whatever problem grabs their attention. In Joubert Park, they focused first on the children. In Rusape, the sewing cooperative began by planting gardens. In India, Mukesh's fellow villagers started with vermi-composting. Once the work begins, more possibilities and interconnections become visible; people focus on what's next, following the call for change wherever it leads them. They end up dealing with a lot of different issues, and, as the work becomes successful, more people join in. Over time, the community becomes energized to take on anything, everything. People transform from resignation to engagement, from dependence to self-reliance, from compliance to creativity.

At the beginning, we don't have to know where we're going. We don't have to build an organization ahead of time. We don't have to have approval, funding, expertise or answers. We just have to get started.

We make our path by walking it. *Caminante, no hay camino, se hace camino al andar. Wanderer, there is no road, the road is made by walking.* These words by Spanish poet Antonio Machado have captivated pioneers and pathfinders the world over. Walk Ons take a leap of faith, they set foot where there is no visible solid ground. It isn't that there is no road; it's that we can't recognize it until we're on it—it reveals itself step by uncertain step. The twenty-five journeyers on the cycle yatra throw themselves into the arms of strangers and passersby, trusting that they'll discover the patterns and practices of gift culture along the way. At the Art of Learning Centering in Greece, participants stumble along a toilet-papered path, twisting and turning uncomfortably until they find their way together. The indigenous learners at Unitierra-Chiapas practice a pedagogy of learning as they go, walking out of ready-made education, jobs and expectations and walking on to a path of self-determination, discovery, and interdependence.

If the road looks familiar, if we've walked it before, if we feel comfortable knowing where we're going, then we aren't walking on, we aren't pioneering something new. Walk Ons make their path by walking.

We have what we need. *Resources are finite. There's not enough to go around. We must fight for what we need and protect what we have.* This is the world according to scarcity, a mindset that dominates most cultures. It breeds competition and aggression, where neighbors and co-workers compete for limited access, power, influence, and material goods. We become grasping and distrustful, afraid we'll lose what little we have. We notice what's missing, but not what's present.

How paradoxical, then, to discover that among the communities we visited—most of which really do suffer from a lack of resources—scarcity has been replaced by abundance, a mindset that declares: *We have what we need. Our creativity produces infinite wealth. We share what we have, and there's more than enough to go around.* The Warriors Without Weapons and the residents of Paquetá look through eyes of abundance at a ruinous warehouse and see a cultural center; they look at a foul heap of rubble and trash and see a children's garden. The Kufundees embrace the brilliant solution of arborloos by shifting their attention from what they lack (sufficient water and healthy soil for planting food) to what they have (renewable organic waste). The residents of Clintonville in Columbus experiment with their community's health care assets—dentists, nutritionists, compassionate neighbors—rather than waiting for an intractable system they can't influence. When we look in new places for the resources that are always abundantly available in community, we realize that we have what we need. We give up waiting for rescue, we stop feeling victimized or betrayed, and we enthusiastically get to work solving our own problems.

The leaders we need are already here. *I thought that because I was one of the poorest people in my community, I had no role to play.* Remember Anna Marunda's words? Perhaps she gave voice to our own doubts that we don't know enough, don't have enough, and aren't good enough to step forward and provide leadership in our communities. How many of us still cling to the belief that we have to wait for the experts, that we can't move without the support of those with power and influence? How many of us keep hoping that some charismatic leader will appear to save us?

At Kufunda, I learned that each one of us has something special to give. . . . I have learned that I am a strong woman. . . . I am trustworthy, so people are coming to me. These, too, are the words of Anna Marunda, after she bravely stepped forward and began working on what she most cared about. She is one woman among many in Rusape who are eagerly engaged, discovering that they *are* leaders, serving their community in many different ways to make it function better. So, too, are the mothers of Joubert Park; they stepped forward to create a day care center, then they invited friends and neighbors to learn to read. Twelve-year-old Rohit who collects gobar in India is a leader, as are the children who design their own jardim das crianças, the upcyclers and urban gardeners at Shikshantar, the bicimáquina makers, the hosts of World Cafés focused on ending hunger and homelessness.

The pattern here is simple: People see something in their world that needs to change, and they step forward to take that first action. They don't declare themselves "a leader"; they just start acting to change things. A leader is anyone willing to help, anyone willing to take those first steps to remedy a situation or create a new possibility. How many more leaders are already here in our organizations and communities, just waiting for the opportunity to serve?

We are living the worlds we want today. How would you describe the world you wish for? The participants at the Art of Learning Centering described their new world as a place where people feed themselves in ways that nourish their bodies and renew the earth, where everyone is a learner, everyone is creative, where families consume enough to support their livelihood and offer surpluses to neighbors, where the people lead and the leaders serve. It is a world that engages all of its members—women, men, elders, youth, ancestors—in stewarding their community to be healthy and resilient.

This is the world the Zapatistas are creating, though they give it different names and practices. It is the world the Kufundees are creating. It is the world the Warriors Without Weapons are creating as they partner with the people of Paquetá. It is the world of the Pirate Ship, where young men experiment with using their hands to build what they can imagine. In every case, these Walk Outs Who Walk On begin living the worlds they want today. They let go of complaints, arguments, and dramas; they place the work at the center, invite everyone inside and find solutions to problems that others think unsolvable. With their dedication and experiments, they are creating a world that has a place for all of us.

We walk at the pace of the slowest. *The Zapatistas say we walk to make the road better, we must listen as we walk, and we must walk at the pace of the slowest.* If we wish to build healthy and resilient communities, we can't leave anyone behind. So we take the journey as slowly as we need to. We forgo shortcuts in favor of the learning that comes when we travel the long way round. Daniel or Carlos of Maya Pedal could have created a bicimáquina manual for the replication of their inventions; instead they invited each learner to figure out what might work, stumbling into his or her own local expression and unique designs. This also is the spirit of swaraj that permeates Shikshantar as it rejects the ready-made world in favor of self-directed learning—a path that is often slow, laborious, and inefficient by conventional standards. To walk at the pace of the slowest is to practice solidarity, like the women of Grameen Bank's lending circles, who are committed to the success of each member repaying her loan, no matter how far she may be lagging behind.

Speed is not our goal. Growth is not our purpose. Winning is not evidence of our success. What gifts do we discover as we slow down, look around, invite more people in, and enjoy our well-companioned journey?

We listen, even to the whispers. Which voices do we listen to? Are they the familiar voices of power—those with position and authority, influence and wealth, expertise and training? Or do we make the road to the future by listening to the voices of everyone: the faceless, the nameless, the invisible, the indigenous people of Chiapas, the squatters in Brazil's cortiços and favelas, the dalits of India, the homeless in Columbus, and, everywhere, the voices of women, elders, children.

We hear these voices only if we create the spaces to listen. We hear the voices of the homeless at Barb Poppe's World Cafés, where they sit side-by-side with professionals and policy makers to shape their future. We hear these voices at the Art of Learning Centering as people work together tilling soil, digging holes, and preparing food, in conversations that expose new ideas, disagreements, and discoveries. We hear these voices when we invite people to self-organize around the issues they care most about, such as the invitation extended by the Transition Town movement for citizens to experiment in rebuilding their world.

When we listen to the whispers, we free ourselves from the limiting belief that only some people have the answers, that only some people are worth listening to. As we tune into this chorus of whispers, as their voices become more confident and clear, we discover we are an incredibly talented choir, able to take on more challenging music.

We turn to one another. *Whatever the problem, community is the answer. There is no power greater than a community discovering what it cares about.* Only when we turn to one another do we discover the wisdom and wealth that is so abundantly present in us, our traditions and our environment. The residents of Joubert Park turn to one another to create a sense of safety, care for their children, educate adults, empower youth, grow their own food, and make wise use of their waste. In Rusape, the community invites its elders to sit together in circle and recall traditional practices for maintaining a resilient food system. Warriors Without Weapons gather from many different countries to playfully engage with the residents of Paquetá to create gardens and a community center. Art of Hosting practitioners throughout Columbus form a community of practice to strengthen their courage and capacity to disrupt and enliven bureaucratic institutions.

A community that turns to one another creates a spirit of welcome for all its members. It relies on the fact that people want to be engaged, that they want to learn and contribute to their community. It recognizes that people will step forward as leaders when they discover an issue they care about. It pays attention to the web of relationships, and works to include, not exclude. It keeps inviting in more people for their rich diversity of ideas, heritage, perspectives. As it does all this, a miraculous gift reveals itself. It doesn't matter if no one is coming to help. We have what we need, right here, right now, among us all.

WILL YOU WALK ON?

Even as we discover principles and practices that promise so much more, as we see more clearly what the future could be, as we aspire to step forward to create a new world, it's difficult to maintain clarity and focus. The old world keeps yanking us backward. When we tell people what we've just experienced and learned is possible, we sound like wide-eyed, foolish dreamers. Friends and colleagues are more likely to smile and change the conversation than to explore what has us so excited. Our loved ones may feel left out or left behind. At times, we ourselves will doubt that a new world is possible or that it's worth the trouble to try living the future now. And then there's the day-to-day practicalities of living in this world, earning a living, taking care of our families—needing to appear normal, predictable, not crazy.

Yet a new world must be made, and if we don't do it, who will? At Berkana, we've struggled with the dilemmas and challenges of pioneering, edge-walking work for many years now. In company with our friends worldwide, we've developed simple practices for sustaining ourselves as Walk Ons and for resisting the strong gravity of familiar ways. These practices are: Name, Connect, Nourish, Illuminate.

Naming is being able to claim publicly who we are and what we're walking on to. Whenever we give ourselves a new name, it's a way of making visible our intentions. What are you walking out of, and why? By walking on, who are you choosing to be? However you name yourself, choose a name that encourages you to move forward, that challenges you to be fearless. I am a Zapatista. I am a Walk Out. I am an edge-walker. I am a leader. I am daring to live the future now.

How will you name yourself?

Connecting is finding others who share our purpose, who hear our new name and say, "Me, too!" None of us can do this work alone—we need each other to support, encourage, and console one another. We need companions to think with, celebrate with, cry with, dance with. We need companions to lessen the loneliness, to keep us going when the work gets hard, when the world tells us we're lunatics. Skilled pioneers never venture forth alone, and neither can you.

Whom will you connect with?

Nourishing is turning to one another for ideas, knowledge, practices, and dreams. Among us, we already have a great deal of experience and expertise. When we affiliate with other Walk Ons, we inspire, provoke, and support each other. Ideas and inventions flow among us, like the bicimáquinas, the Oasis Game, the arborloos. When we gather together, we learn quickly from one another, discovering new ideas and solutions, like at the Art of Learning Centering, as in the Art of Hosting communities of practice. Together we discover that we have what we need.

Where will you turn for nourishment?

Illuminating is sharing our stories so many more people can know we're out there and join in. Walking out is never easy, and walking on is often invisible. Our work comes from the future and is difficult to see through current lenses. By shining a light on our pioneering efforts, we bring the future into focus. Little by little, our work becomes recognizable as evidence of what's possible, of what a new world could be. This book has been an experience of illuminating that future.

What stories will you illuminate?

STEPPING ONTO THE INVISIBLE PATH

Walking out is an act of bravery, one that requires companions, compassion, determination, and perseverance. Yet if we're brave enough to take that leap, we are richly rewarded. We walk out of confining ideas and places, we remove the limits and barriers—and our world becomes wide open to possibilities. We feel creative again, sometimes outrageously so. It's intoxicating to feel this alive. And it's wonderful to discover that we're not alone, that the world is filled with interesting, courageous Walk Outs. We have companions for the journey.

As Walk Outs, we can start anywhere—we can go to a community meeting that we've avoided in the past, we can speak up at work, we can talk to a few friends about what we care about, we can decide to learn more about an issue that troubles us rather than ignoring or denying it. When we take these first steps, we have no idea where they will lead, what we'll do or who we'll become.

Yet our first actions, no matter how small, are a declaration of our new identity: We're Walk Outs Who Walk On. We accept the risk, step onto the invisible path and walk into the unknown. And there, much to our delight, we discover the many beautiful people already bringing this new world into form.

> You thought I knew where the road was and you followed me.
> But no. I didn't know where the road was.
> We had to make the road together.
> And that is what we did.
> That's how we got where we wanted to be.
> We made the road. It wasn't there.[104]
>
> —*Subcomandante Marcos*

PART IV
REFLECTIONS

CHOOSING TO ACT

Deborah Frieze

I began hosting Learning Journeys in 2004, when I took my first group of fourteen participants to South Africa and Zimbabwe. Within six months of that trip, four participants had quit their jobs—the life they returned to just didn't make sense anymore—and I became curious. What about our journey was creating this disturbance? What were we seeing now that hadn't been visible to us before? I began paying attention to our Walk Out statistics. Sure enough, within six to twelve months of each journey, about 30 percent of the participants would walk out of their previous lives, declaring that something more must be possible.

These Learning Journeys have been working on me relentlessly ever since. I've discovered that the real work of the journey only begins once you have returned home and you see your familiar world through new eyes. Patterns and choices that once had been indistinguishable suddenly come into high relief. Until now, these patterns have been operating in the background, invisible and unintentional—Meg and I call this a *system of influence*, the dominant forces of our culture that have us unconsciously embracing the collective assumptions about how we should live. But a Learning Journey interrupts that unconsciousness and moves those patterns to the foreground, where we are confronted with choice. Let me give you some examples of where that has happened to me.

During one visit to Kufunda, I remember taking a bath at Marianne's cottage. She instructed me when I was finished not to drain the tub, but rather to collect my bathwater in buckets to be poured over the water-starved plants in her small garden plot. I haven't started collecting my bathwater here at home—in my downtown Boston apartment, I wouldn't know what to do with it. But now each time I watch it swirl down the drain—uselessly, wastefully—I'm confronted with the question of how else it might have served. My daily complicity in a system of influence that invites us to mindlessly consume and waste as much as we can afford to is no longer invisible to me. My fellow Bostonians shared this experience briefly in May 2010 when a broken water pipe disrupted the region's water system. For several days we boiled water and showered with our mouths closed—hardly a crisis, but one that knocked people off center (featuring shoving matches and price gouging for bottled water), revealing the fragility—the lack of resilience—in our system. And then the water main was repaired, and most of us Bostonians went back to our mindless consumption. But that experience of watering the plants with my bathwater has remained in the foreground, prompting me to continue asking, How do I choose to act on what I now see? What behaviors am I willing to walk out of? Which ones will make a difference?

When I was traveling in India, I became excited about the upcycled crafts the learners at Shikshantar were creating. It aroused the entrepreneur in me, and I dreamed up a business of importing upcycled jewelry, handbags, and sculptures, which I pitched to Manish. Not only would this bring additional income to Shikshantar, I proposed, but it would be an excellent way to share their story and the important work of upcycling, the practice of reimagining our waste, with a U.S. audience that needed to wake up to its own wastefulness. Manish was unimpressed. My proposition would merely reinforce a culture of consumption in the United States and of dependency in India: Upcyclers would be required to craft their creations for the tastes of a faraway and anonymous consumer rather than focus on their own learning and local community. For Manish, walking on to sustainable lives and livelihoods means local production for local consumption. It was astounding to me that he would walk away from a viable and socially responsible opportunity to generate income . . . at first. And then I began to see how my assumptions about growth, economic security, and international development were driving my entrepreneurship. Shikshantar's upcyclers did not need access to a foreign market; they did not need U.S. dollars to improve their lives and livelihoods. There was no problem for me to solve— no matter how well intentioned I might have been.

Sergio of Unitierra took this lesson one step further when he handed me a speech to read entitled "To Hell with Good Intentions." It was an address by Ivan Illich to American students who had come to Mexico in 1968 as volunteer service workers. Illich said:

> I do have deep faith in the enormous good will of the U.S. volunteer. However, his good faith can usually be explained only by an abysmal lack of intuitive delicacy. . . .

> Next to money and guns, the third largest North American export is the U.S. idealist, who turns up in every theater of the world: the teacher, the volunteer, the missionary, the community organizer, the economic developer, and the vacationing do-gooders. Ideally, these people define their role as service. Actually, they frequently wind up alleviating the damage done by money and weapons, or "seducing" the "underdeveloped" to the benefits of the world of affluence and achievement. Perhaps this is the moment to instead bring home to the people of the U.S. the knowledge that the way of life they have chosen simply is not alive enough to be shared.[105]

Here, even the most basic tenets of our society—the desire to help, aid, assist, solve, fix—move from the shadows of our assumptions and into the light. The culture I was raised in taught me to solve problems, pursue success, maximize profit, gain influence, leverage power, and be compensated well for doing so. If I choose to walk out of that worldview, what then will guide my actions? For many Walk Outs, for me, there comes a stage of paralysis. How can I make a contribution when I know that the familiar ways don't work—that success often comes at the cost of other people's lives and livelihoods? Where then shall I put my attention? How shall I now act?

There are no easy answers, only a long string of unanswerable questions that slam into us once we return home from our journeys and discover that we're no longer comfortable where we are. Questions like:

How do I hold what I now know?

How do I live in integrity with my beliefs?

How can I hold my own hypocrisy with compassion?

When do I engage and stay—and when do I walk out?

What am I willing to walk on to?

A Learning Journey has never given me answers to these questions. It gives me the practice of clear seeing, of bearing witness to my choices. That has meant noticing when I discard plastic rather than upcycle it, when I opt for the anonymity of transacting rather than gifting, when I bemoan imperfect efficiency, when I choose speed over inclusion, when I take the replication shortcut because it gives me more control.

It's not about making myself wrong for what I choose; it's about choosing consciously—and sometimes challenging myself to stand in the discomfort of abandoning the familiar. Here in the United States, the system we live in hasn't collapsed. For most of us, there's food on the table, water in the taps, teachers in the schools, medicine in the hospitals—unlike in Zimbabwe. And yet, our food is creating a pandemic of obesity and diabetes, our cities are rationing water, our schools are failing our children, and our pharmaceuticals are generating disease. We don't have to wait for collapse to decide that it's time to let go of our dying systems, to walk out and walk on to create the world we wish for.

Alas, the path forward is never clear or easy. I'm reminded of the scene in *Raiders of the Lost Ark* when Indiana Jones crosses the chasm on an invisible bridge. It isn't that there is no bridge; it's that the path forward reveals itself one step at a time—and only *after* we've committed ourselves to moving ahead. Sometimes we find ourselves moving ahead in ways that seem infinitely insignificant—we bring our bags to the store, we take public transportation, we buy local food. And sometimes we take terrifying plunges—we walk out of our jobs, we pull our kids out of conventional schools, we simplify our needs and give away most of our possessions. What matters is not *what* we choose, but *that* we choose. Whether we walk on to affirm our participation in what was already there or we find ourselves in the great unknown, either way we make a choice, we participate, we act—rather than be acted upon.

But we can't act alone. One of the reasons I helped to create the Berkana Exchange is that I needed a community of fellow pioneers, people willing to experiment with groundbreaking work, people willing to fail over and over again and yet to persevere in their yearning to create a new future. People who would understand that Walk Ons feel perpetually on the edge of chaos, swinging back and forth between hope and hopelessness, possibility and resignation, triumph and frustration. Some days, everything we do feels insufficient—*Nothing will change. I can't make a difference. Why bother?* Other days, we are graced with the clarity that we're doing exactly what is ours to do—*This is what's in front of me. I trust my contribution. And it is enough.* Not a single Walk On in this book got started by doing anything more than what was in front of them—not Edgard, not Dorah, not Mukesh. Not even Wangari Maathai or Muhammad Yunus. In the company of fellow Walk Ons, I am reminded that we never know what difference our contribution might make. Our work is to see what's right in front of us and to step forward to claim it. And then to keep seeing, to keep paying attention, to stay with the hard places, the uncomfortable relationships, the unanswerable questions.

A story is told of a student who traveled a long distance to meet with a famous rabbi. The student humbly asks, "Rebbe, how do I become wise?" The rabbi looks carefully at the student and answers, "From making good choices." "But rebbe, how will I know how to make good choices?" The rabbi responds, "From experience." "But," the student continues, "How do I get that experience?" The rabbi smiles and answers, "From bad choices."

Our work is, over and over and over again, to choose to act.

WE NEVER KNOW WHO WE ARE

Meg Wheatley

We never know who we are
(this is strange, isn't it?)
or what vows we made
or who we knew
or what we hoped for
or where we were
when the world's dreams
were seeded.

Until the day just one of us

sighs a gentle longing
and we all feel the change
one of us calls our name
and we all know to be there
one of us tells a dream
and we all breathe life into it

one of us asks "why?"
and we all know the answer.

It is very strange. We never know who we are.

NOTES

1. Explore the history and current work of the Walkouts Network (*Swapathgami*) at http://www.swaraj.org/shikshantar/walkoutsnetwork.htm. *Swapathgami* is Hindi for "making our own paths of learning and living."

2. For more information about The Berkana Institute, see p. 265 or visit www.berkana.org.

3. Gratitude to Myron Rogers, who first coined the phrase "Start anywhere, follow it everywhere."

4. Guillermo Bonfil Batalla, *México Profundo: Reclaiming a Civilization* (Austin: University of Texas Press, 1996), 5.

5. To learn more about co-motion, read Gustavo Esteva, "Back from the Future," http://gustavoesteva.com/english_site/back_from_the_future .htm#_ftn1.

6. CIDECI stands for Centro Indigena de Capacitación Integral.

7. Dr. Raymundo Sánchez Barraza shared this in an interview with Nic Paget-Clarke published in *In Motion Magazine*. See "Interview with Raymundo Sánchez Barraza: A University Without Shoes," http://inmotion magazine.com/global/rsb_int_eng.html, September 2005 (accessed August 17, 2010).

8. Opening remarks by Subcomandante Marcos at the First Intercontinental Encuentro for Humanity and Against Neoliberalism, July 27, 1996. Subcomandante Marcos and Juan Ponce de León, *Our Word Is Our Weapon* (New York: Seven Stories Press, 2003), 102.

9. Gustavo Esteva and Madhu Suri Prakash, *Grassroots Postmodernism* (London: Zed Books, 1998), 6.

10. Gabriel Szulanski and Sidney Winter, "Getting It Right the Second Time," *Harvard Business Review*, January 2002.

11. Opening remarks at the First Intercontinental Encuentro for Humanity and Against Neoliberalism, July 27, 1996. Marcos and Ponce de León, *Our Word Is Our Weapon.*

12. Email correspondence with Daniel Perera.

13. Transition Network, "Transition Initiatives Directory," www.transition network.org/initiatives (accessed July 30, 2010).

14. Subcomandante Marcos, "Old Antonio's History of the Upholder of the Sky," translated by irlandesa, *The Narco News Bulletin*, www.narconews .com/Issue31/article832.html (accessed August 17, 2010).

15. By nominal GDP, according to the World Bank's 2009 list, "Gross Domestic Product (2009)." The World Bank: World Development Indicators database, http://siteresources.worldbank.org/DATASTATISTICS/Resources/GDP.pdf (accessed July 05, 2010).

16. Canadian International Development Agency. "A Synthesis of Canada's Cooperation Strategy in Brazil," http://www.acdi-cida.gc.ca/inet/images.nsf/vLUImages/Brazil/$file/Brazil-country-strategy-FINAL.pdf, March 2005 (accessed August 17, 2010).

17. Myles Horton and Paulo Freire, *We Make the Road by Walking: Conversations on Education and Social Change*, ed. Brenda Bell, John Gaventa, and John Peters (Philadelphia: Temple University Press, 1990), 56.

18. In his book, *The Careless Society* (p. 154), John McKnight characterizes the conventional approach to community organizing, which emerged in the 1940s, as one that encourages neighborhoods to organize against "enemies" whose power can be manipulated.

19. The term *upcycling* is most commonly attributed to the 2002 publication of *Cradle to Cradle,* the pioneering book on ecologically intelligent design by William McDonough and Michael Braungart. Earlier citations of the word have been identified from 1996 on (see WordSpy at www.wordspy.com/words/upcycling.asp), although it's unclear exactly where it was first coined.

20. As of April 2010. In 2009, it was 127,000.

21. Many of the voices of possibility are actual quotes from Paquetá community members, particularly Kátia dos Santos. Watch 2007 Warriors Without Weapons film at http://warriorswithoutweapons.wordpress.com/www-2011.

22. Barbara Ehrenreich, *Dancing in the Streets: A History of Collective Joy* (New York: Holt, 2006), 18.

23. The Zulu word *indaba* has many meanings in South Africa. Traditionally, it referred to a council or meeting of indigenous peoples to discuss an important matter. Informally, it is used to gather people together for discussion.

24. This Zulu origin story is adapted from Credo Mutwa, *Zulu Shaman: Dreams, Prophecies and Mysteries* (Rochester, VT: Destiny Books, 2003), 33–35.

25. From the journals of Thomas Richard Adlam. See Maryna Fraser, Edmund Bright, Thomas Richard Adlam, *Johannesburg Pioneer Journals, 1888–1909* (Cape Town: Van Riebeeck Society, 1986), 77.

NOTES

26. These scenes from Joubert Park come from recorded personal recollections from residents of Johannesburg.

27. Nelson Mandela, *Long Walk to Freedom* (New York: Back Bay Books, 1995), 149.

28. Ibid., 111.

29. Desmond Tutu, *No Future Without Forgiveness* (London: Rider Books, 1999), 34–35.

30. According to the Institute for Security Studies (www.iss.co.za, accessed August 17, 2010), the murder rate in Johannesburg Central could be as high as 1,000 per 100,000 residents—which is off the charts compared with an international average of 9.6 murders per 100,000 people.

31. The larger neighborhood that the government recognizes as Joubert Park covers about one hundred city blocks. Its official population is estimated to be nearly thirty thousand, although residents say the figures are much higher. City of Johannesburg E-Services, www.joburg.org.za (accessed August 17, 2010).

32. HIV statistics vary for age, gender, and race. According to the 2008 South African National HIV survey, while the overall infection rate in South Africa is about 11 percent, for black Africans in their twenties and thirties, the infection rate leaps as high as 29 percent—and likely higher in the Central Business District. And even higher in the late 1990s. O. Shisana, T. Rehle, L. C. Simbayi, K. Zuma, S. Jooste, V. Pillay-van-Wyk, N. Mbelle, J. Van Zyl, W. Parker, N. P. Zungu, S. Pezi, and the SABSSM III Implementation Team, "South African National HIV Prevalence, Incidence, Behavior and Communication Survey, 2008," HSRC Press, www.mrc.ac.za/pressreleases/2009/sanat.pdf (accessed August 17, 2010).

33. These rankings come from www.NationMaster.com (accessed August 17, 2010), which sources data from the *CIA World Factbook*, the United Nations, and the International Centre for Prison Studies, among others.

34. While the official unemployment rate in South Africa peaked at 37 percent in 2003–2004 and is today closer to 22 percent, the unofficial rate—particularly among black Africans in the inner city—is much higher. Statistics South Africa, www.statssa.gov.za (accessed August 17, 2010).

35. John McKnight, *The Careless Society* (New York: Basic Books, 1995), 105–106.

36. Tutu, *No Future Without Forgiveness,* 213.

37. Adapted from interviews with Dorah and quotes from *The Green-*

House Project film featured on Global Oneness (www.globalonenessproject
.org/videos/thegreenhouseproject).

38. The GreenHouse Project has had a turbulent relationship with its
primary funder, the National Lotteries Board, and is focused on developing
income-generating activities that will lead to greater economic self-reliance.

39. Quote from Masupatsela Series 11, Episode 12, a film about The
GreenHouse Project (www.freerangefilms.co.za/Masupatsela2/episodes/
episode12agreenerworld/).

40. www.transitiontowns.org.

41. www.transitionnetwork.org/welcome (July 2010).

42. The annual inflation rate in Zimbabwe as of November 2008. Steve
H. Hanke, "New Hyperinflation Index (HHIZ) Puts Zimbabwe Inflation at
89.7 Sextillion Percent," The Cato Institute, www.cato.org/zimbabwe (accessed August 18, 2010).

43. According to the World Food Program Zimbabwe Country Report,
www.wfp.org/countries/zimbabwe (accessed August 18, 2010).

44. This means the HIV rate is 15.3 percent, which is 1 in 7. Daniel Howden,
"Zimbabwe's Bad Practice: 3,500 Dead Each Week as Meltdown Looms," *The
Independent*, December 1, 2006, www.independent.co.uk/news/world/
africa/zimbabwes-bad-practice-3500-dead-each-week-as-meltdown-looms-
426580.html (accessed August 18, 2010).

45. While toilet trivia fanatics abound on the Internet, no one has run
an exact figure here. Estimates are that gallons per flush range from 1.6 to
5 (averaging 3); flushes per day average 4 to 5; and the U.S. population is
more than 309 million. Which leaves us with an average of, say, 4.2 billion
gallons per day.

46. Vandana Shiva points out that on average, Green Revolution agriculture requires ten times more water input than nonchemical agriculture.
And today, industrial agriculture requires three hundred times more chemical inputs than when it was first introduced. Watch "A Critique of the
Green Revolution" on YouTube at www.youtube.com/watch?v=UfKi47Vfriw.

47. Vandana Shiva, *The Violence of the Green Revolution: Third World
Agriculture, Ecology and Politics* (London: Zed Books, 1992), 15.

48. World Bank Zimbabwe Country Report, http://data.worldbank.
org/country/zimbabwe (accessed August 18, 2010).

49. Several years later in 2008, Kufunda did install a drip irrigation
system (funded through a grant). At the time, frequent power cuts compromising their ability to pump water made gardening increasingly difficult. To feed themselves and continue gardening, they decided to install

the system with the intention of learning from it how to design similar systems using cheaper and recycled materials that would be more affordable for their partner communities.

50. Direct experience and Kufunda 2005 annual report.

51. The film *Power of Community* depicts the story of the agricultural revolution in Cuba. www.powerofcommunity.org.

52. Brian Walker and David Salt, *Resilience Thinking: Sustaining Ecosystems and People in a Changing World* (Seattle: Island Press, 2006).

53. Ibid., 9.

54. Jeffrey D. Sachs, *The End of Poverty: Economic Possibilities for Our Time* (New York: Penguin Books, 2005), 213.

55. United Nations, "The Millennium Development Goals Report 2009," www.un.org/millenniumgoals/pdf/MDG_Report_2009_ENG.pdf (accessed August 18, 2010).

56. Ibid., 3.

57. For more on this perspective on Haiti, read "What You're Not Hearing About Haiti (But Should Be)" by Carl Lindskoog, Common Dreams, January 14, 2010, www.commondreams.org/view/2010/01/14-2 (accessed August 18, 2010).

58. Walker and Salt, *Resilience Thinking,* 14.

59. Mahatma Gandhi (1869–1948) was the political and spiritual leader of India during the Indian independence movement. Jiddu Krishnamurti (1895–1986) was a prolific philosopher and spiritual teacher known worldwide for his practice of challenging assumptions. Rabindranath Tagore (1861–1941) was a Nobel Prize–winning poet, novelist, playwright, and musician. Vandana Shiva (born in 1952) is an environmental activist and ecofeminist who has catalyzed a worldwide movement against industrial agriculture. Arundhati Roy (born in 1961), best known for her novel *The God of Small Things*, is an activist focused on social justice and economic inequality.

60. This dialogue is based on quotes drawn directly from the work of each leader and assembled to create this fictional conversation.

61. Sri Aurobindo (1872–1950) was a philosopher who was said to have integrated Eastern and Western cultures in his work; he was also a political activist, spiritual leader, poet, and yogi. Vinoba Bhave (1895–1982) was the spiritual successor of Gandhi and an advocate of nonviolence and human rights.

62. PBS, "Holy Cow: Hinduism's Sacred Animal," Thirteen/WNET New York and Icon Films, 2004,www.pbs.org/wnet/nature/holycow/hinduism.html (accessed August 18, 2010).

63. According to Chetan Singh Mehta in his book *Environmental Protection and the Law* (New Delhi: APH Publishing, 2009). Cattle figure adjusted from Mehta's estimate of 300 million to 280 million.

64. Learn more about producing *amrit jal* and *amrit mitti* from Natueco City Farming, http://natuecocityfarming.blogspot.com.

65. From *You Are, Therefore I Am,* by Satish Kumar, cited in *Reclaiming the Gift Culture*, a 131-page booklet produced by Shikshantar.

66. Stuart Kauffman, *Reinventing the Sacred: A New View of Science, Reason, and Religion* (New York: Basic Books, 2008), 9.

67. Adapted from Rabbi Joseph Telushkin, *Jewish Wisdom: Ethical, Spiritual and Historical Lessons from the Great Works and Thinkers* (New York: Morrow, 1994), 183.

68. Manish Jain and Shilpa Jain, eds., *Vimukt Shiksha: Reclaiming the Gift Culture* (Rajasthan: Shikshantar, 2009), 78–80.

69. To learn more about the Berkana Fellows program, read *The Leaders We Need Are Already Here,* by Nitin Paranjape, a booklet and accompanying video available at www.berkana.org. This program was a prototype for Swaraj University (www.swarajuniversity.org), a two-year self-directed learning program.

70. Bernard Lietaer, *The Future of Money: Creating New Wealth, Work and a Wiser World* (Post Falls, ID: Century, 2001), 146.

71. To illustrate, in the United States, banks are required to hold 10 percent of a loan in reserve. If the bank receives a $100 deposit, it may lend out $90 of that deposit. When the borrower uses that loan to pay someone else who deposits the $90 in the bank, the bank can now lend out $81. The cycle continues until the bank turns that original $100 deposit into up to $1,000 in loans ($100 + 90 + 81 + 72.90 + . . . = $1,000). And this is how $900 is created out of thin air.

72. Thomas Greco, *The End of Money and the Future of Civilization* (n.p.: Green Press Initiative, 2009), 55.

73. Mahatma Gandhi, *Trusteeship* (Ahmedabad: Navajivan Publishing, 1996).

74. Lietaer, *Future of Money*, 159, and direct interview. When Lietaer last did a "hard inventory" of currency systems, he found a minimum of 2,500 in operation. His estimate (as of 2010) is that there are between 2,500 and 5,000 community currencies operating in the dozen countries he is tracking.

75. Rabindranath Tagore, "Prisoner," in *Gitanjali* (Charleston, SC: BookSurge Classics, 2003), 20.

76. Iamblichus, *On the Pythagorean Life,* trans. Gillian Clark (Liverpool: Liverpool University Press, 1989), 50.

77. Nassim Nicholas Taleb, *The Black Swan: The Impact of the Highly Improbable.* New York: Random House, 2007), xx.

78. Professor James Chace of Bard College shared his views about the emergence of interventionism in a 2002 interview on *NewsHour* with Jim Lehrer: "History of Intervention." PBS, July 31, 2002, www.pbs.org/newshour/bb/middle_east/july-dec02/historians_7-31.html (accessed August 18, 2010).

79. Dambisa Moyo, *Dead Aid: Why Aid Is Not Working and How There Is a Better Way for Africa (New York: Farrar, Straus and Giroux, 2009), xviii.*

80. Ibid., 35.

81. Peter Kenyon, "Obscured by War, Water Crisis Looms in Yemen," NPR, November 20, 2009, www.npr.org/templates/story/story.php?storyId=120619082 (accessed August 18, 2010).

82. Richard Harris, "Reef Conservation Strategy Backfires," NPR, November 18, 2009, www.npr.org/templates/story/story.php?storyId=120536304 (accessed August 18, 2010).

83. Oxfam Briefing Papers, "Stop the Dumping: How EU Agricultural Subsidies Are Damaging Livelihoods in the Developing World," Oxfam International, October 2002, www.oxfam.org.uk/resources/policy/trade/downloads/bp31_dumping.pdf (accessed August 18, 2010).

84. Moyo, *Dead Aid*, 46.

85. Plato, *Symposium*, 175d. In *The Collected Dialogues,* ed. Edith Hamilton and Huntington Cairns (Princeton, NJ: Princeton University Press, 1961), 530.

86. Estimates range from $2.4 to as high as $6 billion. Linda Rodriguez, "Toilet Paper History: How America Convinced the World to Wipe," Mental Floss, November 7, 2009, www.mentalfloss.com/blogs/archives/40088 (accessed August 18, 2010).

87. Toilet Paper History, "Toilet Paper Fun Facts," www.toiletpaperhistory .net/toilet-paper-facts/toilet-paper-fun-facts (accessed August 18, 2010).

88. Leslie Kaufman, "Mr. Whipple Left It Out: Soft Is Rough on Forests," *New York Times,* February 25, 2009, www.nytimes.com/2009/02/26/science/earth/26charmin.html?_r=1&em (accessed August 18, 2010).

89. Cottonelle slogan.

90. Christopher Alexander, *A Timeless Way of Building* (Oxford: Oxford University Press, 1979), 236.

91. In *Tools for Conviviality*, Illich chooses an unconventional use of the

term *convivial*. He writes, "I have chosen 'convivial' as a technical term to designate a modern society of responsibly limited tools."

92. Ivan Illich, Jerry Brown, and Carl Mitcham, "Land of Found Friends," *Whole Earth*, Summer 1997, http://ournature.org/~novembre/illich/1997_ friendship.html (accessed October 27, 2010).

93. Defined by Grameen as living on less than $1 per day. In 2008, the World Bank revised the poverty line figure to $1.25.

94. Muhammad Yunus, *Creating a World Without Poverty* (New York: PublicAffairs Books, 2007), 114.

95. Liz Osborn, "Cloudiest Cities in America," Current Results Nexus, www.currentresults.com/Weather-Extremes/US/cloudiest-cities.php (accessed August 19, 2010).

96. For years, Columbus consistently ranked as a top test market for consumer products. Recent studies indicate that the city may no longer be equally representative of the U.S. population. Business First of Columbus, "Study: Columbus Not So Good as Test Market." www.bizjournals .com/columbus/stories/2004/05/31/daily2.html (accessed August 19, 2010).

97. See www.artofhosting.org. This quote is in Margaret Wheatley, *Turning to One Another: Simple Conversations to Restore Hope to the Future,* 2nd ed. (San Francisco: Berrett-Koehler, 2009), 177.

98. From www.osu.edu/osutoday/stuinfo.php and elsewhere at www .osu.edu.

99. Open Space: www.openspaceworld.org.

100. PeerSpirit: www.peerspirit.com.

101. Interview with Toke Møller, March 2010.

102. Quotes from Phil come from direct interviews and from a workshop he and Toke hosted in Nova Scotia where they told the Columbus health care story. See www.youtube.com/watch?v=AxK51N_IwIY&NR=1.

103. These statistics come from Our Optimal Health documents and are based on 2004 figures.

104. From *Zapatista Stories*, translated by Dinah Livingstone, www .katabasis.co.uk/pantonio.html.

105. Ivan Illich, "To Hell with Good Intentions," www.swaraj.org/illich_ hell.htm (accessed November 10, 2010).

BIBLIOGRAPHY

Here are the primary resources we used for this book. If you wish to learn more about the people, places and issues introduced here, please visit www.walkoutwalkon.net, where we provide many additional resources.

Alexander, Christopher. *A Timeless Way of Building.* Oxford: Oxford University Press, 1979.

Art of Hosting, www.artofhosting.org.

Axladitsa-Avatakia, www.axladitsa.org.

The Berkana Institute, www.berkana.org.

Bonfil Batalla, Guillermo. *México Profundo: Reclaiming a Civilization.* Trans. Philip A. Dennis. Austin: University of Texas Press, 1996.

Brown, Juanita, and David Isaacs. *The World Café: Shaping Our Futures Through Conversations That Matter.* San Francisco: Berrett-Koehler, 2005.

Cass, Phil, and Toke Møller. "Affordable, Sustainable Healthcare in Columbus, Ohio." Ravi Tangri, July 19, 2007, www.youtube.com/watch?v=AxK51N_IwlY&NR=1 (accessed October 27, 2010).

Centro Indígena de Capacitación Integral (CIDECI), http://cideci.blogspot.com.

Community Shelter Board, www.csb.org.

Ejército Zapatista de Liberación Nacional (EZLN). *EZLN: Otro Mundo Es Posible.* Imagen MX. (Acquired in 2007 from Zapatista movement.)

Esteva, Gustavo. "Back from the Future." http://gustavoesteva.com/english_site/back_from_the_future.htm#_ftn1 (accessed October 27, 2010).

Esteva, Gustavo, and Madhu Suri Prakash. *Grassroots Postmodernism.* London: Zed Books, 1998.

Gandhi, Mahatma. *Hind Swaraj.* Ahmedabad: Navajivan Trust, 1938.

Gandhi, Mahatma. *Trusteeship.* Ahmedabad: Navajivan Publishing, 1996.

Global Oneness Project. *The GreenHouse Project* (film). www.globalonenessproject.org/videos/thegreenhouseproject (accessed October 27, 2010).

Goerner, Sally J., Bernard Lietaer, and Robert E. Ulanowicz. "Quantifying Economic Sustainability: Implications for Free-Enterprise Theory, Policy and Practice." *Ecological Economics,* November 15, 2009. www.lietaer.com/images/Quantifying_Economic_Sustainability_Published_Final_pdf.pdf (accessed October 27, 2010).

Greco, Thomas. *The End of Money and the Future of Civilization.* N.p.: Green Press Initiative, 2009.

Hawken, Paul. "Commencement: Healing or Stealing?" Commencement address at University of Portland, May 3, 2009. University of Portland, www.up.edu/commencement/default.aspx?cid=9456 (accessed October 27, 2010).

Hopkins, Rob. *The Transition Handbook: From Oil Dependency to Local Resilience.* Foxhole, U.K.: Green Books, 2008.

Horton, Myles, and Paulo Freire. *We Make the Road by Walking: Conversations on Education and Social Change.* Edited by Brenda Bell, John Gaventa, and John Peters. Philadelphia: Temple University Press, 1990.

Hyde, Lewis. *The Gift.* New York: Vintage Books, 2007.

Illich, Ivan. "To Hell with Good Intentions," April 20, 1968, www.swaraj.org/illich_hell.htm (accessed October 27, 2010).

Illich, Ivan. *Tools for Conviviality.* London: Marion Boyars, 2001.

Illich, Ivan, Jerry Brown, and Carl Mitcham. "Land of Found Friends." *Whole Earth*, Summer 1997, http://ournature.org/~novembre/illich/1997_friendship.html (accessed October 27, 2010).

International Honors Program and Centro de Encuentros y Diálogos Interculturales. *Indigenous Perspectives 2005 Mexico Reader.* Produced for the International Honors Program in affiliation with Boston University, 2005.

Jain, Manish, and Shilpa Jain, eds. *Vimukt Shiksha: Reclaiming the Gift Culture.* Rajasthan: Shikshantar, 2009.

Kauffman, Stuart. *Reinventing the Sacred: A New View of Science, Reason, and Religion.* New York: Basic Books, 2008.

Korten, David. *Agenda for a New Economy: From Phantom Wealth to Real Wealth.* San Francisco: Berrett-Koehler, 2009.

Krishnamurti, Jiddu. *The First and Last Freedom.* New York: HarperOne, 1975.

Kufunda Learning Village, www.kufunda.org.

Kumar, Satish. *You Are, Therefore I Am: A Declaration of Dependence.* Foxhole, U.K.: Green Books, 2002.

Lietaer, Bernard. *The Future of Money: Creating New Wealth, Work and a Wiser World.* Post Falls, ID: Century, 2001.

Lietaer, Bernard. "Quantifying Economic Sustainability: Implications for Free-Enterprise Theory, Policy and Practice." *Ecological Economics,* November 15, 2009, www.lietaer.com/images/Quantifying_Economic_Sustainability_Published_Final_pdf.pdf (accessed August 18, 2010).

Mandela, Nelson. *A Long Walk to Freedom.* New York: Back Bay Books, 1995.

Maraire, J. Nozipo. *Zenzele: A Letter for My Daughter.* Peaslake, U.K.: Delta, 1997.

Marcos, Subcomandante (author), and Juan Ponce de León (editor). *Our Word Is Our Weapon.* New York: Seven Stories Press, 2003.

Marcos, Subcomandante. *Zapatista Stories.* Trans. Dinah Livingstone, www.katabasis.co.uk/pantonio.html (accessed October 27, 2010).

Masupatsela Series 11, Episode 12: *A Greener World* (film). Jacqueline van Meygaarde. Free Range Films, www.freerangefilms.co.za/Masupatsela2/episodes/episode12agreenerworld/, October 2009 (accessed October 27, 2010).

Maya Pedal, www.mayapedal.org.

McDonough, William, and Michael Braungart. *Cradle to Cradle: Remaking the Way We Make Things.* New York: North Point Press, 2002.

McKnight, John. *The Careless Society.* New York: Basic Books, 1995.

Mid-Ohio Foodbank, www.midohiofoodbank.org.

Moyo, Dambisa. *Dead Aid: Why Aid Is Not Working and How There Is a Better Way for Africa.* New York: Farrar, Straus and Giroux, 2009.

Mutwa, Credo. *Zulu Shaman: Dreams, Prophecies and Mysteries.* Rochester, VT: Destiny Books, 2003.

Natueco City Farming, http://natuecocityfarming.blogspot.com

The Ohio State University, www.osu.edu.

Open Space Technology, www.openspaceworld.org.

Paranjape, Nitin. *The Leaders We Need Are Already Here.* Spokane, WA: Berkana Publishing, 2010.

PeerSpirit, www.peerspirit.com.

"The Power of Community: How Cuba Survived Peak Oil" (film). Faith Morgan. Arthur Morgan Institute for Community Solutions, 2006, www.powerofcommunity .org (accessed August 18, 2010).

Powers of Place Initiative, www.powersofplace.com.

Reader, John. *Africa: A Biography of the Continent.* New York: Vintage Books, 1997.

Sachs, Jeffrey D. *The End of Poverty: Economic Possibilities for Our Time.* New York: Penguin Books, 2005.

Shikshantar, www.swaraj.org/shikshantar.

Shiva, Vandana. *Water Wars: Privatization, Pollution and Profit.* Boston: South End Press, 2002.

Shiva, Vandana. *The Violence of the Green Revolution: Third World Agriculture, Ecology and Politics.* London: Zed Books, 1992.

Shiva, Vandana. "A Critique of the Green Revolution," YouTube, www.youtube .com/watch?v=UfKi47Vfriw (accessed October 27, 2010).

Sparks, Allistair. *Beyond the Miracle: Inside the New South Africa.* Chicago: University of Chicago Press, 2003.

Swaraj University, www.swarajuniversity.org.

Tagore, Rabindranath. *Gitanjali.* Charleston, SC: BookSurge Classics, 2003.

Taleb, Nassim Nicholas. *The Black Swan: The Impact of the Highly Improbable.* New York: Random House, 2007.

Transition Towns Wiki, www.transitiontowns.org.

Tutu, Desmond. *No Future Without Forgiveness.* London: Rider, 1999.

Unitierra, www.unitierra.org.

Upcycling: Re-imagining Our Waste, Berkana, www.trunity.net/upcycling (accessed October 27, 2010).

United States Interagency Council on Homelessness, www.ich.gov.

Walker, Brian, and David Salt. *Resilience Thinking: Sustaining Ecosystems and People in a Changing World*. Seattle: Island Press, 2006.

Warriors Without Weapons, http://warriorswithoutweapons.wordpress.com (accessed August 17, 2010).

World Café, www.theworldcafe.com.

Yunus, Muhammad. *Creating a World Without Poverty* (New York: PublicAffairs Books, 2007).

ACKNOWLEDGMENTS

From Meg

I started working in the world in 1966, beginning as a Peace Corps volunteer in South Korea. Now, as I think about whom I'd like to thank, I realize that I need to thank all of you.

To all of you who've used my ideas, who've experimented, who've pioneered, who've persevered, I say thank you. Without you, I would have given up long ago. Your continuing support, your courage, your curiosity, have given me a life of rich, meaningful work that I hope to continue well into the future. The risks you've taken have been more costly than mine; the challenges you've faced are greater than what I've encountered. (It's much easier to be a "thought leader" than a real leader.) Thank you.

To my teachers who attempt to keep me humble, my family who keeps me grounded and happy, my friends who never leave, and to all those whose shoulders I stand on, thank you.

From Deborah

Although I didn't know it at the time, this book began in February 2004 when Manish Jain and I launched the Berkana Exchange, and there was no turning back. I am indebted to the members of our trans-local learning community for offering me a wake-up call, an invitation to aliveness, the companionship of pioneers. For all of you—dear friends and fellow pathfinders from Unitierra in Mexico, from the Elos Institute in Brazil, from Joubert Park in South Africa, from Kufunda Learning Village in Zimbabwe, from Shikshantar in India, from Axladitsa-Avatakia in Greece, and from everywhere a member of the Berkana Exchange today walks on—I am grateful.

As for the Berkana family here at home—Bob, Lizzie, Tenneson, Teresa, Tim, Tom, Tuesday—thank you for your wisdom, your discernment, your commitment, and your patience. This book has emerged through your willingness to be bold, to experiment over and over again. You are devoted stewards of the irrepressible spirit of life. As for you, Meg, we have truly journeyed together, haven't we? Thank you for inviting me to join you and for being a wise and compassionate guide.

Aerin and Lauren, it would be impossible to fully acknowledge what you have contributed to my learning and growth—and certainly to this book. I relied on you to remember things I had forgotten, to test out ideas, and to support me in moments of doubt. And you always kept me laughing (mostly at myself). The same goes for you, Manish, dear brother. You have inspired me time and again to unlearn, to widen my lens, and to step more boldly into the unknown.

Thank you to everyone who read and reread parts of this manuscript and helped keep it accurate and true. These are your stories, and I honor your generosity in sharing them so freely: Aerin Dunford, Sergio Beltrán, Daniel Perera, Rodrigo Alonso, Edgard Gouveia Júnior, Dorah Lebelo, Mabule Mokhine, Jackie Cahi, Lauren Parks, Manish Jain, Shilpa Jain, Maria Scordialou, Monica Nissén, Phil Cass, Sarah Whiteley, and Tuesday Ryan-Hart.

In this long, quiet year of book writing that kept me off the road and mostly in Boston, I have a crew of support to acknowledge. Thank you Samantha, Robin, Kate, Julie, and Jane for the friendship, listening and nourishment of Hagalaz. . . . To Elena, Gibran, Nick, and again Samantha for the brilliant stimulation and timely compassion of our Emergence Learning Circle. . . . To Sib and Judy Wright for lovingly hosting me in the inspired space in which this book worked its way into the world. . . . And to David, Donna, Ken, and Tamar for giving me the best gifts ever throughout this process—Talia, Sloane, and Jacob who bring me continuous joy and put everything back in perspective.

And finally, to my parents: Thank you for inviting me to take risks and discover the world my own way. Thank you for teaching me *tikkun olam*. Thank you for your love, your patience, and your unparalleled generosity. If you like what you read, go ahead and take some credit!

ACKNOWLEDGMENTS

CREDITS AND SOURCES

150, Courtesy of Shikshantar
150, Deborah Frieze
163, Carla Kimball, Photographer
    (www.revealedpresence.com)
163, Carla Kimball
164, Deborah Frieze
164, Carla Kimball
167, Sarah Whiteley
167, Carla Kimball
173, Lauren Parks
173, Carla Kimball
175, Deborah Frieze
175, Deborah Frieze
183, Meg Wheatley
185, Lauren Parks
187, Deborah Frieze
192, Courtesy of the Mid-Ohio
    Foodbank
192, Courtesy of the Mid-Ohio
    Foodbank

194, Meg Wheatley
194, Courtesy of the ALIA Institute
197, Courtesy of Knowlton School of
    Architecture Digital Library.
    Photographer: Danni Chen
197, Deborah Frieze
200, Hazel Morrow-Jones
200, Monica Nissén
203, Monica Nissén
203, Hazel Morrow-Jones
205, Courtesy of the Community
    Shelter Board
205, Image by Kelvy Bird, graphic
    facilitator, www.kelvybird.com
211, Meg Wheatley
213, Deborah Frieze
215, Deborah Frieze
216, Deborah Frieze
228, Aeron Miller

SOURCES

ix, Pema Chödrön, *When Things Fall Apart*, Shambhala, 1997

xii, Members of the Berkana community, clockwise from top left: Tuesday Ryan-Hart, Maria-Elena Letona, Jackie Cahi, Nomonde Mokhine, Cynthia Wiggins, Aerin Dunford, Edgard Gouveia Júnior, Jeanne Dasaro, Manish Jain, Alexis Schroeder

2, Rabbi Lawrence Kushner, *Honey from the Rock: An Introduction to Jewish Mysticism*, Jewish Lights Publishing, 1999

50, Kaká Werá Jecupé spoke this to the Warriors Without Weapons.

74, Archbishop Desmond Tutu, *No Future Without Forgiveness*, Doubleday, 1999

102, J. Nozipo Maraire, *Zenzele: A Letter for My Daughter*, Dell, 1997

123, Poem by Bev Reeler

160, Henry David Thoreau, *Walden; or Life in the Woods*, Ticknor & Fields, 1854

188, Paul Hawken, *2009 Commencement Address*, University of Portland, May 3, 2009

218, Adrienne Rich, from the poem *Natural Resources*, in *The Dream of a Common Language: Poems 1974–1977*, Norton, 1978

INDEX

256

WEBSITE

www.walkoutwalkon.net

We're eager to provide many ways for you to continue to get to know these communities, to follow their continuing work, their successes, failures, learnings. We've created a second space for that, a website that accompanies this book. For each community, you can go online to hear their music, watch videos of their efforts, listen to interviews, and discover what's happened in the time since we wrote about them. You also can explore any of the issues raised here in much greater depth, with links to people engaged with these issues, to articles, books, videos, and other resources.

We hope you'll continue to journey with these people and issues online. But be assured that the book is complete in itself, so if you're not web-inclined, you'll still have a rich and full experience of these people and places.

ABOUT THE AUTHORS

Margaret (Meg) Wheatley, Ed.D.

Margaret Wheatley writes, teaches, and speaks about how we can organize and accomplish work in chaotic times, sustain our relationships, and willingly step forward to serve. She is co-founder and President Emerita of The Berkana Institute.

Since 1973, Meg has worked with an unusually broad variety of organizations. Her clients and audiences range from the head of the U.S. Army to twelve-year-old Girl Scouts, from CEOs and government ministers to small-town ministers, from large universities to rural aboriginal villages. All of these organizations and people wrestle with a common dilemma: how to maintain their integrity, focus, and effectiveness as they cope with the relentless upheavals and rapid shifts of this troubling time. But there is another similarity: a common human desire to find ways to live together more harmoniously, more humanely, so that more people may benefit.

She has written several best-selling books. Her most recent book was *Perseverance,* published in 2010. Her other books are *Leadership and the New Science* (now in eighteen languages and a third edition); *Finding Our Way: Leadership for an Uncertain Time; Turning to One Another: Simple Conversations to Restore Hope to the Future* (seven languages and a second edition); *A Simpler Way* (with Myron Rogers). Her numerous articles appear in both professional and popular journals and may be downloaded free from her website. Explore her website for a rich variety of resources: DVDs, articles, Conversation Starter Kits, and other products. www.margaretwheatley.com

Meg earned her doctorate in Organizational Behavior from Harvard University, and a master's in Media Ecology from New York University. She also studied at University College London, England. She has been a global citizen since her youth, serving in the Peace Corps in Korea in the 1960s, and has taught, consulted, or served in an advisory capacity on all continents (except Antarctica). She began her career as a public school teacher and also has been a professor in two graduate management programs (Brigham Young University and Cambridge College Massachusetts).

Meg has received several awards and honorary doctorates. In 2002, the American Society for Training and Development (ASTD) honored her for her contribution "to workplace learning and development" and dubbed her "a living legend." In April 2005, she was elected to the Leonardo da Vinci Society for the Study of Thinking for her contribution to the development of the field of systems thinking. In 2010, she was appointed by the White House and the Secretary of the Interior to serve on the National Advisory Board of the National Parks System; her primary responsibility is to support the growth of a twenty-first-century culture of adaptation and innovation throughout the system.

She returns from her frequent global travels to her home in the mountains of Utah and the true peace of wilderness. She has raised a large family now dispersed throughout the United States and is a very happy mother and grandmother.

Deborah Frieze

In 2001, Deborah Frieze walked out of her career as an executive in the high-tech industry. She was disillusioned by a business culture that emphasized short-term results, looked upon growth as an end rather than a means, and cared more about compliance than community. A year later, she met Meg Wheatley and a community of pioneering leaders who, like her, were walking out of organizations and systems that were failing to contribute to the common good. These were friends and colleagues of The Berkana Institute.

Deborah joined Berkana full-time in 2004 when, in partnership with Manish Jain of Shikshantar in India, she proposed a new initiative to the Berkana Board. The Berkana Exchange would be a trans-local learning community of people who were walking on to build healthy and resilient communities. These people are the subject of this book.

In 2005, Deborah became Meg Wheatley's successor as co-president of Berkana (in partnership with Bob Stilger). She served in that capacity for four years, deepening the work of the Berkana Exchange and launching many new initiatives with partners across the globe. In partnership with Berkana's board, she developed a transition plan for the Institute to become more powerfully aligned with its core commitments and to experiment with the future form of nonprofits. In 2009, Deborah and the board successfully dissolved the co-presidency and declared Berkana a self-organizing system.

She currently serves as a board member and is leading several Berkana initiatives, including Feeding Ourselves Sustainably, a youth-driven community of practice in North America; Swaraj University, an alternative learning institute in India; several Sharing Our Learning projects, including publications and online media; and consulting as part of the Berkana Collaborative.

Previously, Deborah was a partner and founding member of ZEFER, an Internet services firm that integrated business strategy, experience design, technology, and program management. Earlier in her career, she was an editor for *Snow Country* magazine, and she continues to count skiing and winter sports among her greatest passions.

She has worked in partnership with the Mastery Foundation, leading peace and reconciliation programs in Northern Ireland and Israel. She serves as a consultant and adviser to numerous grassroots organizations both locally and abroad. Deborah has an MBA from Harvard Business School and a bachelor's degree from Amherst College.

She currently lives in Boston but can more often be found visiting friends and colleagues around the world who are creating healthy and resilient communities. Learn more at www.deborahfrieze.com.

ABOUT BERKANA

The Berkana Institute works in partnership with a rich diversity of people around the world who strengthen their communities by working with the wisdom and wealth already present in their people, traditions and environment. As pioneers, we do not deny or flee from our global crisis. We respond by moving courageously into the future now, experimenting with many different solutions.

Berkana and our partners share the clarity that whatever the problem, community is the answer. We prepare for an unknown future by creating strong and sustainable relationships, by wisely stewarding the Earth's resources, and by building resilient communities. We rely on the belief that human beings are caring, generous, and want to be together.

Each of our initiatives is based on a coherent, in-depth theory of how life organizes in cooperative, generous, and interdependent systems—work we've developed with hundreds of colleagues over many years of dialogue, think tanks, and practical applications in all kinds of settings.

Berkana's work is in three major areas: Pioneering Initiatives, Consulting and Learning Services, and Sharing Our Learning.

A portion of the proceeds of this book supports the work of Berkana. We welcome your interest and curiosity about our work. www.berkana.org.

Also by Margaret Wheatley

Perseverance

In this inspiring and beautifully illustrated book, Margaret Wheatley offers guidance to people everywhere for how to persevere through challenges in their personal lives, with their families, at their workplaces, in their communities, and in their struggles to make a better world. In a series of concise and compassionate essays, Wheatley names a behavior or dynamic—such as fearlessness, guilt, joy, jealousy—that supports or impedes our efforts to persevere. She puts each in a broader human or timeless perspective, offering ways to either live with or transcend each one. *Perseverance* includes poems and quotations drawn from traditions and cultures around the world and throughout history, all of which underscore her essential message: human beings throughout time have persevered. We're just the most recent ones to face these challenges, and we can meet them as those who came before us did.

Paperback, 168 pages, ISBN 978-1-60509-820-3
PDF ebook, ISBN 978-1-60509-854-8

BK® Berrett–Koehler Publishers, Inc.
San Francisco, *www.bkconnection.com*

800.929.2929

Leadership and the New Science
Discovering Order in a Chaotic World, Third Edition

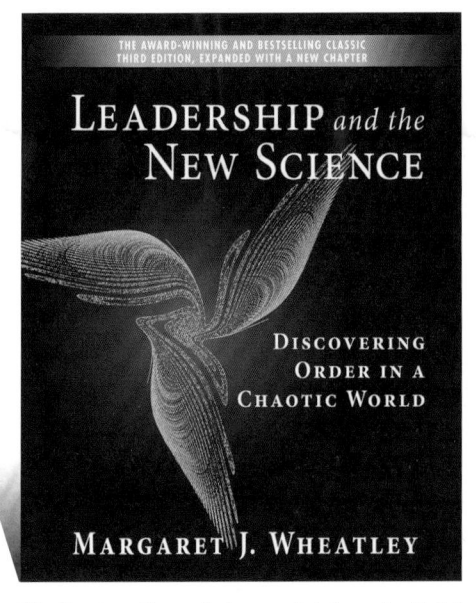

We live in a time of chaos, rich in potential for new possibilities. We need new ideas, new ways of seeing, and new relationships to help us. Recent discoveries in biology, chaos theory, and quantum physics offer this guidance. This is the bestselling, most acclaimed, and most influential guide to applying these discoveries to management and leadership. It will teach you how to move with greater certainty and easier grace into the new forms of organizations and communities that are taking shape.

Paperback, 248 pages, ISBN 978-1-57675-344-6
PDF ebook, ISBN 978-1-60509-147-1

BK® Berrett–Koehler Publishers, Inc.
San Francisco, *www.bkconnection.com*   800.929.2929

Turning to One Another
Simple Conversations to Restore Hope to the Future, Second Edition

Real social change, both local and global, will not come from governments or corporations but from the ageless process of people thinking together in conversation. *Turning to One Another* explores the power of conversation and the conditions—simplicity, personal courage, real listening, and diversity—that support it. It contains quotes and images to encourage the reader to pause and reflect, as well as ten "conversation starters"—questions that lead people to share their deepest beliefs, fears, and hopes.

Paperback, 192 pages, ISBN 978-1-57675-764-2
PDF ebook, ISBN 978-1-57675-984-4

BK Berrett–Koehler Publishers, Inc.
San Francisco, *www.bkconnection.com*

800.929.2929

❄ Berrett–Koehler
BK Publishers

Berrett-Koehler is an independent publisher dedicated to an ambitious mission: *Creating a World That Works for All.*

We believe that to truly create a better world, action is needed at all levels—individual, organizational, and societal. At the individual level, our publications help people align their lives with their values and with their aspirations for a better world. At the organizational level, our publications promote progressive leadership and management practices, socially responsible approaches to business, and humane and effective organizations. At the societal level, our publications advance social and economic justice, shared prosperity, sustainability, and new solutions to national and global issues.

A major theme of our publications is "Opening Up New Space." Berrett-Koehler titles challenge conventional thinking, introduce new ideas, and foster positive change. Their common quest is changing the underlying beliefs, mindsets, institutions, and structures that keep generating the same cycles of problems, no matter who our leaders are or what improvement programs we adopt.

We strive to practice what we preach—to operate our publishing company in line with the ideas in our books. At the core of our approach is stewardship, which we define as a deep sense of responsibility to administer the company for the benefit of all of our "stakeholder" groups: authors, customers, employees, investors, service providers, and the communities and environment around us.

We are grateful to the thousands of readers, authors, and other friends of the company who consider themselves to be part of the "BK Community." We hope that you, too, will join us in our mission.

A BK Currents Book

This book is part of our BK Currents series. BK Currents books advance social and economic justice by exploring the critical intersections between business and society. Offering a unique combination of thoughtful analysis and progressive alternatives, BK Currents books promote positive change at the national and global levels. To find out more, visit **www.bkconnection .com**.

Berrett–Koehler
Publishers

A community dedicated to creating
a world that works for all

Visit Our Website: www.bkconnection.com

Read book excerpts, see author videos and Internet movies, read our authors' blogs, join discussion groups, download book apps, find out about the BK Affiliate Network, browse subject-area libraries of books, get special discounts, and more!

Subscribe to Our Free E-Newsletter, the *BK Communiqué*

Be the first to hear about new publications, special discount offers, exclusive articles, news about bestsellers, and more! Get on the list for our free e-newsletter by going to www.bkconnection.com.

Get Quantity Discounts

Berrett-Koehler books are available at quantity discounts for orders of ten or more copies. Please call us toll-free at (800) 929-2929 or email us at bkp.orders@aidcvt.com.

Join the BK Community

BKcommunity.com is a virtual meeting place where people from around the world can engage with kindred spirits to create a world that works for all. BKcommunity.com members may create their own profiles, blog, start and participate in forums and discussion groups, post photos and videos, answer surveys, announce and register for upcoming events, and chat with others online in real time. Please join the conversation!